From the Local to the Global

From the Local to the Global

Key Issues in Development Studies

Edited by
Gerard McCann and Stephen McCloskey

Pluto Press

LONDON • STERLING, VIRGINIA

First published 2003 by Pluto Press
345 Archway Road, London N6 5AA
and 22883 Quicksilver Drive,
Sterling, VA 20166–2012, USA

www.plutobooks.com

British Library Cataloguing in Publication Data
A catalogue record for this book is available from the British Library

ISBN 0 7453 1813 4 hardback
ISBN 0 7453 1812 6 paperback

Library of Congress Cataloging in Publication Data
applied for

10   9   8   7   6   5   4   3   2   1

Designed and produced for Pluto Press by
Chase Publishing Services, Fortescue, Sidmouth EX10 9QG, England
Typeset from disk by Stanford DTP Services, Towcester, England
Printed in the European Union by
Antony Rowe Ltd, Chippenham and Eastbourne, England

Contents

Acknowledgements

A publication of this nature would simply not have been possible without the support and encouragement of our respective organisations. We commend the staff and Management Board of the One World Centre (NI) and St. Mary's College, Queen's University, Belfast for facilitating this initiative. The commitment of both organisations to this publication made it possible. We also thank those non-governmental organisations that financially support the One World Centre – Christian Aid, Concern Worldwide, Mercy Justice Centre, Save the Children Fund and Trócaire – for encouragement throughout the process of compiling this text. Particular mention should also be made of a number of development agencies – the Jubilee 2000 Debt Campaign, Oxfam and the World Development Movement – for providing us with invaluable source material.

We valued the insightful comments and improvements made to the book by Roger van Zwanenberg and Julie Stoll at Pluto Press. Their unending patience in the face of slipping deadlines was much appreciated. The contributors to the text deserve our thanks for working to difficult deadlines and delivering quality manuscripts that made our role as editors much easier. Special thanks are owed to Paul Hainsworth for useful and friendly editorial advice, and assistance in conceiving the format of the text. We also relied on the goodwill and support of a number of individuals who diligently went through full drafts or sections of the text, particularly Nathalie Caleyron, Karen Muldoon and Birgit Schippers. Of course, as editors, we take full and ultimate responsibility for the content of this publication.

Gerard McCann
Stephen McCloskey
March 2003

Abbreviations

AASM	Associated African and Malagasy States
ACP	Africa, the Caribbean and the Pacific
AFTA	ASEAN Free Trade Area
AMF	Asian Monetary Fund
AMICC	American Coalition for the ICC
AMUE	Association for Monetary Union in Europe
AOA	Agreement on Agriculture
APEC	Asia-Pacific Economic Co-operation
ARF	Asia-Pacific Regional Forum
ASEAN	Association of Southeast Asian Nations
ASPA	American Service Members' Protection Act
CACM	Central American Common Market
CAFOD	Catholic Agency for Overseas Development
CAP	Common Agricultural Policy
CASA	Co-ordinating Action on Small Arms
CCP	Common Commercial Policy
CEDAW	Convention on the Elimination of All Forms of Discrimination Against Women
CET	Common External Tariff
CFSP	Common Foreign and Security Policy
CICC	Coalition for an International Criminal Court
CIT	Countries in Transition
COMESA	Common Market for Eastern and Southern Africa
CPAG	Child Poverty Action Group
DAC	Development Assistance Committee
DEA	Development Education Association
DECs	Development Education Centres
DFA	Department of Foreign Affairs (Ir)
DFID	Department for International Development (UK)
DTI	Department of Trade and Industry (UK)
EAC	East African Co-operation
EBRD	European Bank for Reconstruction and Development
ECHO	European Community Humanitarian Office
ECA	Economic Commission for Africa
EC	European Community (EEC, EU)

EDF	European Development Fund
EEC	European Economic Community (EU, EC)
EES	Enabling Effective Support
ELD	Export-Led Development
ELI	Export-Led Industrialisation
EMU	Economic and Monetary Union
EP	European Parliament
ERT	European Round Table of Industrialists
ESAF	Enhanced Structural Adjustment Facility
ESD	Education for Sustainable Development
EU	European Union
EURODAD	European Network on Debt and Development
FAO	Food and Agriculture Organisation
FDI	Foreign Direct Investment
FOCUS	Focus on the Global South
FTA	Free Trade Agreement
FTAA	Free Trade Area of the Americas
GATS	General Agreement on Trade in Services
GATT	General Agreement on Tariffs and Trade
GDP	Gross Domestic Product
GPF	Global Policy Forum
GMPs	Genetically Modified Products
GNP	Gross National Product
HDI	Human Development Index
HIPCs	Heavily Indebted Poor Countries
IBRD	International Bank for Reconstruction and Development
ICC	International Criminal Court
ICTFY	International Criminal Tribunal for the Former Yugoslavia
IDA	International Development Association
IDPs	Internally Displaced Persons
IDTs	International Development Targets
IFC	International Finance Co-operation
IFG	International Forum on Globalisation
IFIs	International Financial Institutions
IGAD	Intergovernmental Authority on Development
IGOs	International Governmental Organisations
ILC	International Law Commission
ILO	International Labour Organisation
IMF	International Monetary Fund

IPRs	Intellectual Property Rights
ISI	Import-Substitution Industrialisation
ITO	International Trade Organisation
LAFTA	Latin American Free Trade Association
LDCs	Least Developed Countries
MAI	Multilateral Agreement on Investment
MFN	Most Favoured Nation
MNCs	Multinational Corporations
MSF	Médecins Sans Frontières
NAFTA	North American Free Trade Agreement
NATO	North Atlantic Treaty Organisation
NCDE	National Committee for Development Education
NCH	National Children's Home
NGOs	Non-Governmental Organisations
NGDOs	Non-Governmental Development Organisations
NICs	Newly Industrialised Countries
OCTs	Overseas Countries and Territories
ODA	Overseas Development Administration
ODA	Official Development Assistance
ODCCP	Office for Drug Control and Crime Prevention
OECD	Organisation for Economic Co-operation and Development
OPEC	Organisation of Petroleum Exporting Countries
OWC	One World Centre (NI)
PCAs	Partnership and Co-operation Agreements
PRGF	Poverty Reduction and Growth Facility
PRSP	Poverty Reduction Strategy Papers
SAFTA	Southern African Free Trade Area
SAPs	Structural Adjustment Programmes
STABEX	Stabilisation of Export Earnings from Products
SWIFT	Society of Worldwide Inter-bank Financial Telecommunications
TNCs	Transnational Corporations
TRIMs	Trade Related Investment Measures
TRIPs	Trade Related Intellectual Property Rights
TWN	Third World Network
UN	United Nations
UNCED	United Nations Conference on Environment and Development
UNCHR	United Nations Commissioner for Human Rights
UNCRC	United Nations Convention on the Rights of the Child

UNCTAD	United Nations Conference on Trade and Development
UNDDA	United Nations Department for Disarmament Affairs
UNDP	United Nations Development Programme
UNHCR	United Nations High Commissioner for Refugees
UNICEF	United Nations Children's Fund
UNMAS	United Nations Mine Action Service
UNSC	United Nations Security Council
WDM	World Development Movement
WHO	World Health Organisation
WID	Women in Development
WRI	World Resources Institute
WSSD	World Summit on Sustainable Development
WTO	World Trade Organisation

Introduction:
Whither Development in
the Age of Globalisation?

Stephen McCloskey

Understanding development issues is essential to enable all of us to play an effective role as global citizens in working toward the eradication of poverty, injustice and social exclusion in both local and global contexts. With over a billion people consigned to subsistence lifestyles and living on less than a dollar a day, we have secure grounds on which to question the Western-led model of development that has characterised the past 50 years. During this period, development has become synonymous with globalisation and regarded as encompassing rapid industrialisation, global trade in goods and services, laissez-faire economics and capital transfer. In fact, some commentators on globalisation have traced its origins to the earliest colonisation of the Americas initiated by Columbus 500 years ago and view post-war development as an extension of that process. The current phase of globalisation has adopted new technologies and institutions to maintain the old hegemonic control of the leading Western powers that has spanned centuries. While many corrupt and compliant Third World leaders have played a significant role in economically disadvantaging their own people, the development model advocated by Western governments in the aftermath of the Second World War has been largely responsible for the deepening underdevelopment that has enveloped the majority of the world's people.

This introduction will examine the concepts of globalisation and development in historical and contemporary contexts. It will highlight the importance of development issues in equipping learners with the skills and knowledge necessary to analyse how the modern world is ordered and to address the latent inequalities of globalisation. This chapter will also outline the main institutional and ideological instruments of globalisation whilst charting a future course for development in the context of the new popular movements for change that have emerged in recent years.

1

GLOBALISATION AND DEVELOPMENT

Development issues have accrued increasing importance in the period of renewed globalisation that has characterised the post-Cold War era. The collapse of state command economies in the Eastern bloc in 1989 was to herald a 'new world order' of greater prosperity, security and equality. The United States (US) emerged from the Cold War as the world's last remaining superpower, confident that its dominant neo-liberal model of economic development had eclipsed the failed alternative path of socialism. Throughout the 1990s, neo-liberalism became an unchallenged article of faith proclaimed by Western governments and preached to the poor. This ideological dominance was manifested in a sharp swing to the right in political institutions across Europe and North America, and provided an ideological context for an accelerated form of globalisation which was promoted as the only legitimate pathway to development.

The contemporary form of globalisation has been characterised by new innovations in telecommunications, increased interdependence amongst states, enhanced cultural awareness and, more negatively, by a rampant private sector dominated by Transnational Corporations (TNCs). The political philosophy underpinning globalisation advocates greater trade liberalisation, reduced state intervention in the economy, and the derogation of increasing levels of control over our public services to the private sector. As globalisation has reached new levels of technical development, production and profit, the poverty gap between rich and poor has widened between (and within) developed and developing countries.[1]

In assessing progress toward the eradication of poverty in the ten years following the collapse of the eastern bloc, the United Nations *Human Development Report (2000)* found that by the late 1990s the fifth of the world's people living in the highest income countries controlled 86 per cent of the global Gross Domestic Product (GDP) – the bottom fifth controlled just 1 per cent.[2] Thus, the profits generated by globalisation have been largely accumulated by a wealthy elite rather than redistributed according to social need. Global inequalities increased in the twentieth century 'by orders of magnitude out of proportion to anything experienced before' whereby the distortion in income between the richest and poorest countries grew from 34 to 1 in 1970 to 70 to 1 in 1997.[3] Moreover, the combined wealth of the top 200 billionaires in 1999 reached a staggering $1,135 billion compared to the collective incomes of $146 billion for the 582 million people living in the least developed countries.[4] The human cost of globalisation has been immense and largely poverty related. Some 30,000 children die every day from preventable diseases mostly caused by food shortages and a lack of clean water. Over 1.2 billion people live on less than a dollar a day whilst 2.4 billion people lack basic sanitation.[5] The technological advances that have been the flagship of globalisation underline the unevenness of development when contrasted with the medieval environs of some sub-Saharan African states gripped in poverty and continually threatened by famine or drought.

The role of globalisation in the development process has been hotly contested by governments and non-governmental organisations (NGOs). For example, in 2000, the British government's Department for International Development (DFID) published a White Paper, *Eliminating World Poverty: Making Globalisation Work for the Poor*, which argued that 'globalisation creates unprecedented new opportunities for sustainable development and poverty reduction'.[6] In a critique of DFID's position, the Catholic Agency for Overseas Development (CAFOD) suggested that 'equity and redistribution are increasingly recognized as the "missing link" between globalisation and poverty reduction... What is good for poor people is good for the economy as a whole. Yet up to now, globalisation has frequently been linked with inequality.'[7] Western governments, therefore, argue that globalisation can be an agent of development by generating growth and investment in developing countries and integrating their economies into the global market of commodities and services. However, NGOs and civil society activists believe that globalisation is exacerbating poverty levels in developing countries and effectively dictating their engagement with the global economy on terms favourable to the developed world. Third World countries have been particularly critical of the institutional instruments of globalisation.

THE INSTITUTIONAL INSTRUMENTS OF GLOBALISATION

The Bretton Woods Institutions.

The concepts of development and globalisation can be sourced to the post-Second World War period of reconstruction led by the United States. The economic philosophy associated with the modern and renewed form of today's globalisation has its origins in the Bretton Woods Institutions – the International Monetary Fund (IMF) and the World Bank – established in 1944 to 'support post-war rehabilitation and promote international trade'.[8] These bodies have been the vanguard of globalisation for almost 60 years, primarily through the disbursement of conditional loans to developing countries. While the post-war period was characterised by resurgent nationalism and the fragmentation of old colonial empires, the combined efforts of the World Bank and the IMF resulted in an insidious recolonisation process by economic means. The World Bank was charged at Bretton Woods with providing 'longer term loans to developing countries to support their development' whilst the IMF was given the role of supporting an 'orderly international monetary system'.[9] Beneath the façade of this laudable rhetoric, however, the IMF and the World Bank have orchestrated economic indebtedness throughout the Third World by facilitating a 'bonanza' of irresponsible borrowing by developing countries in the 1970s. Loans from the IMF became conditional on the implementation of structural adjustment programmes (SAPs) that 'covered social policies, financial policy, corporate laws and governance'.[10] In short, SAPs represented a neo-liberal reform programme designed to dictate economic policy to Third World governments.

Over the past 30 years the debt crisis has strangled Third World economies and prevented meaningful development for the world's poor. According to the Drop the Debt Campaign, the combined debt of developing countries currently exceeds $2.4 billion and thereby forces Third World governments to drastically cut social expenditure in order to meet loan repayment schedules.[11] Developing countries are locked in a vicious cycle of debt repayment, rescheduling loans when faltering on payments, and fresh borrowing to repay old debt. The poorest countries are forced to channel more than 50 per cent of their GDP into repaying debt, which necessitates a massive austerity programme encompassing cuts in health, education, welfare, housing and public utilities. The burden generated by this neo-liberal agenda is most acutely felt by the vulnerable in developing countries: the elderly, children and, especially, women who often combine onerous domestic chores (unpaid labour) with intensive, low-paid employment in either rural or urban contexts. Debt also traduces the impact of multilateral (from international organisations like the United Nations) and bilateral (country-to-country) aid as agents of development. For every $1 donated in grant aid to developing countries, more than $13 is returned in debt repayments to the developed world.[12] While long-term aid delivered in partnership with communities and NGOs in developing countries can effectively address social needs, this process is continually undermined by the downsizing of governments by the debt crisis.

World Trade Organisation

A third key agent of the contemporary form of globalisation is the World Trade Organisation (WTO) which, together with the World Bank and the IMF, makes up a triumvirate of international financial institutions (IFIs) that effectively control the policy agenda for global trade and economic development. The WTO was established on 1 January 1995 as a successor to the General Agreement on Tariffs and Trade (GATT) with the aim of liberalising trade and reducing state protectionism of domestic markets. The US was initially reluctant to devolve meaningful powers to an international regulatory body on trade so GATT evolved through a series of trade negotiations that culminated with the Uruguay Round from 1986–94. Although GATT focused primarily on manufactured goods, its successive trade rounds reduced tariffs on commodities from 'an average of 40 per cent in the 1940s to 4 per cent today'.[13] The Uruguay Round agreed the establishment of the WTO to carry forward the GATT agenda which was broadened to include agriculture, services (such as telecommunications and finance) and intellectual property rights that governed the patenting of commodities. The WTO also has the power to arbitrate in trading disputes between its members and, if necessary, impose sanctions on nations in breech of its regulations.

Negotiating and implementing the rules of global trade provides the WTO with enormous influence over the economic development of Third World countries. Development NGOs consider the WTO an undemocratic institution designed to propagate a profit-driven model of development that mostly benefits developed countries and private companies. With 144 members, the WTO should, in theory, arrive at decisions favouring developing countries, which represent some 80 per cent of the world's population. In practice, however, negotiations are rarely concluded by democratic procedures, but rather involve bruising exchanges in which poorer nations are arm-twisted into accepting terms tabled by Western governments. Moreover, many developing countries lack the resources and expertise to properly negotiate their case in the WTO on a level playing field. Negotiations represent a web of legalistic jargon and intricate detail that require regular monitoring and expert representation. Government delegates to the WTO are regularly lobbied by TNCs equipped with batteries of lawyers contracted to enhance the privatisation of public utilities and maximise the investment conditions for private companies. However, developing countries are woefully under-represented and, thereby, sidelined in negotiations that regularly result in outcomes that benefit the developed world.

Developed countries proclaim the benefits of free trade economics as a badge of honour and, yet, protect their domestic markets from Third World imports by applying tariffs and quotas to specified commodities. By contrast, developing countries are browbeaten into accepting foreign direct investment by TNCs on terms that threaten domestic productivity and services, and increase unemployment. The 'open economy' mantra of the WTO can be disastrous for developing countries. For example, the dumping of cheap food imports into Mexico from the US created a collapse in local maize prices and impoverished Mexican farmers who saw their income slashed and livelihoods threatened.[14] The WTO sustains the trading domination of developed countries by employing loopholes to circumvent regulations. An example is the WTO Agreement on Agriculture, which is designed to reduce subsidies to farmers and protect members' domestic markets from cheap food imports. However, the European Union (EU) and US government continue to subsidise farmers at an annual rate of $360 million which, consequently, undermines agribusiness in developing countries.[15] According to the United Nations (UN), this form of protectionism in developed countries costs the Third World 'an export income of $2 billion a day, many times more than the total inflows of aid'.[16]

GATS and TRIPS

The decision-making mechanisms of the WTO are dominated by 'the Quad' – Canada, the European Union, Japan and the US – with a view to securing maximum advantage for their economies and facilitating the creeping privatisation of the public sector in the Northern and Southern Hemispheres. The EU and the US sometimes make uneasy transatlantic bedfellows and have occasionally engaged in mutual recrimination over protectionist policies that have disadvantaged imports. However, 'the Quad' has been unified in its pursuit of WTO agreements designed to open up public sector services to private investment and control. The Multilateral Agreement on Investment (MAI) was formulated in the 1990s and offered unprecedented powers to TNCs in challenging the rights of national governments to protect public utilities and employment sectors from private takeover and competition. The MAI was defeated in December 1998 through the vigorous and sustained campaigning efforts of hundreds of NGOs around the world. The privatising impulse of MAI has been resurrected, however, in the guise of the General Agreement on Trade in Services (GATS) which was originally ratified in 1994 and is currently under debate at the WTO with a view to extending its remit. Described by the WTO Secretariat as 'the world's first international investment agreement', GATS is designed to remove any restrictions and internal government regulations in the area of service delivery that are considered to be 'barriers to trade'.[17]

The services vulnerable to privatisation under the GATS agreement include education (schools and colleges), health (hospitals), public libraries, and municipal services such as the supply of water. The main danger for the poor, of course, lies in public services becoming profit-making entities under the control of TNCs that will then demand payment at the point of delivery. The quality of essential services will steadily decline without government intervention and be priced beyond the reach of the poorest communities in developing countries. Unsurprisingly, it is the TNCs that have driven the GATS negotiations in the WTO and it is they who are primed to become its chief beneficiaries. The foothold of TNCs in developing countries has also been secured by the Agreement on Trade Related Intellectual Property Rights (TRIPS), which was one of the main outcomes of the Uruguay Round of trade talks.

TRIPS is a particularly damaging agreement for developing countries in that it enables TNCs to patent 'intellectual property' that includes medicines and agricultural seeds indigenous to the South. As the South African activist Mohau Pheko stated, TRIPS enables 'bio-pirates to steal from your land, patent your seeds and then sell them back to you'.[18] Under the auspices of TRIPS, Western-based corporations can monopolise new technologies and stifle indigenous industrial development in developing countries. Most crucially, however, intellectual property rights (IPRs) enable TNCs to patent and market drugs and agricultural products that will hinder food and commodity production, and exacerbate medicinal shortages in developing countries. With the spiralling AIDS crisis reaching epidemic proportions in Southern Africa, the TRIPS agreement will deepen the suffering of its victims.

Transnational Corporations

TNCs have been the vanguard of globalisation in the post-war era. Like modern manifestations of the Spanish Conquistadors, who first brought a missionary and military zeal to empire building over five centuries ago, TNCs are international conglomerates which use the force of capital to capture new markets. TNCs such as McDonald's and Starbucks have become totems of accelerated globalisation and driven its expansion into areas such as Eastern Europe that are ripe for investment following the end of the Cold War. With their headquarters normally based in Western Europe or North America, TNCs have proliferated their operations in developing countries under the auspices of favourable trading terms agreed in the Uruguay Round. Accountable only to stockholders and the international share index, TNCs reflect the capacity of trade rules to open up governments and markets to the advantage of developed countries and private capital. The operations of TNCs have been criticised on the grounds that they:

- Relocate most of their profits to their countries of origin (usually industrialised nations)
- Regularly prevent the unionisation of their labour force
- Exploit child and women workers in poor developing countries to maximise their profits
- Pay low wages to employees who are forced to work long hours to earn a living wage
- Create environmental problems through the use of unsafe and polluting methods of production, particularly, in the oil industry
- Breach environmental and labour standards in host countries, especially poor nations in the greatest need of internal investment

The world's top ten TNCs exercise immense political influence and accumulate annual revenues that dwarf the earnings of many developed and developing countries. For example, the car manufacturer General Motors has an annual turnover greater than Norway and the US-based oil company Exxon can boast an annual income that is more than double the Gross National Product of Venezuela – one of the world's leading oil exporting countries.[19] TNCs are, therefore, developing an alarming level of political impunity in their operations, facilitated by the profit-driven ethos of neo-liberalism, favourable trading conditions, and the prescriptive economic measures foisted by the World Bank and the IMF on vulnerable developing world economies. The World Development Movement (WDM), an NGO that has successfully campaigned on trade justice issues, states that:

> ... multinationals could play a valuable role in pro-poor economic development providing jobs, capital and technical know-how, but in reality their positive impact is limited. Their full potential is not realized. Moreover, there is mounting evidence that multi-nationals, registered in the North, are actually causing harm in the Third World. Transgressions include: abusing workers' rights and causing bodily harm; destroying local lands and livelihoods; promoting harmful products to consumers; breaking national laws and undermining local democracy.[20]

Thus, TNCs could generate positive investment in developing countries but, instead, effectively asset-strip natural resources from the Third World while exploiting a labour force that receives in wages a fraction of the profits made by TNCs on commodities sold in developed countries.

The WDM has urged industrialised countries to take responsibility for the activities of corporations based and registered under their jurisdictions that operate in developing countries. In an ideal scenario, TNCs would be self-regulating bodies measuring their operations against a firmly enforced code of conduct which addresses issues relating to the environment, working conditions, wages and trade unions. However, many leading corporations, such as Nike and Gap, continue to manufacture their products in conditions that contravene international labour standards despite using a code of conduct in promoting their products in developed countries.[21] The WDM has argued for binding regulations to be introduced that will properly police the activities of corporations under the auspices of an International Investment Treaty 'promoting quality investment and core standards for corporate responsibility'.[22] Given the influence of TNCs over some national governments in the context of WTO nego-tiations, the regulation of such a treaty should be handled by independent specialist bodies such as the International Labour Organisation (ILO) and the World Health Organisation (WHO).

THE IDEOLOGICAL INSTRUMENTS OF GLOBALISATION

Development and Underdevelopment

The international financial institutions have been the battleground on which the contemporary debate on development has been fought. Third World networks, NGOs and development organisations regard the IFIs as partners in globalisation, working in tandem to pursue a neo-liberal agenda that masquerades as development but, in fact, deepens poverty levels in developing countries. The lending policies of the World Bank and the IMF have prised open Third World economies to inward investment from countries and corporations in the developed world, while the WTO has locked developing countries into unfair trade agreements that compound their difficulties. The IFIs and Northern governments regard development as integrating poor countries into the globalising economy. This is achieved by export-led economic regeneration, attracting inward investment, dropping protectionist tariffs, and enhancing private control of public services. However, the prescriptive policies of the IFIs raise fundamental questions about the appropriateness of neo-liberalism in a developing world context and what actually constitutes meaningful development.

Wolfgang Sachs has sourced the concept of development to an inaugural address by US President Harry Truman on 20 January 1949 in which he described the Southern Hemisphere as comprising 'under-developed areas'.[23] Sachs regarded Truman's description of underdevelopment as having four basic premises:

1. That industrialised nations stood at the top of the 'social evolutionary' scale and, therefore, represented the apex of development – the model to which underdeveloped nations should aspire. The 2001 *Human Development Report*, however, points to increasing levels of poverty in the wealthy member states of the Organisation for Economic Co-operation and Development (OECD) in which:

   - 15 per cent of adults are functionally illiterate
   - 130 million people are living in income poverty
   - 34 million people are unemployed
   - 8 million people are undernourished[24]

2. That the development process would enable the US to enlist the support of developing countries in the ideological battle with

Eastern bloc countries during the Cold War. The US, therefore, represented a 'comforting vision of development' which poor countries could ape in their eagerness to 'develop'. However, Sachs suggests that the US has run out of 'ideological steam' in the aftermath of the Cold War and that the East–West rivalry has now been superseded by the rich–poor divide, with under-developed countries largely blamed for their own poverty.

3. That in the race to develop, poor countries would ultimately match their counterparts in the North by adopting the same model of development and swallowing the strong medicine of neo-liberal reform. The 'one-size-fits-all' doctrine of the Truman years continues to underpin the model of development espoused by Northern governments today. The IFIs apply the same neo-liberal template to all developing countries without due consideration of their particular social, economic and political needs. Southern countries that have bravely embraced alternative paths to development which encompass the redistribution of wealth and land, and tackle social problems such as health and education, are bullied, threatened or overthrown by the US. Chile, Cuba, Nicaragua, and more recently, Venezuela, are examples of countries that challenged US hegemony within its own hemisphere and, consequently, suffered varying levels of US intervention.

4. That development will result in the westernisation of the world. Sachs argues that the Truman 'project' aimed to create a mirror image of the US in the development of poor countries. This fear has been realised to an extent in the cultural imperialism attending the pervasive export of Hollywood films (the biggest export earner for the US economy), and brand names like Nike and Coca-Cola. These icons of globalisation collectively threaten cultural diversity, standardise material expectations and margin-alise traditional life in terms of customs, clothing, language, and identity. Westernising the world, however, reinforces the old monetarist hierarchy of countries and the ideological dominance of the US. It also stifles debate on alternative models of develop-ment that are both sustainable and consistent with social justice and equality.[25]

The Truman Doctrine

A dictionary definition of a developing country states that it is a 'poor or non-industrial country seeking to develop its resources by industrialisation'.[26] Thus, the concept of development is equated with industrialisation or, as Gustavo Esteva suggests, is reduced to the accrual of economic growth.[27] Truman's coinage of 'under-developed' as a new description of poor regions prefaced a commitment to a 'program of development based on the concepts of democratic fair dealing' ... 'The old imperialism,' he said, 'has no place in our plans.'[28] Truman's speech heralded over 50 years of deepening global underdevelopment in which many developing countries, such as Indonesia and Vietnam, became pawns in a Cold War over markets, control of resources, strategic dominance and ideological supremacy.

Indonesia provides a prescient example of the human cost of the Cold War. In 1965, the US and its Western partners turned a blind eye to the 1965 military *coup d'état* led by General Suharto that resulted in the slaughter of 1 million Indonesians and a 30-year dictatorship which plunged the country into communal division, corruption, political repression and widespread human rights abuses.[29] The US embraced the new military regime, which conveniently disposed of a communist 'bogeyman', President Sukarno, who had led a reformist government that took a leadership role among developing countries to co-ordinate united action towards effecting meaningful development for poor nations. Sukarno was sacrificed to satisfy the strategic interests of the US in South-East Asia, where it now had a foothold to repel the spread of communism and, most importantly, an ally conducive to Western investment and neo-liberal 'reform'. Truman's promise of development as 'democratic fair dealing' became an example of Orwellian double-speak that characterises how development is defined by today's leading agents of globalisation. Truman's 'development' consigned millions to poverty, insecurity, repression, hunger and social marginalisation – the antithesis of development – through a renewal of the 'old imperialism' that had no place in 'his plans'.[30] Development, therefore, signalled a deepening underdevelopment which prioritised selfish strategic and economic interests over the welfare of the world's poor.

THE INSTRUMENTS OF CHANGE

Charting the Future

Despite the social polarisation of wealth and inequality that has attended accelerated globalisation over the past 50 years, there are grounds for optimism regarding development in this new millennium. In December 1999, the Ministerial Council of the WTO met in Seattle and faced vehement protests from an international coalition of campaign groups: NGOs, development agencies, women's organisations, environmentalists, socialist groups, trade unions and other civil society organisations. The aim of the protesters was to demand 'trade justice' for developing countries, including: the cancellation of Third World debt; abolition of trade rules that hobble developing world economies; meaningful and binding controls on environmental pollution; and the democratic accountability of TNCs. The protesters successfully collapsed the WTO talks but, more significantly, drew worldwide public attention to the undemocratic operations of the IFIs and their exacerbation of poverty in developed and developing countries. While similar protests had been organised in developing countries along similar lines in the past, the formulation of a trade justice agenda and campaign movement in the North reflected a deepening public awareness of development issues within industrialised countries. Moreover, civil society in the North demonstrated a preparedness to take action that would address poverty-related issues in solidarity and in partnership with developing countries on the doorstep of the IFIs.

The trade justice coalition is arguably the most significant popular movement to emerge in the North since the civil rights and anti-Vietnam protests of the 1960s. It indicates the often underestimated capacity of the public to digest complex economic issues and formulate strong opinions on the causes of underdevelopment. Since Seattle, protests have been organised in cities throughout the developed world, including Bonn, Genoa, London, Madrid and Seville, to coincide with the meetings of international financial and policy-making bodies like the EU, the Group of Eight leading industrialised countries (G8), the UN, the World Bank and the WTO. Although the mainstream media and Western governments have often been dismissive of the protests as anti-democratic and harbouring violent intent, in reality the trade justice movement represents a revitalisation of democracy on the streets rather than a threat to democratic order. The protesters recognise the culpability of Western governments in facilitating the privatisation of the public sector largely to the benefit of powerful corporations. Civil society has consequently become increasingly alienated from Northern governments and been prepared to bypass 'democratic' institutions to seek justice for a silent majority disempowered and marginalised by government bodies. As the journalist and broadcaster John Pilger points out, the British general election in May 2001 produced the lowest turnout in electoral history: '24 per cent of the electorate voted for Tony Blair and this is described as a landslide victory.' As Pilger suggests, the low turnout was less an indication of public 'apathy' than a demonstration of 'public protest'.[31]

The trade justice movement has successfully monitored and challenged the policies and negotiations of the IFIs, played an important educational role in raising awareness of development issues in the public domain, and illustrated the value and power of popular democracy as an effective vehicle for change. The protesters have also recaptured the concept of development from the distortion of Truman's definition to encompass:

- The redistribution of wealth to address social needs
- The regulation of trade and investment to developing countries to ensure that it enhances their technological development and promotion of indigenous industry
- Greater Third World participation in, and influence over, international finance and trade bodies
- The establishment of national development strategies to promote pro-poor growth
- Sustained public investment in health, education and welfare services
- The introduction of an effectively monitored International Investment Agreement
- The cancellation of Third World debt
- The implementation of effective controls over environmental pollution and the protection of biodiversity[32]

These are baseline measures that can begin to arrest the poverty gap within and between developed and developing countries. The alternative vision of development advocated by leading world powers will not only perpetuate social divisions and inequalities but also absorb natural resources at an unsustainable rate. Sustainability has become increasingly debated in the context of development, particularly since the 1992 United Nations Conference on Environment and Development in Rio de Janeiro which raised concerns about the increasing demands made of the natural environment to fuel the global trade in commodities.[33] The follow-up to the Rio conference, the World Summit on Sustainable Development, held in Johannesburg from 26 August to 4 September 2002, tested the commitment of developed countries in setting aside national economic interests to ensure sustainable development on a global scale.

World Summit on Sustainable Development

In the ten years since the Rio conference, poverty levels have worsened in the developing world, overseas aid from some developed countries has receded, the number of people living without clean water and sanitation has risen to over 2 billion, and 28 million people in sub-Saharan Africa have contracted HIV/AIDS (an estimated 60,000 Africans died of AIDS during the ten-day summit).[34] The Johannesburg summit, therefore, presented a challenge to all the participating countries to display the political will necessary to address the world's immense social problems and the main causes of environmental denudation. The key environmental concerns discussed at the summit included arresting the depletion in fish stocks, increasing renewable energy sources to reduce pollution caused by fossil fuels, protecting biodiversity, and tackling the causes and effects of adverse climate change. The World Summit consequently had a formidable agenda that required universal consensus to end what Thabo Mbeki, the South African president, described as a 'global apartheid' between rich and poor.[35]

A total of 45,000 delegates representing 187 countries attended the summit, which was addressed by 104 world leaders – although President George Bush refused to lead the US delegation at the conference. Bush's decision was apparently influenced to some extent by a letter (leaked to Friends of the Earth) from 31 right-wing political groups in the US – seven of which are funded to the tune of over $1 million by the oil giant Exxon Mobil – which advised the president that 'the least important global environment issue is potential global warming, and we hope your negotiators keep it off the table and out of the spotlight'.[36] In fact, the US negotiators were conspicuously successful in preventing the summit establishing new targets and timetables in respect of key development and environment concerns. Frustration with the US position over the ten days of the summit boiled over on the final day when Colin Powell, the US Secretary of State, was roundly booed by delegates for his country's intractability on key issues.

Before the summit had even begun it was clear that delegates would find it difficult to reach consensus on a plan of action to take away from Johannesburg. Preliminary negotiations designed to structure an agenda for the conference identified more than 400 points of disagreement between delegates. Thus, the fact that the summit managed to agree a 65-page plan of action at end of the event was considered by many as nothing short of miraculous – though NGO and Third World delegates were bitterly disappointed by the final text. The most significant new target agreed at the summit was a pledge to halve the number of people (about 1.2 billion) living without basic sanitation by 2015, which in itself was a restatement of an earlier International Development Target (IDT) set at a UN Millennium Summit in 2000 to halve the number of people without safe drinking water.

Securing US support for the basic sanitation target came at a price however: the vetoing of an EU-led proposal to increase the proportion of global energy supplies from clean, renewable sources such as wind and sun. The EU's initiative was specifically aimed at over 2 billion people lacking electricity supplies and reliant on alternative polluting sources of fuel such as animal dung. Renewable energy has the capacity of bringing clean energy to the poor without exacerbating global warming through the use of fossil fuels. However, the EU found itself hopelessly isolated on the issue, with Australia, Canada and Japan joining the US in opposing its proposal. Even the group of 77 Third World countries, which normally operates by consensus in the UN as a single bloc, could not reach agreement on renewable energy targets. Third World members of OPEC (Organisation of Petroleum Exporting Countries) were concerned about reduced oil revenues in the event that the EU initiative proved successful. The summit plan of action was, therefore, woefully short of firm timescales and targets for eradicating poverty and undoing the environmental damage caused by unchecked resource consumption over several generations.

In comparing the Johannesburg and Rio summits, delegates pointed to the increased influence and direct involvement of the business sector in the former as partially explaining its failure to arrive at positive and meaningful outcomes. Held in the prosperous and exclusive suburb of Sandton, the Johannesburg summit assumed the appearance of a corporate trade fair with its hi-tech exhibitions housed in a 'plush shopping centre'.[37] Some 8,000 business and pressure group representatives attended the summit and were heavily involved in the preliminary negotiations which agreed the agenda. Naomi Klein, the author and commentator on TNC activity, suggested that 'many of the official "stakeholders" (NGOs and community activists) weren't at the official table but out in the streets or organizing counter-summit conferences to plot very different routes to development'.[38] For Klein and other activists, the business sector had supplanted the interests of the poor in summit negotiations, ensuring that key decisions were either deferred and left in a negotiating limbo, or only paid lip service at the event.

The fact that a conference on sustainable development, which included strong NGO representation, became itself subject to a 40,000 strong counter-demonstration similar to those organised at IFI meetings, reflected the anger and disappointment of development and environment activists with the summit proceedings. Delegates were unequivocal in their condemnation of the US as the main source of the summit's failings, but also apportioned culpability to other developed countries in their lacklustre efforts to make headway on key issues. Whatever the causes of the summit's poorly received plan of action, it seems that the UN is rethinking the organisation of similar large-scale set-piece conferences in the future 'until governments put into practice what they have decided to do'.[39] The reaction to the summit's toothless action plan by NGOs, developing countries and those suffering the effects of underdevelopment will undoubtedly be manifested in greater activism in grassroots development and support for the global coalition for economic and social justice.

Global Interdependence

The trade justice coalition has been labeled an anti-globalisation movement by the media and governments, which suggests that the protestors are opposed to all things global and all aspects of globalisation. In fact, the protest movement is itself a global initiative in the composition of its affiliates, the issues it addresses and the nature of its operations. Therefore, it can hardly be defined as anti-globalisation. Moreover, the benefits of globalisation include new innovations in telecommunications and information technology that have underpinned the mobilisation of trade justice groups. Amartya Sen, the 1998 Nobel Laureate for Economics, suggests that 'over thousands of years globalisation has progressed through travel, trade, migration, spread of cultural influences and dissemination of knowledge and understanding, including of science and technology'.[40] Globalisation has strengthened cultural interdependence between developed and developing countries enabling us to increase our understanding of other societies and develop more meaningful opportunities for cultural exchange.

The challenge of development in the age of globalisation is to promote cultural diversity and interdependence while implementing democratic controls over unfettered trade and reckless forms of investment. A Christian Aid/CAFOD briefing paper on globalisation states that:

> Globalisation is a process of increasing interconnectedness of individuals, groups, companies and countries. The technological, economic and political changes which have brought people closer together have also generated serious concerns over the terms of that globalisation. These concerns have also been generated by the realisation that while globalisation has led to benefits for some, it has not led to benefits for all. The benefits appear to have gone to those who already have the most, while many of the poorest have failed to benefit fully and some have even been made poorer.[41]

The increasing power and influence of international finance and investment organisations over the past half century has compelled some commentators to write the obituary of the nation state as an agent of development. Their concerns are based on a perceived erosion of democracy that has attended the shift of decision-making processes from national governments to regional trading blocs such as the European Union. The danger of regionalisation is that key decisions affecting our everyday lives will be taken by faceless, unelected bureaucrats in Brussels, Geneva or Washington who are unaccountable to national forums and their elected officials. Moreover, the accumulation of wealth and political clout in the boardrooms of major corporations combined with WTO trade rules and the increasing deregulation inherent in the investment policies of the World Bank and the IMF, are limiting the capacity of national governments to implement programmes that are consistent with social justice and equality. These concerns merit serious discussion given that development has to take root at local and national levels to bear fruit in the international arena. However, it may be premature to consider the nation state a spent force in promoting development and effecting positive global change.

For example, the European Union summit held in Seville in June 2002 considered proposals tabled by the British and Spanish governments 'to cut aid to countries such as Turkey and Bosnia that refuse to crack down on asylum seekers passing through their borders'.[42] The Anglo-Spanish plan to tie aid donations to compliance with hardline EU policies on asylum and immigration was vetoed by France and Sweden when a unanimous vote was required. The difficulty in establishing a common position on such contentious issues in international bodies like the EU and the UN is rooted in the pressures felt by politicians at a national level to act in the best interests of the state and the electorate. This was underlined in Seville, where France vetoed the asylum plan advocated by Tony Blair 'to protect its relations with francophone countries in North Africa and the Middle East', while Sweden commendably 'recoiled at the harshness' of the measures on poor countries.[43] Thus, developed countries can significantly influence decisions in the international arena either bilaterally or in tandem with other nation states. Therefore the challenge for the trade justice movement is to ensure that wealthy countries support policies toward eradicating poverty even when such policies might conflict with their own economic interests.

The Text

This text aims to introduce the key issues that are fundamental to our understanding of development. It is offered as a reference text or research aid for those active in the field of development, studying development issues at tertiary level or interested in enhancing their knowledge of the main economic and political forces that influence our lives. The contributors to the book include leading academic commentators in the development field and representatives of some of the main development NGOs that operate in both local and global contexts. While the text is not an exhaustive commentary on all aspects of development it provides useful suggestions (including web sites) for further reading on the issues raised. The chapters are designed both to introduce specific issues and to complement the contributions from other authors, particularly, as many of the themes addressed in the text are interconnected. It is also intended that the chapters can serve as 'stand-alone' introductions to the main issues highlighted in the book. Readers are encouraged to use the text as a manual for increasing their knowledge of development issues and, in the spirit of Freirean discourse, to use their understanding as the basis for action to effect positive change.

NOTES

1. The use of the terms 'developed world' and 'developing world' refer to the so-called First World and Third World. Alternative terms used in this

text include minority (First) and majority (Third) worlds, and North (Northern Hemisphere) and South (Southern Hemisphere). The developed world refers to wealthy, industrialised countries and the developing world to poor, underdeveloped countries. We accept the limitations of all of these terms, which have been used interchangeably in the text. For example, the term Third World is often considered derogatory as if suggesting a third-class status for people living in developing countries. In fact, this term emerged from the Third World during the Cold War, and referred to a possible third path to development which strictly followed neither capitalism nor communism. The terms 'developed' and 'developing' are also flawed in suggesting that poor countries should embrace a Western-led model of development, when social inequalities and divisions are strongly prevalent in industrialised countries. 'North' and 'South' represent a crude demarcation of developed and underdeveloped countries – for example, Australia is a developed country located in the Southern Hemisphere. 'Majority world' and 'minority world' are narrow, one-dimensional terms reflecting the fact that 80 per cent of the world's population live in developing countries and 20 per cent in developed countries. We acknowledge the validity of other terms not used in the text and those outlined above. The terminology of development is usefully outlined in Wolfgang Sachs (ed.), *The Development Dictionary: A Guide to Knowledge as Power* (London and New Jersey: Zed Books, 1992).

2. UNDP, *Human Development Report 1999* (Oxford and New York: United Nations Development Programme, 1999), p. 3.
3. UNDP, *Human Development Report 2001* (Oxford and New York: United Nations Development Programme, 2001), p. 20.
4. UNDP, *Human Development Report 2000*, p. 82.
5. UNDP, *Human Development Report 2001*, p. 9.
6. DFID, *Making Globalisation Work for the World's Poor: An Introduction to the UK Government's White Paper on International Development* (London: Department for International Development, December 2000), p. 4.
7. CAFOD, 'A Development NGO Critique of Globalisation: Submission to the House of Lords Economic Affairs Committee' (London: Catholic Agency for Overseas Development, February 2002).
8. Jean Somers, 'Debt: The new colonialism', in Colm Regan (ed.), *75:25, Ireland in an Increasingly Unequal World* (Dublin: Dochas, 1996), p. 171.
9. Somers, 'Debt: The new colonialism', p. 171.
10. Martin Khor, *Rethinking Globalisation: Critical Issues and Policy Choices* (London: Zed Books, 2001), p. 12.
11. The Drop the Debt Campaign is an extension of Jubilee 2000, a global coalition of NGOs and civil society organisations that vigorously campaigned for complete debt cancellation at the start of the new millennium. The campaign achieved significant successes with some debt liabilities being written off by developed countries; however, anti-debt campaigners regard this approach as piecemeal and insufficient in addressing the larger debt problem. A full analysis of the debt crisis can be accessed on <www.jubilee2000uk.org>.
12. Drop the Debt Campaign, <www.jubilee2000uk.org> (19 July 2001).

13. CAFOD, *CAFOD Guide to the WTO* (London: CAFOD, 2001).
14. CAFOD, *CAFOD Guide to the WTO*.
15. CAFOD, *CAFOD Guide to the WTO*.
16. CAFOD, *CAFOD Guide to the WTO*.
17. World Development Movement (WDM), 'Briefing Paper on GATS', <www.wdm.org.uk/campaign/GATS.htm> (27 January 2002). The WDM was one of the leading campaigning NGOs that ensured the defeat of the Multilateral Agreement on Investment (MAI) in 1998. It has played a valuable role in deciphering the trade jargon used in the WTO and exposing the effects of global trade on the world's poor. The WDM web site is a useful resource for information on global trade and investment issues.
18. Mohau Pheko (Africa Gender and Trade Network) was speaking at the World Development Movement conference 'Whose Rules Rule?' held in the Institute of Education, London (8–9 June 2002).
19. Regan, *75:25*, p. 189.
20. WDM, 'Briefing on Regulating TNCs: Making investment work for people: An international framework for regulating corporations' (London: World Development Movement, February 1999).
21. See the investigative journalism of John Pilger on the impact of globalisation in developing countries recorded in *The New Rulers of the World* (London: Verso, 2002). Pilger gathered evidence of human rights abuses and widespread exploitation of workers in factories in Indonesia manufacturing products for Western-based multinationals that claimed to operate a code of practice. The codes seem designed to allay the fears and salve the consciences of customers concerned that they may be purchasing goods produced by exploited workers rather than provide a modus operandi for corporations.
22. WDM, 'Briefing on Regulating TNCs'.
23. Sachs, *Development Dictionary*, p. 2.
24. UNDP, *Human Development Report 2001*.
25. Sachs, *Development Dictionary*, pp. 2–4.
26. *Collins Pocket English Dictionary* (Glasgow: HarperCollins, 1989).
27. Gustavo Esteva, 'Development', in Sachs, *Development Dictionary*, p. 12.
28. President Truman's Inaugural speech delivered on 20 January 1949, quoted in Gustavo Esteva, 'Development', p. 8.
29. Pilger, *New Rulers of the World*, pp. 15–45. Pilger describes events surrounding the *coup d'état* in 1965 and the consequences of the Suharto dictatorship for today's Indonesia – which has been a 'model pupil' of the World Bank and IMF.
30. Quoted in Esteva, 'Development', p. 6.
31. John Pilger quoted from his input to the World Development Movement conference 'Whose Rules Rule?', held in the Institute of Education, London (8–9 June 2002).
32. WDM, 'Briefing on Regulating TNCs'.
33. OWC, *Education for Sustainable Development in Northern Ireland* (Belfast: Environmental Education Forum and One World Centre, 2000).
34. *Irish Times* (7 September 2002).
35. *Guardian* (31 August 2002).

36. *Guardian* (24 August 2002).
37. Geoffrey Lean, 'They Came. They Talked. And Weasled. And Left', *Independent on Sunday* (8 September 2002).
38. *Guardian* (4 September 2002).
39. *Independent on Sunday* (8 September 2002).
40. Amartya Sen, 'Slicing up the Spoils', *Guardian* (19 July 2001).
41. Christian Aid and CAFOD, 'A Human Development Approach to Globalisation' (June 2000) <www.cafod.org.uk/policy/polhumdevglobsum1.shtml> .
42. *Observer* (23 June 2002).
43. *Observer* (23 June 2002).

WEB SITES

Catholic Agency for Overseas Development	www.cafod.org.uk
Christian Aid	www.christian-aid.org.uk
Development Education Association	www.dea.org.uk
Drop the Debt Campaign	www.jubilee2000uk.org
One World Centre (NI)	www.belfastdec.org
World Development Movement	www.wdm.org.uk
World Summit on Sustainable Development	www.worldsummit.org

Part I

Development Issues and Definitions

1   Measuring Development

Andy Storey

Underdevelopment is shocking: the squalor, disease, unnecessary deaths, and hopelessness of it all! No man [sic] understands if underdevelopment remains for him a mere statistic reflecting low income, poor housing, premature mortality or underemployment. The most empathetic observer can speak objectively about under-development only after undergoing, personally or vicariously, the 'shock of underdevelopment'. This unique culture shock comes to one as he is initiated to the emotions which prevail in the 'culture of poverty'. The reverse shock is felt by those living in destitution when a new self-understanding reveals to them that their life is neither human nor inevitable... The prevalent emotion of underdevelopment is a sense of personal and societal impotence in the face of disease and death, of confusion and ignorance as one gropes to understand change, of servility toward men whose decisions govern the course of events, of hopelessness before hunger and natural catastrophe. Chronic poverty is a cruel kind of hell, and one cannot understand how cruel that hell is merely by gazing upon poverty as an object.[1]

Measuring development presupposes defining what development entails. Only after touching on this issue of definition does this chapter move on to examine the most conventional measures of economic development – notably Gross Domestic Product (GDP) and Gross National Product (GNP). These remain the standard inter-national measures of economic development but, arguably, encompass only a limited understanding of how development affects the way in which people actually live. As a consequence GDP and GNP have had many criticisms levelled against their usage. As a method of measuring development the best known 'alternative' is the Human Development Index (HDI), which relies upon multiple (not solely economic) criteria. There are also concepts of under-development that point towards the potential impossibility of quantitatively measuring development (or its absence) at all; and, according to some theorists, the very *attempt* at measurement may result in, or reinforce, Western domination of the so-called 'Third World'. This chapter concludes by emphasising the necessarily inconclusive and open-ended nature of the topic, one that raises numerous questions but offers few, if any, answers.

DEFINING DEVELOPMENT

Measures of development are inextricably linked to definitions of development, highlighting the need for a better understanding of what development is before seeking to measure it. For many years this understanding seemed fairly unproblematic. For most economists and policy analysts, development was seen as equivalent to economic growth, of which growth of GNP – discussed in detail below – served as the main indicator. This was (and still is) usually expressed in 'per capita' (per person) terms, i.e., the gross, or total, national product was divided by a country's population to give an average figure for a country's level of economic development. Comparing GNP per capita from year to year provided a measure of economic growth relative to population size, and this, therefore, was the measure of development. This view of development still underlies much current official thinking. For example, until recently, the World Bank's annual *World Development Report*, in the presentation of its authoritative world development indicators, ranked countries from highest GNP per capita down to the lowest.

For many years also, development was officially seen not only as growth in the economy, but also as a transformation or shift of the economic structure away from primary goods (agriculture and raw material production) towards manufacturing and service activities. This was most famously articulated by Walt Rostow in 1960 in the *The Process of Economic Growth*, in which he developed the notion of 'stages of growth'. Rostow's stages were:

1. Traditional society
2. Preconditions for take-off
3. Take-off
4. Drive to maturity
5. Age of high mass consumption[2]

This crude, linear model came under increasing challenge, particularly in the 1960s and 1970s. The notion of 'growth without development' became dominant, with reference to countries like Brazil where impressive GNP per capita growth – and indeed a degree of Rostow-style structural transformation – seemed to co-exist with growing inequality and poverty for many. As a Brazilian politician remarked at the time, 'Brazil is doing well, but its people are not.' For the British economist Dudley Seers, alternative definitions of development were required:

> The questions to ask about a country's development are therefore: What has been happening to poverty? What has been happening to unemployment? What has been happening to inequality? If all three of these have declined from high levels then beyond doubt this has been a period of development for the country concerned. If one or two of these central problems have been growing worse, especially if all three have, it would be strange to call the result 'development' even if per capita income doubled.[3]

The development criteria suggested by Seers can be discerned, at least in part, in the later method introduced by the United Nations Development Programme (UNDP) in the form of the Human Development Index (HDI). The HDI encapsulates a concept of development as a process of enlarging people's choices, allowing them the opportunity to live longer, to acquire knowledge, etc. Thus, the narrow focus on economic growth and transformation is widened to embrace a variety of other (economic but also non-economic) factors. The 1980s saw a further crucial variable thrown into this definitional pot, that of environmental sustainability. In its most famous articulation from the Brundtland Commission, 'Development is sustainable when it meets the needs of the present without compromising the ability of future generations to meet their own needs.'[4] The central challenge of the environmental critique of 'traditional' development is to question whether unlimited access to narrowly defined economic development is sustainable within the constraints of a finite ecosystem.[5]

Beyond the standard measurement systems which are utilised by international agencies, there are many more contested definitional issues. Some writers, for example, see societies which have developed materially, but which have lost touch with traditional spiritual or cultural values, as having 'maldeveloped'. Others see the absence of political freedom and democracy as invalidating any claim to development regardless of levels of economic growth (sustainable or not) and the improvement of social indicators. One attempt to tie together some of these diverse strands of development was made by J.G. Speth:

> Sustainable human development is development that not only generates economic growth but distributes its benefits equitably; that regenerates the environment rather than destroying it; that empowers people rather than marginalising them. It gives priority to the poor, enlarging their choices and opportunities, and provides for their participation in decisions affecting them. It is development that is pro-poor, pro-nature, pro-jobs, pro-democracy, pro-women, and pro-children.[6]

This is a heroic summary, but it begs as many questions as it answers, including: Is it possible to have unlimited economic growth without, ultimately, destroying the environment? And, if the poor participate in *all* decisions affecting them, can an economy or society function effectively? Leaving aside these issues of principle, the definition of development suggested by Speth does not, to say the least, lend itself to easy measurement! This ultimately may be why many commentators still seek to measure development in a narrower and less holistic sense. It is to these narrower measurements that we first turn.

MEASURING DEVELOPMENT: STANDARD ECONOMIC DEVELOPMENT MEASURES

For most economists and policy-makers, development has usually been seen as equivalent to growth in economic activity. A basic measure of economic activity is Gross Domestic Product (GDP) – the total output of goods and services in an economy measured at market prices. It is important to note that this measurement should, ideally, only include the *final* output produced and not *intermediate* production. For example, if a factory produces screws that subsequently contribute to the value of a car also produced in the same country, then only the final value of the car should be included in GDP – to count the value of the screws separately would be to double-count. GDP, essentially, measures the total productive capacity (in use) of an economy. However, it does not measure the extent to which resources are *available* in that economy, in that not all that is produced is necessarily available to the residents of the country.

To order to capture the actual level of resource availability it is necessary to adapt GDP. One way to do this is to engage in a process of addition and subtraction. One could subtract from GDP certain outflows of resources. Some of these resources are related to capital – chiefly, profits remitted out of an economy by companies (often, though not necessarily, foreign ones) resident in that economy. Other resource outflows are related to labour – such as the percentage of wage income remitted home by migrant workers resident in the economy. Because capital and labour are often described as the 'factors of production', such outflows are referred to as factor outflows. Conversely, one could add to GDP certain inflows of resources. These would include capital-related flows, such as the profits remitted *into* an economy from a company operating externally – for example, in the case of the United States, the profits sent back to the United States from a US multinational company's operations in, say, Nigeria or Colombia. There will also be labour-related inflows, such as the portions of wages sent home to India or Bangladesh by workers from those countries labouring in the Gulf states or in Europe. Taken together, these are referred to as factor inflows.

For any given economy, there will be both factor outflows and factor inflows. Balancing out these different flows will yield what is called 'net factor income' – which can be either positive or negative. GDP plus or minus net factor income generates Gross National Product (GNP), the most commonly used measure of economic development. As mentioned earlier, the World Bank uses GNP (relative to population size) as the principal criterion for classifying countries according to their level of development. The main argument in favour of using GNP per capita as a measure of development is that unless there is an increase in the availability of goods and services then development is unlikely to be occurring – that is, a rising GNP per capita is, at least, a *precondition* for development. Moreover, the method of calculating GNP is reasonably well understood and widely recognised – most people know what is being measured and how. Also, all countries produce GNP estimates so international comparisons can be facilitated.

The arguments against using GNP per capita as a measure of development merit greater discussion because they have fed into the emergence of alternative measures of development. Firstly, and most fundamentally, GNP is an *economic* measurement and, by definition, does not take account of non-economic criteria. If, as discussed above, one's definition of development incorporates social, cultural or political considerations then any solely economic measurement has obvious limitations. Secondly, GNP, when expressed in per capita terms, takes no account of how resources are distributed. GNP per capita is a statistical average that has no necessary relationship to the actual resources available to any person in a country. A society with a highly unequal distribution of resources could have a high GNP per capita, while the majority of its population live in extreme poverty or even destitution. It was precisely this anomaly that prompted Seers (see above) to suggest instead an emphasis on factors such as unemployment and poverty as the proper criteria of development.[7]

Thirdly, GNP (as with GDP) is based on market prices. Non-market transactions are not necessarily covered. A variety of economic activities, especially in poorer economies, may not be included in GNP calculations. These typically include: the cultivation of food; the processing and cooking of food; the maintenance or repair of domestic equipment and clothing; the provision of household fuel and water; caring for children, the elderly and the sick; and participation in community activities. A common thread unites these disparate activities, namely that they are usually performed by women. Thus, GDP and GNP emerge as gender-biased indicators of development.[8] But it is not only women's work that may be undervalued or excluded from GDP and GNP. Activities taking place in the so-called 'informal' economy – perhaps involving barter or, at least, not passing through official market channels – are also usually underestimated or completely ignored by the standard measures of economic development.

Fourthly, market prices – the foundation stones of GDP and GNP – may not reflect the real social value or cost of producing an economic resource. For example, a chemical factory may produce (and thus make available) a drug that is valued at a certain market price and which is included in GDP/GNP on that basis. But this production may simultaneously generate considerable pollution and, strictly speaking, the cost of that should be reflected in the market price of the drug. In practice this is unlikely to be the case, and the pollution remains what economists call a 'negative externality', which should be somehow factored into any true measure of overall societal development but is often excluded under existing conventional practice.

Still on this fourth point, and even more critically, there is no guarantee that the economic activity comprising GDP/GNP is really a positive contribution to society at all. If a production activity involves serious environmental depletion and damage, then it might be more accurately considered a hindrance to society's development, whereas the GDP/GNP measure will automatically regard the marketed output as a boost to development. This point is underlined in the extreme example of a country that cut down all its trees, sold them for wood and then gambled the proceeds: GNP per capita would register a significant increase, whereas real societal development would clearly have been seriously impaired. In order to counter this sort of gross distortion some commentators have sought to develop environmentally adjusted measures of economic development.[9]

The issues of resource distribution (described above) and the environment have been tied together in the pithy observation of Edward Goldsmith that 'GDP growth is the rate at which the powerful are expropriating the resources of the weak to create garbage'.[10] This is a generalisation insofar as GDP (or GNP) growth could equally represent improved welfare for the poor and the production of socially useful goods, but it illustrates the potential dangers of a crude reliance on such indices as measures of development. In summary, there are significant arguments against any simplistic usage of GNP per capita as a measure of a country's development. Most of these arguments have been around for some time, but a difficulty has often been the formulation of any alternative measure of development that would tackle some of GNP's shortcomings, and simultaneously match it in terms of wide usage and relative ease of comprehension. Therein lies the significance of the Human Development Index (HDI), probably the only such alternative measure that has come close to matching GNP in those terms.

THE HUMAN DEVELOPMENT INDEX

Since 1990 the United Nations Development Programme (UNDP) has produced an annual publication called the *Human Development Report*. The centrepiece of this report is the Human Development Index (HDI), which ranks countries on the basis of developmental criteria extending well beyond economic indices alone. Specifically, the HDI is an amalgam of three variables for each country:

- Per capita income or output
- Life expectancy
- Educational attainment – itself an amalgam of each country's adult literacy rate and the average number of years spent at school

These three variables were chosen on the basis of their being proxies for, and/or means to achieve, other aspects of human development. Thus, a relatively high life expectancy is a good thing in itself, but it is also reflective of the quality of a country's health care, sanitation, etc. Educational attainment is likewise something to be valued for its own sake, but is also a means through which people are empowered to pursue other goals – such as economic progress or cultural self-assertion. Income is itself useful and, again, is a tool through which people may pursue social objectives. Each of these variables is converted into a ranking index (where 0 is the lowest and 1 the highest), which facilitates the calculation of an aggregate measure of human development for each country. Countries are classified as:

- Low human development (an index of 0.0 to 0.5)
- Medium human development (an index of 0.51 to 0.79)
- High human development (an index of 0.8 to 1.0)

Over the years this classification system has helped draw attention to the fact that some countries that appear very 'developed' in GNP per capita terms fare considerably less well on the HDI ranking. This is often as a result of their unequal resource distribution and correspondingly poor societal standards of life expectancy and educational attainment. Many of the Arab states of the Middle East (such as Kuwait) fall into this category. On the other hand, some countries with relatively low levels of GNP per capita emerge creditably on the HDI scale due to their comparatively high levels of social expenditure – Cuba and Costa Rica are examples of this. While the HDI is, like GNP per capita, a societal average, life expectancy or years spent at school simply cannot reflect income-style inequalities. For example, a rich person will usually live longer than a poor person but not by a factor of several million, as can be the case with income differentials. Thus, the HDI is much less vulnerable than GNP per capita to the problem of distortion by gross inequality – more egalitarian countries tend to do better on the HDI scale than they do on the GNP per capita league table.

While the HDI is still the centrepiece of the *Human Development Report*, the report's focus has broadened over the years, as described by Martinussen:

> … human development [was defined] as a process of enlarging people's choices. At first, attention was concentrated around the

choices in three essential areas: the opportunity to lead a long and healthy life; the opportunity to acquire knowledge; and the opportunity to have access to resources needed for a decent standard of living ... To these were later added considerations regarding political freedom and human rights; human development for women as well as for men; environmental and other aspects of sustainability; and themes regarding citizens' participation and opportunities to affect the political decisions in society.[11]

While the HDI itself is still built on the basis of the 'three essential areas', the supporting data and textual documentation of the annual reports have increasingly drawn attention to these wider issues of politics, gender relations and sustainability.

However, there are still some obvious shortcomings or limitations in using the HDI as a measure of development. One concerns the weighting of the three variables. The UNDP assigns each of the three an equal weight, which makes for relative simplicity but is inevitably somewhat arbitrary: for example, could it not be argued that life expectancy should be considered more important than educational achievement or level of income? Another limitation is the perennial issue of data reliability. For many countries, the data available on life expectancy, let alone other indicators, are very unreliable. Even where reasonably good data are at hand, information on the *quality* of, for example, education is not necessarily provided – one may know how many years, on average, children spend at school, but not how much has been learned during those years. Also, the HDI is vulnerable to the allegation of a certain Eurocentrism: average years' schooling refers to Western-type classroom schooling, thus implicitly devaluing other forms of education that might take place in, say, the African countryside.

A more radical concept of the way in which a measure of development may itself become a form of oppression is returned to in the discussion on post-development theory below. It relates to a wider debate about whether development can be captured in any meaningful sense by the tools and techniques of quantification. Indeed, *under*development may not lend itself to measurement based on quantification at all.

STRUCTURAL VIOLENCE

The condition of structural violence – which can be seen as a very broad-based measure of *under*development – has been examined by

Peter Uvin in relation to pre-genocide (pre-1994) Rwanda. This condition is characterised by extreme poverty – Rwanda, proportionately, may have had more absolutely poor people (perhaps 90 per cent of the population) than anywhere else in the world – but the concept cannot be limited to poverty alone.[12] Structural violence in Rwanda was also characterised by inequality, injustice, discrimination, corruption, and treatment of the poor with contempt. The poor – the vast majority of the population – were subjected to humiliation and a state of permanent exclusion from the benefits of 'development', benefits that neither they nor their children could ever hope to attain but which were flaunted in their faces by wealthy locals and foreigners. 'The poor were considered backward, ignorant, and passive – almost subhuman – and were treated in a condescending, paternalistic and humiliating manner', by both the Rwandan elite and by expatriates.[13]

> Long before the 1990s, life in Rwanda had become devoid of hopes and dreams for the large majority of people: the future looked worse than the already bad present... Peasant life was perceived as a prison without escape in which poverty, infantilisation, social inferiority, and powerlessness combined to create a sense of personal failure.[14]

Uvin's argument is a very convincing one in relation to the specific case of Rwanda. A key feature is his emphasis on dreams, perceptions and senses of personal failure – themes strongly alluded to in the opening quotation to this chapter from Denis Goulet. By their very nature these aspects of experience do not lend themselves to easy (if any) quantification, and yet they do clearly signify important dimensions of development or the lack of it. This shift away from quantification has been taken a stage further by a group of writers who have come to see all existing measurements of development as not only flawed, but as positively oppressive.

POST-DEVELOPMENT THEORY AND THE MEASUREMENT OF DEVELOPMENT

For some writers, dissatisfaction with the idea of development has led to a dissatisfaction with *any* attempt to measure development, and indeed to a rejection of the very concept of development itself. This line of thinking can be broadly classified as the 'post-development' approach, which draws from wider currents of postmodern philosophy and also from post-colonial theory.[15]

The largest intellectual debt of post-development theory is owed to the work of the French philosopher Michel Foucault. Following Foucault, post-development theory views development as a *discourse*:

> This theory argues that development constitutes a specific way of thinking about the world, a particular form of knowledge. Development is, in the Foucauldian sense, a particular discourse which does not reflect but actually *constructs* reality. In doing so, it closes off alternative ways of thinking and so constitutes a form of power.[16]

Thus, Foucault's discourse raised a key question: What effect does this form of power generate?

According to the post-development approach, the principal effect generated by development discourse is to legitimise and reinforce Western dominance over the 'Third World', in part through its very definition or categorisation of the 'Third World' as being in *need* of Western-style development, and constituting an *object* of/for development.[17] The 'Third World' is subject not only to the economic but also to 'the definitional power of the West.... Development... [is] a standard by which the West measures the non-West.'[18] For example, the absence of Western forms of technology is treated as a criterion not of difference but of underdevelopment, as is the absence of Western-style education in relation to the HDI (see above). 'Development discourse, from this perspective, is about disciplining difference, establishing what the norm is and what deviance is.'[19] Thus, the standard measures of development become instruments of oppression, tools whereby one group of people exercise power over others.

The essence of the argument being made by the post-development approach may be illustrated by means of a specific example. Ferguson, in his 1990 analysis of the World Bank's depiction of the economy of Lesotho, found a recurrent Bank emphasis on certain putative features of the Lesotho economy. One Bank formulation was that Lesotho was, allegedly, an 'aboriginal' economy, largely unexposed to commercial markets and the money economy – that it was a classically 'underdeveloped' (or 'deviant') economy. Ferguson shows how each of the alleged characteristics was wildly at variance with the historical record. Indeed, Lesotho had been part of a cash economy for centuries. Ferguson goes on to argue that the Bank's stylised portrayal of the Lesotho economy was inaccurate but not irrational, its purpose dictated by the Bank's need to find a role for itself in the 'development' ('disciplining') of that economy – through the financing of rural cattle markets, the building of rural roads, and other such 'development' projects.

As Ferguson documents, almost all these projects failed dismally to achieve their stated objectives, but criticism on those grounds is, he claims, pointless – because the projects did fulfil what he interprets as the (unstated) objective of justifying Bank involvement in Lesotho. Lesotho was constructed, defined and painstakingly *measured* as 'underdeveloped' in order to legitimise, and facilitate the exercise of, Western dominance over it. Institutional self-interest demanded that a certain *measured* view be taken of the Lesotho economy, and the necessary view was therefore taken – because those taking the view operated within a particular discursive framework of, to them, 'acceptable statements and utterances'.[20] One of the criteria of what constitutes 'acceptability' is the appearance of precision in measurement.

Ferguson is sceptical about whether the development discourse can be combated by pointing out its divergences from the reality of Lesotho or elsewhere, by pointing to the illusory nature of the precise measurements cited within the 'acceptable' discourse. For Foucault, '...the problem does not consist in drawing the line between that in a discourse which falls under the category of scientificity or truth [the realm of measurement], and that which comes under some other category, but in seeing historically how effects of truth are produced within discourses which in themselves are neither true nor false'.[21] A certain form or exercise of power cannot be undermined by 'truth' – an alternative measurement to get at some 'true' essence – in some objective sense. Development 'talk'/discourse has its own self-contained rationale and internal logic – its set of 'acceptable statements and utterances' – that is not amenable to challenge on 'objective' or measurable grounds. According to Foucault, 'it's not a matter of a battle "on behalf" of the truth, but of a battle about the status of truth and the economic and political role it plays'.[22]

Furthermore, to demonstrate the measurable 'failure' of development to reduce poverty is also to miss the point, because the real purpose of the development exercise (measurement included) is to discipline and dominate. This is, in Foucault's terms, 'the economic and political role it plays'. To call for policy change within the terms of the dominant development discourse, it is argued, simply reinforces the power of dominant institutions such as the World Bank because they can then rationalise further interventions in the name of 'corrective' action. As Crush puts it in *Power of Development*, 'development is always the cure, never the cause'.[23] For post-development theorists, the 'Third World' thus remains objectified, and its people's needs externally defined. The very act of measurement is inextricably tied to the act of domination. Not only do 'reformist' critiques misunderstand the point of the development exercise, they may also encourage the adaptation and extension of the underlying power relationship. Development, however revised, 'can only lead to further subjugation of the non-West'.[24]

Escobar argues for a fundamental reconceptualisation of the very meaning of underdevelopment 'if the power of the development discourse is to be challenged or displaced'.[25] What seems to be required is a willingness somehow to step outside the dominant world of what Ferguson terms 'acceptable statements and utterances' – the realm of measurement – and to prioritise and valorise other statements and worldviews, views of 'people beyond modernity' and their 'sagas of resistance and liberation'.[26] The extent to which post-development writers tend to deploy romanticised language when talking about non-Western communities is striking and problematic, but it conveys the extent to which the very logic of measurable 'development' is being rejected by some in favour of a radically different frame of reference and perspective.[27]

CONCLUSION

The question of measurement covers a very wide field. It moves from questions of how development might be defined, through some of the more conventional measures of development, to a questioning of whether the very act of measurement contributes to the perpetuation of oppression. More questions than answers are inevitably thrown up by a discussion of this sort. By way of conclusion, we might usefully bear in mind the dangers of undue attention to measurement, as humorously parodied in a quote from Robert Chambers:

> Economists have come to feel
> What can't be measured isn't real
> The truth is always an amount
> Count numbers, only numbers count.[28]

Even if we do not go so far as to see measurement as itself always part of the problem of 'underdevelopment', we could usefully take on board Chambers' caution against excessive reliance on quantification. His argument may be summarised as follows – what can be measured may not be what is most important, and an admission of imprecision (or approximation) is better than a bogus claim to exactitude. Chambers approvingly quotes John Maynard Keynes' observation that: 'It is better to be approximately right than precisely wrong', and these are indeed words to which development scholars and activists might well pay greater heed.[29]

NOTES

1. Denis Goulet, *The Cruel Choice: A New Concept in the Theory of Development*, cited in M.T. Todaro, *Economic Development*, seventh edition (Reading, Mass.: Addison-Wesley, 2000), p. 15.
2. W.W. Rostow, *The Process of Economic Growth* (Oxford: Clarendon Press, 1960), cited in Todaro, *Economic Development*, pp. 79-80.
3. Dudley Seers is cited in Todaro, *Economic Development*, p. 15.
4. Brundtland Commission, 1987, cited in J. Martinussen, *Society, State and Market: A Guide to Competing Theories of Development* (London and New Jersey: Zed Books, 1997), p. 150.
5. H. Daly, 'Sustainable Growth: An impossibility theorem', *Development*, Vol. 40 (1997), pp. 121–5; R. Douthwaite, 'Is it Possible to Build a Sustainable World?', in R. Munck and D. O'Hearn (eds), *Critical Development Theory: Contributions to a New Paradigm* (London and New York: Zed Books, 1999), pp. 157–77. Whether economic measures of development can be adapted or refined to take better account of these ecological constraints is discussed briefly in note 9.
6. J.G. Speth, 'Foreword', in UNDP, *Human Development Report 1994* (New York and Oxford: Oxford University Press, 1994), p. iii.
7. One measure of poverty is the 'poverty line', a minimum amount of money necessary for a person to acquire their most basic needs – people who fall 'below' this line would be classified as poor in an *absolute* sense. Alternatively, poverty could be measured in a *relative* sense, i.e., relative to other people in one's own society, in which case someone whose basic needs were satisfied could still be considered poor in the sense that they were unable to participate fully in the normal life of their society.
8. L. Benería, 'Towards a Greater Integration of Gender in Economics', *World Development*, Vol. 23, No. 11 (1995), pp. 1839–50.
9. Daly, 'Sustainable Growth'; Douthwaite, 'Is it Possible to Build a Sustainable World?'. 'Green GDP' or 'sustainable GDP' represent potential alternatives to simple GDP indicators as measures of development. 'Green GDP' is an aggregate measure of conventional GDP minus depletion of environmental assets, and minus costs of environmental degradation. Such an aggregate figure can reveal substantial losses of environmental resources which would be hidden in standard GDP

accounts; see Panos, 'Economic Forever: Building sustainability into economic policy', *Media Briefing*, No. 38 (2000). Similarly, Carley and Christie argue that natural capital needs to be factored into any discussion of national levels of development and endorse the replacement of GNP with a measure of 'Gross *Natural* Product'; M. Carley and I. Christie, *Managing Sustainable Development* (London and Sterling, Va: Earthscan, 2000), p. 30.

10. Edward Goldsmith, cited in A. Starr, *Naming the Enemy: Anti-Corporate Movements Confront Globalisation* (London: Zed Books, 2000), p. 1.

11. Martinussen, *Society, State and Market: A Guide to Competing Theories of Development*, p. 38.

12. P. Uvin, *Aiding Violence: The Development Enterprise in Rwanda* (West Harford, Conn.: Kumarian Press, 1998), p. 117.

13. Uvin, *Aiding Violence*, p. 128. Uvin pays particular attention to the role of aid in creating or compounding this condition of structural violence, for example: 'Aid financed much of the machinery of exclusion, inequality and humiliation; provided it with legitimacy and support; and sometimes directly contributed to it.' Uvin, p. 231. This last point is a reference to, for example, the expropriation of peasant land for aid-funded development projects.

14. Uvin, *Aiding Violence*, p. 117.

15. C. Sylvester, 'Development Studies and Postcolonial Studies: Disparate tales of the "Third World"', *Third World Quarterly*, Vol. 20, No. 4 (1999), pp. 703–21.

16. R. Kiely, 'The Last Refuge of the Noble Savage? A critical assessment of post-development theory', *The European Journal of Development Research*, Vol. 11, No. 1 (1999), p. 31. Emphasis in original.

17. M. Hobart, *An Anthropological Critique of Development: The Growth of Ignorance* (London and New York: Routledge, 1993); A. Escobar, 'Imagining a Post-Development Era', in J. Crush (ed.), *Power of Development* (London and New York: Routledge, 1995), pp. 211–27.

18. Z. Sardar, 'Development and the Locations of Eurocentrism', in Munck and O'Hearn, *Critical Development Theory*, pp. 44, 49. Also, pp. 44–62.

19. R. Munck, 'Dependency and Imperialism in the New Times: A Latin American perspective', *The European Journal of Development Research*, Vol. 11, No. 1 (1999), p. 68.

20. J. Ferguson, *The Anti-Politics Machine: 'Development', Depoliticisation and Bureaucratic Power in Lesotho* (Minneapolis and London: University of Minnesota Press, 1990), p. 18.

21. M. Foucault, in C. Gordon (ed.), *Power/Knowledge: Selected Interviews and Other Writings 1972–1977 by Michel Foucault* (New York: Pantheon Books, 1980), p. 118.

22. Cited in Gordon, *Power/Knowledge*, p. 132.

23. J. Crush, 'Introduction: Imagining development', in J. Crush (ed.), *Power of Development* (London and New York: Routledge, 1995), p. 10.

24. Sardar, 'Development and the Locations of Eurocentrism', p. 53.

25. A. Escobar, 'The Making and Unmaking of the Third World through Development', in M. Rahnema and V. Bawtree (eds), *The Post-Development Reader* (London and New Jersey: Zed Books, 1997), p. 92.

26. G. Esteva and M.S. Prakash, 'Beyond Development, What?', *Development in Practice*, Vol. 8, No. 3 (1998), p. 290.

27. A. Storey, 'Post-Development Theory: Romanticism and Pontius Pilate politics', *Development*, Vol. 43, No. 4 (2000), pp. 40–6; J. Nederveen Pieterse, 'My Paradigm or Yours? Alternative development, post-development, reflexive development', *Development and Change,* Vol. 29 (1998), p. 364.

28. R. Chambers, *Whose Reality Counts? Putting the Last First* (London: Intermediate Technology Publications, 1997), p. 42.

29. Chambers, *Whose Reality Counts?* pp. 41, 38–42.

WEB SITES

United Nations	www.un.org
UN Development Programme	www.undp.org
Statistics on Human Development	www.ids.ac.uk
Earth Summit	www.earthsummit2002.org
Information about aid agencies	www.aidagency.com
World Bank Data	www.worldbank.org/data
UNESCO	unescostat.unesco.org
OECD Development Indicators	www.oecd.org/dac/indicators/index.htm

2 The Colonial Legacy and the European Response

Gerard McCann

The European Union (EU) is the largest trading bloc in the world. It can boast greater economic strength than the United States (US) and Japan, and with the deciding vote at the G8 summits on global development, it has become the world's most powerful non-military alliance. The EU contains 6 per cent of the world's population, yet with only 370 million people, its combined Gross Domestic Product (GDP) accounts for over a quarter of the world's wealth. In terms of trade relations, the member states which make up this political and economic network account for 19 per cent of all global exports and a similar percentage of imports.[1] EU member states also represent the majority of former colonial powers and, as a consequence, the interaction with former colonies has altered significantly since the common market was founded at the Treaty of Rome in 1957. Since then, EU relations with developing countries have evolved from early policies typified by colonial trade agreements, to the sophisticated exchanges which now accompany the process of globalisation. These 'third country' policies – as the EU describes its contact with developing countries – have served to deepen EU involvement in the development process, yet have often resulted in negative outcomes for the developing world.

The relationship between the EU and developing countries has largely been informed by historical links between the key players in the integration of the European market system and the developing world, particularly countries in Africa, Indo-China and South America. Consequently, one of the key features of the debate around 'EU – third country relations' has been that sense of paternalism that has characterised trading and political agreements with developing countries since the 1950s. These agreements have subsequently tied many former colonies to the economic and political designs and fortunes of key EU member states. During periods of economic growth this interaction has had some positive effects, but conversely, when Europe suffers an economic downturn, as in the mid-1990s,

41

its dependent former colonies in the developing world are severely affected. Similarly, when economic theory and culture in the developed countries change, as they did in the 1980s with the emergence of a more purist neo-liberal ideology, the impact is immediately felt across the southern hemisphere.

Three pillars of policy have come to dominate the interaction between the EU and developing countries since the signing of the Treaty of Rome. First, *trade*: where developing countries now account for around 30 per cent of EU export markets and with the EU depending on southern hemisphere producers for commodities such as rubber, cocoa, uranium and copper. Second, *aid*: corruption in the distribution of EU aid to developing countries led to the collapse of the EU Commission (in 2000), and yet the EU remains the largest, most involved aid contributor to the developing world. Third, *the movement of people*: this issue was addressed in the controversial Treaty of Nice, framed in 2000, and covering the vexed and linked issues of 'immigration, asylum seekers and a common security policy'.[2] The role of the EU in relation to developing countries has been summarised in the European Commission's strategic document *Agenda 2000*:

> The Union must increase its influence in world affairs, promote values such as peace and security, democracy and human rights, provide aid for the least developed countries, defend its social model and establish its presence on the world markets ... prevent major damage to the environment and ensure sustainable growth with an optimum use of world resources. Collective action by the European Union is an ever increasing necessity if these interests are to be defended, if full advantage is to be taken of the benefits of globalisation and if the constraints it imposes are to be faced successfully.[3]

In terms of financial commitment, 9 billion euros were designated by the EU in 2001 for developing many of the most impoverished countries in the world. This increased to 10 billion euros in 2002. In emergency aid alone, the Humanitarian Aid Office of the EU (ECHO) allocated a total of 491.7 million euros in 2000 to 121 designated humanitarian crisis situations across the globe.[4] This financial commitment has steadily widened since the establishment of the common market, but the relationship has maintained an awkward *quid pro quo* character involving investment and support based on political and economic austerity measures in developing countries. Aid programmes have, however, tended to continue to prioritise those regions 'favoured' by member states, almost exclusively the former colonies. In this context, the process of globalisation – within which the EU is a central agent – has come to be regarded by some observers as a system of recolonisation across the developing world based on neo-liberal economics.

YAOUNDÉ AND INFRINGING GLOBALISATION

The origins of the EU's relationship with developing countries can be traced back to the earliest days of the integrating European trade system.[5] The feeder report on trade co-operation, the Spaak Report of May 1956, omitted references to third countries. However, the French government insisted during subsequent negotiations on the report that any new arrangements with third countries must include overseas territories as an implicit part of the French economic bloc. The French government approached the debate from the perspective that levels of dependency from associated overseas countries and territories (OCTs) were becoming burdensome in terms of aid and trading responsibilities, and set about seeking to share this responsibility with the other European countries. After the Treaty of Rome, relations between the European Economic Community (as the EU was known prior to 1992), and its former colonies was largely based on the Common Commercial Policy (CCP), which regulated trade with external countries. The central implementation mechanism of the CCP was the Common External Tariff (CET), which detailed the rules governing trade between the EU and developing countries. Article 110 of the Treaty of Rome stated that the CCP should aim to 'contribute, in the common interest, to the harmonious development of world trade, the progressive abolition of restrictions on international trade, and the lowering of customs barriers'. Attendant institutional arrangements were also a key aspect of this 'associationism'.

The European Commission, the executive wing of the EU system, was given the remit of negotiating with third countries on issues of mutual interest. The Commission acted with instruction from the so-called '133 Committee', which was named after the article in the Treaty of Rome regulating trade with developing countries. From 1957 onwards, the concept of 'special relations' with poorer nations, both in trade and aid, was built into plans for economic expansion. The Treaty also established the European Development Fund, which had the objective of targeting those regions most in need of support. The six signatories of the Treaty agreed to set aside $581.25 million for the fund, of which $511.25 million was allocated to French dependencies.[6] However, the drive for a financial association at this stage was not entirely Eurocentric.

In the early stages of development co-operation, anti-colonial and pan-African movements voiced concern about the emergence of the European Community and its potential effects on the development of the southern hemisphere. EC negotiations with African states in 1958 resulted in a Convention of Association and mechanisms which enabled 18 African states, and Madagascar, to benefit from the new developments in Europe. Indeed, by 1960, these new arrangements meant that 80 per cent of trade from the developing countries involved was with the six states of the EC, while 98 per cent of all aid contributions went to these states.[7] All the participants involved in the formation of this free trade system were aware at an early stage of the necessity of support for developing countrics and the possible impact of a new EC driven market system, particularly on former colonies. A Memorandum on 'Free Trade and its Conditions' (26 February 1959) – the first memorandum from the Commission of the EC to the Council of Ministers – noted that:

> ... it would seem necessary that any large-scale elimination of customs barriers and quotas between highly developed countries on the one hand and developing countries on the other, should be accompanied by a concerted and active development policy. In point of fact, the experience shows that free trade of itself does not lead to the elimination of disparities in levels of development.[8]

This sentiment formed the basis of the first major multilateral arrangement between developing states and the EC, named after the Cameroonian capital, Yaoundé, where the representatives met. The objective of this association was to enhance existing trade relations between the EC and developing countries, and work towards a mutually beneficial trading system. This agreement was later re-negotiated and enhanced in 1969 under the Yaoundé II Convention, which served to engage the (by then) 24 developing states in a process of economic exchange and political contract. Under the auspices of this Convention, the Associated African and Malagasy States (AASM) made representations to the European Parliament and succeeded in generating debate and action on a raft of development issues. The outcome of these discussions, combined with the increasing efficiency in the production of key commodities such as copper and other primary products, strengthened the relationship between developing countries and the EC to a point where the former could secure more favourable agreements from the latter. The expansion of EC development programmes combined with the Yaoundé Convention, encouraged other African states to enter into trading negotiations with the EC. For the developing countries engaging in this trade circle at this time, the benefits were quantifiable and activating growth within their economies.

Three factors, however, changed the relationship between the EC and the developing world in the early 1970s, and significantly altered the working partnership. The first factor was pressure from richer oil-producing countries in the developing world, under the auspices of the Organisation of Petroleum Exporting Countries (OPEC), on the lesser developed nations to accept serial increases in the cost of crude oil. This had an immediate and detrimental effect on the global economy. The EC needed to invest rapidly in 'friendly' oil-producing states in the developing world, or produce its own oil – which it eventually did through its North Sea oil fields. Second, the Cold War had polarised political allegiances within the developing world and proliferated conflicts and anti-imperialist struggles across the world, the most intense occurring in Vietnam and Angola. Thus, the stability of many regions, which were regarded as strategically crucial for global market sustainability, was threatened throughout the world. Third, the enlargement of the EC in the early 1970s increased the number of member states which had existing ex-colonial trading relations. For example, when the UK joined the EC in 1973 it brought with it a large network of developing world and commonwealth trading partners representing a market network in its own right. Similarly, both Spain and Portugal brought colonial partners into the EC with their accession in 1986. These factors cumulatively led to an overhaul of the Yaoundé system and set the scene for the comprehensive negotiations which led to its replacement by the Lomé Convention on 28 February 1975.

EC sensitivity to the unevenness of global development manifested itself on a number of occasions in the expansion debates and statements of the late 1960s. For example, a 1968 declaration by the Commission on 'The Achievement of the Customs Union' stated that:

Europe bears major international responsibilities ... It is the leading importer of products from the countries of the third world. Today, in its present form, it already has major responsibilities to the developing countries – and these will be even more important tomorrow when Europe is a larger entity ... it is Europe's duty to organize cooperation and association with the other main groups in the world.[9]

The Yaoundé protocol had outlined the procedures for interaction between the EC and developing countries in the area of development co-operation. This protocol established, in theory, a process that enabled developing countries to negotiate with the EC as joint stakeholders in development policy. The renegotiation of the Yaoundé Convention offered a new context for including more developing countries within the sphere of EC development programmes, and these states were increasingly adopting the view that independence could pay dividends by broadening the potential for exchange. Consequently, the first Lomé Convention proved a very positive forum for the 46 associates involved in negotiations, from Africa, the Caribbean and the Pacific region (ACP).

Signed in Lomé, the capital of Togo, the association was to operate in a capacity which maximised trade potential, while enhancing sustainable economic support initiatives. From the outset there was an acknowledgement of the need for a more equitable political and trading system between the EC and developing countries. The Preamble of Lomé asserts the necessity for 'a new model for relations between developed and developing States, compatible with the aspirations of the international community towards a more just and more balanced economic order'.[10] EC participation in Lomé was based to a large extent on its relationship with colonies, or former colonies, and the belief that it had a responsibility for the development of these states – especially during a period which would see the reconfiguration of the EC market system and European political structures. Furthermore, the accession of the UK as a member state in 1973 meant that new demands were being made from its former colonies. In addition, the British Commonwealth had a different understanding of development from that espoused by the former French colonies which had negotiated at Yaoundé. It introduced a concept of partnership.

The political imperative during this period of the 'special relationship' was to actively support ex-colonies. Under the terms of

the Convention, development assistance would be given to specifically enhance the economic infrastructures of developing countries.
Priority in trading relations would be given to ACP states with their
products given free access to the EC market. Moreover, ACP export
prices were protected from fluctuating markets by the awkwardly
named System for the Stabilisation of Export Earnings from Products
(STABEX). ACP states also received technical assistance from the EC
in certain fields of development to enhance their market competitiveness, while aid programmes were established to act as baseline
support for development. In return, the ACP states had to prioritise
and formalise their trading relations with EC member states. The idea
of the common interest was an important component of trade, aid
and economic agreements reached between representatives from the
ACP countries and the Commission. Thus, ACP countries could
operate in such a manner as to give parity to the exchange of trade
between the EC and developing countries. It is worth noting though
that many developing countries were excluded from this trade loop,
including some of the most impoverished developing states, such as
India, Bangladesh, Pakistan and Sri Lanka.

The first Lomé agreement meant that the ACP countries were
offered a partnership arrangement which enabled them to deal with
their own internal developmental, strategic and political concerns
without external interference. Furthermore, the Convention established an institution which would represent the interests of the ACP.
The operational title of this body was the Committee of Ambas-
sadors, which worked with the Commission on implementing the
detailed provisions of the Convention. This body ultimately
included the ACP–EC Council – made up of members from the
Council of Ministers, the Commission, and a government minister
from each of the ACP states – and an ACP–European Parliament joint
assembly. In general terms, the Lomé system was recognised as a
positive departure from the traditionally exploitative relationship
between European nations and the developing world. It was also
championed as evidence of the EC Commission's potential in
stabilising global market relations. Charlotte Bretherton and John
Vogler stated that 'the Lomé system, with its complex provisions and
strengthened institutions, consolidated a distinctive, Community
approach to development cooperation'.[11] Lomé I was, however, to
represent a highpoint in EC development co-operation. With
hindsight, the German government later regarded the Lomé I
arrangement as 'one of the greatest achievements' of the EC.[12]

Subsequent EC agreements were weighted increasingly on the side of the EC member states, and were recognisably less favourably disposed towards the developing countries.

Lomé was to be renegotiated on a five-yearly basis: Lomé I spanned 1975 to 1980; Lomé II, 1980 to 1985; Lomé III, 1985 to 1990; and Lomé IV was given a ten-year timescale from 1990 to 2000. At the completion of Lomé IV the number of ACP countries involved had increased to 71. The actual provisions of Lomé did not dramatically change over time, but fundamental shifts in the global economy strengthened the influence of European interests over developing countries. Furthermore, changes were evident not only in the composition of the association, but also in the enlarged membership and enhanced economic position of the EU which culminated with the political unification of member states through the 1992 Maastricht Treaty, the Treaty on European Union. The post-Maastricht EU had a more rationalised perspective on market liberalisation and a declining interest in the needs of the developing world. The market expansion and neo-liberalism of the 1980s, and the acceptance of these theories by the larger EU states, saw the relationship with the ACP countries and their need for a more stable system of trade – particularly with regard to their exports – causing tensions between the EU and the ACP states. ACP representatives were fully aware that trade liberalisation would leave the ACP economies open and vulnerable to EU imports. Restrictions were generally subject to Common Agricultural Policy (CAP) priorities which explicitly protected EU agriculture against competitive imports. By the 1990s, 10 commodities (coffee, rubber, etc.) accounted for approximately 80 per cent of ACP exports and 35 per cent of ACP countries were dependent on a single product for over 50 per cent of their export earnings. They were all products that the EU could not produce itself.

With the accession of the three new Mediterranean states to the EU – Greece, Spain and Portugal – the stabilisation of that region became ever more important to the EU's understanding of its own position in global terms. This shifting balance of power in Europe and a resurgent nationalism resulted in events, such as the breakup of Yugoslavia, which became central to the stability of the region. As a consequence, the EU began redirecting aid and prioritising development programmes in states on the immediate rim of the Mediterranean, rather than in former colonies.

External factors were also impacting on the EU–ACP 'special relationship' agreed in 1975, including powerful economic pressures from international financial institutions such as the World Trade Organisation (WTO) and transnational corporations (TNCs) within the EU itself. These agencies were critical of obstacles to market liberalisation or the single market system advocated by the EU, and portrayed 'third country' trade deals as an obstruction to the unification of market forces within the 15 member states. The flaw in the system – divergence – had been flagged up during the negotiations on Lomé II and was to persist as an issue into its subsequent rounds. The *Focke Report* to the European Parliament revealed the drifting relationships. It stated that: 'The structure of ACP–EEC trade reveals an acute imbalance ... The rule of free trade is meaningless for countries which, at the present stage, because of their production structures, have practically nothing to export to the Community.'[13] In a system fixated by market competition, a situation where countries had 'practically nothing to export' confused the relationship and the type of development envisaged in Europe.

LOMÉ IV

Developing countries were recurrently suffering from falling commodity prices due to fluctuating markets and an escalating debt crisis which increasingly tied their economies to World Bank loans. This meant that EU projects were becoming ineffective in the more vulnerable developing countries and failing to prevent a process of economic meltdown. These problems were compounded in the late 1980s with the collapse of command state economies in the Eastern bloc. This resulted in the reunification of Germany and the need for the EU to heavily commit resources to struggling economies in Eastern Europe. This militated against the ACP countries, which by the time of the Lomé IV negotiations in 1988–89 had doubled their debt liabilities to developed countries and the World Bank. In quantifiable terms, the poverty gap between ACP and EU countries was widening. In 1981, ACP debt had stood at $65 billion, but by 1986 it had reached a staggering $130 billion.[14] Meanwhile, between the conclusion of Lomé I and the signing of Lomé IV on 15 December 1989, the Lomé II and Lomé III agreements had become largely ineffectual in encouraging a mutually beneficial process of development. The General Agreement on Tariffs and Trade (GATT) Uruguay Round introduced other pressures on the culture of partnership which had typified the original Lomé agreement, with its drive towards establishing tariff-free markets where governments would seek to 'roll back' any intervention in the economy. Significantly, this economic development strategy sought to infringe on the protection which Lomé had afforded the ACP states. Neo-liberal economics disadvantaged less developed markets and producers on a global scale. According to Bretherton and Vogler, 'the principles underlying the entire edifice of Community development co-operation were increasingly challenged by the influence of neo-liberal economic orthodoxy, with its reliance upon non-interventionist, market strategies'.[15]

Lomé IV negotiations resulted in the imposition by the EU of conditionalities on development aid to developing countries. Apart from revising the timescales within which they were operating, from five to ten years, additional aspects were added to the existing Lomé provisions. The new criteria included political provisos such as respect for human rights, democratic principles and the rule of law. Support was subject to the understanding that political criteria underpin 'relations between the ACP states and the Community and all the provisions of the Convention'.[16] However, Article 5 of the Lomé IV Convention on human rights was imposed in such a way as to exclude a number of ACP countries from participating in trade with the EU. New EU criteria imposed on ACP countries included controlling their increasing debt to the financial institutions of the developed world, and ensuring that there was also commitment to environmental protection and 'regional economic integration'. The EU also demanded evidence of sustainable economic and political development policies in ACP countries.[17]

ACP countries were to find it increasingly difficult to export commodities to the EU with the introduction of EU standards and regulations on produce which, without significant investment, the ACP producers could not meet. The EU was particularly preoccupied with the single-market strategy during Lomé IV and the debates reflected the economistic priorities of the Council of Ministers at the time. For many representatives from the developing states the new EU trade and aid regulations meant a return to paternalism. Moreover, accelerated globalisation was reflected throughout the Maastricht Treaty. Post-Maastricht policies, underpinning EU relations with the developing world, were contained in Article 177 of Title XX of the Maastricht Treaty. Under the heading 'Development Cooperation', Article 177 states:

1. Community policy in the sphere of development cooperation, which shall be complementary to the policies pursued by the Member States, shall foster:
   - the sustainable economic and social development of the developing countries, and more particularly the most disadvantaged among them;
   - the smooth and gradual integration of the developing countries into the world economy;
   - the campaign against poverty in the developing countries.
2. Community policy in this area shall contribute to the general objective of developing and consolidating democracy and the rule of law, and to that of respecting human rights and fundamental freedoms.[18]

During the Lomé IV negotiations, the ACP countries' cycle of dependency on Western financial aid, in the context of the spiraling debt crisis, was reflected in the former colonies' declining influence in the EU. The ACP negotiating position was weakened by political and economic instability on the domestic front, and marginal influence on the EU. This imbalance facilitated the EU move away from partnership. The European Development Fund (EDF), the dedicated budget for development policy, increased marginally but the commitment was not proportionate with the problems being endured by the ACP countries.

Throughout the 1990s, the concept of 'Fortress Europe' emerged, reflecting the protectionist policies of EU states regarding the movement of people and products from developing countries to Europe. By 1995, when the review of Lomé IV was signed in Mauritius, the role of the EU in relation to ACP countries was one of benign competitor. The conditions on the relationship were further complicated by the revision of Article 5 to include a need for the 'application of democratic principles, the consolidation of the rule of law and good governance', with the qualification on good governance being 'a particular aim of cooperation operations'. The exclusion of states from the EU programmes for not applying the new EU criteria would become routine, yet there was no agreed interpretation of what good governance would in fact involve. The most visible difficulties regarding trade and aid with the ACP countries came not from developing nations themselves, but emerged between Germany, France and the UK over the extent of involvement in development. This was largely due to the fact that the signatories of the Lomé Convention represented individual EU member states in their own right rather than the total EU membership. For example, during the talks in Mauritius, France was concerned with the low levels of EDF support and urged an increase. Alternatively, Germany and the UK were seeking to reduce their EDF contributions to developing countries. At a particularly strained agreement at the Cannes Intergovernmental Summit of June 1995, original commitments were reduced globally – with the UK reducing its contribution by a staggering 23 per cent.[19]

The revisions to what became known as Lomé IV B (1995–2000) introduced a series of policy objectives for the EU member states. These included a concept of sustainability in which projects would have to become economically self-sustaining; a recommitment to the global market system; a consolidation of the democratic rule of law and human rights, particularly with relation to women's rights; and a focus on poverty reduction. However, institutional bureaucracy was to emerge as a central obstacle to the smooth implementation of these policies, with responsibility for development policy within the EU being divided up amongst three separate commissioners, two directorate-generals (DG IB, covering the Southern Mediterranean, Middle East, Latin America, South and East Asia, and DG VIII on development) and a special office (European Community Humanitarian Office – ECHO). This heavily layered structure was complicated further when the European Parliament (EP) gained an influence over the implementation of policies by attaining approval powers over budgets. With the ratification of the Amsterdam Treaty in 1999, the EP received co-decision-making powers with the Council of Ministers over development policy. Due to conflicting positions over the EDF contributions among the biggest players in the EU at the Mauritius and Cannes summits, the release and implementation of the EDF package was stalled and not finalised until the middle of 2002, owing to the lengthy ratification process for new agreements. By the end of the 1990s, EU links with developing countries were silting up with a heavily layered bureaucracy.

CRISIS, REFORM AND COMMITMENT

The 1999 revelations concerning the mismanagement of funds by the EU Commission represented a nadir in the operations of the European Union. The EU Court of Auditors had been repeatedly claiming that a figure in the region of 10 billion euros of an overall annual EU budget of 100 billion euros was somehow 'unaccountable'. Evidence of mismanagement had been notoriously difficult to trace or prove, given the mammoth bureaucracy within the DGs and across the various EU institutions. Events throughout 1998, however, monitored by the European Parliament and the media, propelled the EU system to the point where certain departments and individuals were seen to be responsible for, as the Commission termed it, continuing 'irregularities'. The Court of Auditors, an extraordinary Commission Committee, and the Belgium police investigated the two portfolios from which development policy is administered – the Directorate General for External Relations and Development (DG IB), and the Directorate General for Education (DG XXII). Subsequent allegations focused on the individual Commissioners involved – Manuel Marín, vice-president of the EU Commission and the head of the development budget, and Édith Cresson, EU Commissioner for Education and former French Prime Minister. Events which aroused suspicion included: in July 1998, the police being called in to look into the dealings of a director of the humanitarian aid programme on allegations of grants received in return for favours; in August the Court of Auditors revealed that the 1997 accounts had, to the date of audit, an estimated 5 billion euros 'misspent'; in September, the Commission's internal auditors accused the Marín department of 'metaphysical accounting' between the years 1993 and 1997; also in September, the internal auditors reported that an estimated 1.5 billion euros had been handed out under the EU's humanitarian aid programme without a request for receipts for expenditure; and in November, the Court of Auditors confirmed that 5 billion euros had been lost through 'mismanagement'.[20]

These difficulties came to a head in December when Paul van Buitenen, a long-established and respected auditor, delivered confidential accounts to a Member of the European Parliament which detailed much of the mismanagement. The evidence of 'irregularities' included the reasons for the resignation of Marín's Head of Internal Audit after warnings of fraud were not acknowledged, and details of aid cash being diverted from Rwanda to bureaucrats' accounts in Brussels. Notwithstanding the customary closing of ranks by colleagues regarding such allegations – with both Commissioners given a reprieve, and van Buitenen suspended from his job – the European Parliament voted on 14 January to establish a Committee to investigate and report on the whole affair. Following this exposure, Jacques Santer, the Commission President, announced the introduction of anti-fraud reforms which would penetrate the 'root and branch' operations of the Union's institutions. The entire Commission, along with Santer, was later encouraged to resign by the European Parliament because of the scale of the scandal.

For those involved in the day-to-day work of the Commission and those organisations – including agencies working in developing countries which are linked to the two implicated departments, DG IB and DG XXII – there was a sense of dismay and disbelief over the affair. Developing countries and development agencies regarded the events as a damaging breech of trust. The practical support initiatives and policies formulated between the EU and the developing countries at the Lomé Convention in 1989 had positioned the EU's member states as the principal supporters of development co-operation between developed and developing countries. The whole basis of this work was called into question by the fraud allegations, fundamentally undermining the EU's work in development policy. There was also the strategic problem of how faith in the EU's operations could be restored. The reform and extension of the Lomé system by 2000 seemed like one method of compensating for mal-adminstration at the highest levels. There were also calls for the EU to do justice to the spirit of co-operation with developing countries and aid agencies, firstly by setting its own house in order, and secondly, by uncovering the defrauded development budgets and directing them towards debt relief.

In addition to the dramatic events which led to the Commission's resignation and the subsequent reform initiatives, the development system was revealing signs of stress in other ways. At an operational level, the drift in commitment to developing countries has been further burdened by an increasing bureaucracy and qualifications attached to EDF and other forms of support. Up to 40 official signatures and accompanying documentation are required to approve the dispatching of emergency aid from the European Union to a crisis region in the developing world. In logistical terms this has meant the debilitation of the aid process and a failure to target the most needy regions in times of need. In effect, the system has led to a life-defeating bureaucracy which undermined the very spirit in which the aid was committed by the member states of the EU. For example, in 1998 Hurricane Mitch killed almost 7,000 people in Central America, tens of thousands were made homeless and a public health crisis created. The EU announced a prompt and seemingly effective package of emergency aid totalling £175 million.

The system failed at this point and the promised aid had still not arrived two years on despite commitments having been made to release £57 million in October 2000.

Moreover, a UK report delivered to the cross-party select committee on International Development at Westminster in 2000 revealed that it takes an average of four years and two months to arrange for the distribution of EU aid to a disaster zone in the developing world.[21] Another problem highlighted by the chair of this committee concerned the way in which the Mediterranean countries were receiving aid in order to stabilise their economies at the expense of Africa and Asia – where aid is most needed. Indeed, while 75 per cent of EU Overseas Development Aid went to the poorer regions in 1986, in 2000 only 54 per cent was allocated. The Mediterranean countries, which are eligible for development support but are not regions in need, received an estimated 1 billion euros, which contrasted sharply with the support given to the whole of Asia with its crippling poverty and debt crisis – it received less than half of that figure. The main factor behind this imbalance was undoubtedly political pressure from member states on the Mediterranean coast, which have a commercial interest in supporting markets on their southern borders. From the perspective of developing countries, the economic shift in the relationship with the EU has been compounded by the EU's treatment and criminalisation of asylum seekers from the developing world. Apart from the mass detention of people from the developing world in prisons across the EU, the example of over 1,000 deaths per year of Africans trying to enter the Canary Islands is an unwritten and unreported indictment of an evolving 'Fortress Europe'.

These revelations regarding the imbalance in aid distribution and the bureaucracy which cripples aid commitments emerged only one month after formal agreements were made between the EU and 77 ACP states in a 20-year partnership on trade, political and aid relations. The ACP states involved were some of the most severely indebted and represented more than 650 million of the world's most disadvantaged people. The Cotonou Agreement of 23 June 2000 resulted from an ongoing dialogue to replace the Lomé Convention, which had underpinned trade co-operation between the ACP states and the EU since 1975.[22] The European Development Fund designated 13.5 billion euros for the first five years of this agreement and is set to position the EU as the foremost provider of official development assistance. Its objective is to 'support the ACP governments in their attempts to create a balanced macroeconomic context, expand the private sector and improve both the quality and coverage of social services'. The revised criteria for involvement – with political qualifications – included integration within the global economy, clauses on equality between men and women, sustainable management of the environment and the traditional battle-cry of the EU, the reciprocal removal of trade barriers.

CONCLUSION

The relationship between the most dynamic market on the globe (the EU) and the poorest regions has undoubtedly deteriorated since the concerted drive towards neo-liberalism by the G8 states and the international financial institutions. The introduction of neo-liberal policies across the globe has been disastrous for the least developed countries, and the reduction in aid commitments from the EU, from 0.33 per cent of donors' GDP in 1988 to 0.23 per cent in 1998, has diminished the development process. Indeed, the ACP countries' share of EU trade alone has declined from 6.7 per cent in 1976 to 3 per cent in 1998, and the economic relationship has also reached a point where 60 per cent of total exports from developing countries to the EU have been limited to only 10 commodities. This has also contributed to a situation where, at the beginning of the new millennium, only 6 per cent of African trade is with other African countries.[23] In effect, the interaction between the EU and the developing world has declined since the 1970s when it was, from the viewpoint of the developing countries, a developmental partnership which was beneficial for both parties. Although in the post-11 September 2001 context there has been an obvious play-off over questions of political qualifications, emigration and the distasteful practice of 'repatriation', the options for beneficial EU investment, structural aid and trade development are still open for debate. At this early stage of Cotonou, the emerging policies seem innovative enough to have the potential of assisting ACP states in developing their own indigenous economic bases, but the institutional and bureaucratic barriers within the EU remain. The problems of EU reform and the weight of its bureaucracy are serious concerns for the ACP countries, and although monitored diligently by a number of non-governmental organisations, any attempt to improve the aid and trade cycle without delivering targeted and efficient outputs could make the whole Cotonou strategy, and EU commitment to the developing world, ineffectual.

NOTES

1. Neill Nugent, *The Politics and Government of the European Union* (London: Macmillan Press, 1999), p. 440. Also see Enzo Grilli, *The European Community and the Developing Countries* (Cambridge: Cambridge University Press, 1993), pp. 137–46; and Martin Holland, *The European Union and the Third World* (London: Palgrave, 2002), pp. 25–51. G8 is the group of eight leading industrial nations.

2. Christopher Stevens, 'EU Policy for the Banana Market: The external impact of internal policies', in H. Wallace and W. Wallace, *Policy Making in the European Union* (Oxford: Oxford University Press, 1997), pp. 325–51. For the Treaty of Nice and all EU treaties, visit the official documentation website <europa.eu.int/eur-lex>.

3. European Commission, *Agenda 2000* (Brussels: EC, 1997), a:27.

4. ECHO, *Humanitarian Crises Out of the Spotlight* (Brussels: Humanitarian Aid Office, 2001), p. 20.

5. The Community has enlarged five times since the original membership (West Germany, France, Italy, the Netherlands, Belgium and Luxemburg) to include the United Kingdom, Denmark and Ireland in 1973; Greece in 1981; Spain and Portugal in 1986; Austria, Finland and Sweden in 1995; and after 2004 it is anticipated that most of the old Eastern-bloc countries, bar Russia, will gain accession.

6. Denis Swann, *The Economics of the Common Market* (Harmondsworth: Penguin Books, 1995), p. 359.

7. Grilli, *The European Community and the Developing Countries*, p. 15.

8. Quoted in David Weigall and Peter Stick (eds), *The Origins and Development of the European Community* (Leicester: Leicester University Press, 1992), p. 118.

9. Weigall and Stick, *The Origins and Development of the European Community*, p. 145.

10. Charlotte Bretherton and John Vogler, *The European Union as a Global Actor*, (London: Routledge, 1999), p. 114. The sequence of Association agreements made by the EU are: Treaty of Rome 1958–63; Yaoundé I 1964–69; Yaoundé II 1969–75; Lomé I 1975–80; Lomé II 1980–85; Lomé III 1985–90; Lomé IV 1990–2000; Cotonou 2000–20.

11. Bretherton and Vogler, *The European Union as a Global Actor*, p. 118.

12. Quoted from *Die Zeit*, by A. Erridge, 'The Lomé Convention', *World Politics*, Paper 12 (Milton Keynes: The Open University Press, 1981), p. 9.

13. European Parliament, *Focke Report* (Strasbourg: European Parliament, 1980), p. 14.

14. J. Ravenhill, 'When Weakness is Strength: The Lomé IV negotiations', in I.W. Zartman (ed.), *Europe and Africa* (Boulder, Colo.: Lynne Reiner, 1993), p. 42. Also Bernard Waites, *Europe and the Third World* (Basingstoke: Macmillan, now Palgrave Macmillan, 1999).

15. Bretherton and Vogler, *The European Union as a Global Actor*, p. 119.

16. *Lomé IV B* (Brussels: EC, 1995). Also, European Commission, 'Industrial and Economic Co-operation between the European Union and the Developing Countries' (Brussels: EC, March 1995); European Commission, 'Development: The Lomé Convention' (Brussels: EC, 2000).

17. Desmond Dinan, *Ever Closer Union* (London: Macmillan, 1999), p. 506. Also see Hazel Smith, *European Union Foreign Policy* (London: Pluto Press, 2002).

18. *Maastricht Treaty* (Brussels: EC, 1992) Title XX, Article 177. Visit site <europa.eu.int/eur-lex> for the treaty and attendant documents.

19. With the election of the New Labour administration in May 1997 a review of international development policy was undertaken which reversed the decline in British government contributions during previous Conservative administrations. See the Department for International Development's White Papers: *Eliminating World Poverty: A Challenge for the Twenty-First Century* (London: DFID, 1997) and *Eliminating World Poverty: Making Globalisation Work for the Poor* (London: DFID, 2000).

20. See Gerard McCann, 'Doing Lomé Justice: Managing EU aid', *Global Issues* (Spring 1999), p. 7. Also for a thorough insight into the role of TNCs in the EU see Belén Balanyá et al., *Europe Inc.* (London: Pluto Press, 2000), pp. 3–49.

21. Cited in a speech by the Parliamentary Under-Secretary of State for International Development, George Foulkes, at a debate on EU development policy in the House of Commons (Hansard, 13 July 2000).

22. The Cotonou Agreement is available at web site <europa.eu.int/comm/development/cotonou>. Also see the ACP site <www.acpsec.org>.

23. European Commission, 'Development: The Lomé Convention' (Brussels: EC, 2000), pp. 6–7. Also see <www.oneworld.org/ecdpm>. For an assessment of the adaptation of economic and monetary union, see Charles Wyplosz (ed.), *The Impact of EMU on Europe and the Developing Countries* (Oxford: Oxford University Press, 2001).

WEB SITES

One World NGO	www.oneworld.org/ecdpm
ACP Secretariat	www.acpsec.org
Development NGO	www.twnside.org.sg/index
Think-Tank Prometheus Europe	www.prom.org
Think-Tank Notre Europe	www.notre-europe.asso.fr
Bond UK NGO	www.bond.org.uk
Centre for Economic Policy Research	www.cepr.org
Cotonou Treaty	europa.eu.int/comm/development/cotonou
EU Treaties	europa.eu.int/eur-lex
Agenda 2000	europa.eu.int/comm/agenda2000
EU online web site	europa.eu.int
European Parliament	www.europarl.eu.int
A weekly EU newsletter	www.european-voice.com

3 Towards the Globalisation of Justice: An International Criminal Court

Paul Hainsworth

Globalisation is Janus-faced. On the one hand, for instance, it has the potential to impoverish the life and rights of individuals in one part of the globe, via decisions made in another part. According to Susan George, 'Globalisation is a process ... [and] a system which is being pushed forward and put in place by the very largest industrial and financial transnational corporations ... it moves wealth from the bottom to the top.'[1] George Monbiot presents a similarly critical doomsday scenario for the future: 'The world will consist of a single deregulated market, controlled by multinational companies, in which laws to protect the environment or human rights will not be allowed to survive.'[2] On the other hand, the universalising reach of globalisation can be utilised as a force of progress, international justice and societal improvement. In this sense, it is part of the process of creating a cosmopolitan citizenship, which endows individuals and states with broader, extra-national rights and responsibilities.[3] Ideally, the quest to establish an effective international criminal court – to prosecute perpetrators of the most heinous crimes – falls into the latter category of classification.

In this chapter, the pathway to set up an international criminal court (ICC) is assessed. The first section, therefore, examines briefly the case of what many observers see as the ICC's early predecessor, that is, the 1946 Nuremberg Tribunal. The next section turns to the more contemporary attempts to create an international system of justice, that is, the ex-Yugoslavia and the Rwanda Tribunals, set up in the 1990s. These bodies, of course, were constructed on an ad hoc basis to pursue justice in specific situations and geographical areas. Unsurprisingly, there have been ongoing calls to set up similar bodies to prosecute individuals for very serious and notorious crimes perpetrated in such places as Cambodia, Chile, East Timor and Sierra Leone. This short list, moreover, is not exhaustive; it could easily be expanded upon.

More recently, though, the debate about international justice has moved markedly away from a resort to ad hoc tribunals covering geographically limited jurisdictions or fixed time-spans. The focus has now turned increasingly towards setting up a truly global and permanent international criminal court. This, a key development issue in today's world, is the principal focus of the chapter. The campaign to establish an ICC, or *the* ICC, has gathered momentum over the past decade or so and culminated in the signing of the 1998 Rome Statute (see below). A process of country-by-country ratification of the Statute has duly followed this event, although one significant global and key player, the United States of America (USA) has been conspicuously reticent here – a theme that is assessed in the next section. The debate about an ICC and the issue of international justice, though, was put into a new context after 11 September 2001, following the fatal attacks on the World Trade Center twin towers in New York and on the Pentagon in Washington. The penultimate section of the chapter, therefore, assesses the relationship between these tragic events and the call for an ICC. The conclusion draws the main points of the chapter together and, at the same time, supports the case for the ICC.

NUREMBERG

An immediate post-war attempt to produce an international mechanism of justice was the Nuremberg Tribunal. The Nuremberg Tribunal was created in 1946, by the victorious Allied powers, in response to what happened during the Second World War. The Nazis were seen to have committed some of the most heinous crimes known to the world, including the 'Final Solution' of the Holocaust. The remit of the Nuremberg Tribunal was to prosecute individuals acting on behalf of a state for war crimes (committed against other nationals) and crimes against humanity (committed internally), with the death penalty serving as the ultimate punishment for those declared guilty. A similar body, the Tokyo Tribunal, was set up to prosecute Japanese perpetrators of serious crimes, notably General Tojo, but significantly and controversially not Emperor Hirohito.

Nuremberg was thus an important step in the process of trying *individuals*; it prioritised international and humanitarian obligations above national ones where crimes against humanity were concerned. This principle would be resuscitated some years later in the setting up of the ex-Yugoslavia and Rwanda Tribunals and during the ICC debate. Unlike these more recent innovations though, Nuremberg was, without doubt, a 'victors' tribunal'. Its working procedures were marked by this reality. For instance, as Geoffrey Robertson points out, only the defeated were being prosecuted for war crimes; all the prosecutors and judges were nationals of the Allied powers and all the defendants' lawyers were German.[4] Nevertheless, despite these failings, Robertson is convinced of the overall positive significance of Nuremberg:

> Nuremberg was a show trial, but one in which the victors' sense of fairness was as much on show as the vicissitudes of the vanquished ... Nuremberg stands as a colossus in the development of human rights law, precisely because its Charter defined crimes against humanity and its procedures proved by acceptable and credible evidence that such crimes had been instigated by some defendants.[5]

The Charter of the Nuremberg Tribunal set a precedent, which later calls for an ICC and other tribunals would follow. It ruled that individuals were responsible for actions – they could not hide behind the sovereignty of states and claim that they were only obeying orders in the perpetration of heinous crimes. The Tokyo Tribunal also established the principle of criminal liability for permitting atrocities; in effect a concept of command responsibility that, later in the 1990s, would be applied to the Serbian leaders Radovan Karadzic and General Mladic. From the outset, the nascent United Nations (UN) recognised the need for a body such as an ICC. Resolution 260 (9 December 1948) adopted the Convention on the Prevention and Punishment of the Crime of Genocide, and asked the International Law Commission (ILC) to investigate the desirability and possibility of setting up a body to try people for genocide. The General Assembly gave some attention to this theme in the 1950s, but no draft statute emerged for a long time, with – in particular – no acceptable definition of aggression being agreed upon. This was to prove a nagging definitional problem even when the Rome Statute for an ICC was agreed upon some 50 years later.

THE EX-YUGOSLAVIA AND RWANDA TRIBUNALS[6]

In the 1990s, the call for international justice was revived to meet the desperate situations in Rwanda and in ex-Yugoslavia. At the same time, in 1998 in the UK, it was significant that the House of Lords recognised that the Chilean ex-dictator, General Augusto Pinochet, then temporarily resident in England, was individually responsible for terrible crimes committed under his stewardship as head of state. In short, in these contexts, arguments of national sovereignty were tried against principles of international law and justice, and the former category was found to be wanting. Amidst widespread global attention, the case against Pinochet collapsed in the UK, on the grounds of the ex-dictator's unfitness to stand trial due to ill health. Nonetheless, the spectacle of him being pursued for human rights abuses whilst residing abroad will surely impact on the thoughts and lifestyles of other individuals and human rights abusers seeking safety and security outside their own country.

The International Criminal Tribunal for the Former Yugoslavia (ICTFY), or Hague Tribunal, was set up by the United Nations Security Council (UNSC) – via Security Council Resolution 808 – on 27 May 1993. The mechanism for establishing this body was Chapter VII of the UN Charter, which was specifically concerned with maintaining or restoring peace. In effect then, the ICTFY was an arm of the UNSC and, essentially, a response to the ethnic cleansing and human rights abuses that had bedevilled the territory in question. As such, it began work slowly – with not a single prosecution until 1997 – and only picked up momentum gradually. In August 2000, the Bosnian Serb leader Radislav Krstic was sentenced by the Tribunal to 46 years for his part in the massacres at Srebenica, perhaps the most shocking and sadistic act of mass killing in post-war Europe. Currently, the ex-President of the former Yugoslavia, Slobodan Milosevic, is before the Hague Tribunal – although he refused to recognise its jurisdiction. It is, though, a significant occasion, since a head of state is being prosecuted for atrocities committed by troops under his overall command.

Moreover, an important contribution to international law and justice was the Hague Tribunal's ruling that war crimes and crimes against humanity did not depend upon an international or internal armed conflict situation being classified as such. These crimes were now legally classified as so serious that they were categorised as capable of being perpetrated at any time, in any situation – thus surpassing the restrictive interpretation of the 1949 Geneva Conventions.

In November 1994, a second ad hoc body, the Rwanda Tribunal, was set up as an appendage to the Hague Tribunal, although it was based largely in Arusha and Kigali. Again, the new tribunal – like its immediate predecessor – was a response to Chapter VII of the UN Charter. In this context, the movement of armed refugees, as a result of the Rwanda crisis, was interpreted as a threat to the international peace and security of nearby states. Significantly, the Rwanda Tribunal recognised that crimes against humanity could be committed in peacetime. Both the Rwanda and ICTFY tribunals also recognised that serious human rights abuses could be committed not only by state actors – as Nuremberg ruled – but also by non-state actors that aspired or claimed to rule. A further important difference between Nuremberg and the two ad hoc bodies of the 1990s was that the latter tribunals did not exact the death penalty. This factor encouraged some perpetrators of serious crimes in Rwanda to opt for international justice rather than the potentially life-threatening rulings of their national courts. The Rwanda Tribunal has had some modest successes in bringing perpetrators of serious crimes to justice, including in 1998 the former Rwandan Prime Minister, Jean Kambanba, who pleaded guilty to the crime of genocide.

It is worth underlining the ad hoc nature of the ex-Yugoslavia and Rwanda Tribunals. They were important steps towards implementing a system of international justice and, at the same time, they provided full recognition of the rights of victims and the protection of witnesses. But a more comprehensive path to addressing questions of impunity, crimes against humanity, war crimes and the like, lay in the creation of a permanent international criminal court, with a wider, global remit. Indeed, those responsible for the operations of an ICC could learn from some of the lessons of its predecessors – for instance, human rights training for top personnel could be improved upon. It was also important that prosecutors and judges should not be housed together and serviced by the same support staff. In short, justice had to be impartially dispensed and seen to be done.

THE INTERNATIONAL CRIMINAL COURT

It was not until 1994 that the International Law Commission (see above) submitted to the UN General Assembly its draft statute for an ICC. The General Assembly then proceeded to set up an Ad Hoc Committee on the Establishment of an International Criminal Court, whose report was then studied by the General Assembly before it set up the Preparatory Committee on the Establishment of an International Criminal Court. The last-named body, in 1996–98, prepared a draft for an international conference, which took place in

Rome. The Rome Statute for an International Criminal Court was then adopted on 17 July 1998, by an overwhelming majority of 120 votes to 7. Among the minority against the Statute were the world's most populous states: the USA, India and China. By December 2000, however, 139 states (including the USA) had signed up to the Statute. The Rome Statute was scheduled to come into force when 60 countries had *ratified* it and this duly happened in April 2002, leading to 1 July 2002 being designated as lift-off day. At the time of writing 79 countries have ratified the Statute.

The ICC is to be a permanent body, which will bring to justice individuals who commit the most serious violations of international humanitarian law: war crimes, crimes against humanity, genocide and (to be defined) aggression. War crimes are serious violations of the 1949 Geneva Conventions and other serious violations committed on a large scale in international armed conflicts. Crimes against humanity are prohibited actions perpetrated against civilian populations – such as murder, extermination, enslavement, deportation or forcible transfer of population, torture, rape, sexual slavery, enforced prostitution, forced pregnancy, enforced sterilisation, enforced disappearance and apartheid. Genocide covers specifically prohibited acts perpetrated with a view to destroying, wholly or partially, a national, ethnic, racial or religious group. The crime of aggression is still to be agreed upon and this definitional work will preoccupy the Preparatory Committee on the ICC, notably the Working Group on the Crime of Aggression. The ICC will be complementary to national jurisdictions, and will only become active if national legal systems are unwilling or unable to pursue suspects.

The Rome Statute was a compromise, since there was much discussion and dispute about the type of ICC to be set up. Robertson, for instance, divides the protagonists here into three groupings. First, there were those countries, including the UK, which wanted a powerful prosecutor, and an ICC genuinely independent of the UNSC with a truly global remit. Second, there were those countries, including the USA, France and China that wanted an ICC beholden to the UNSC. Third, there were those countries, including Iran, Iraq and Indonesia, which did not want an ICC at all.[7] Of course, the discussions surrounding the ICC were not simply the preserve of states and IGOs (international governmental organisations). NGOs (non-governmental organisations) too – such as Amnesty International and Human Rights Watch – became closely involved in the campaign for an ICC. The main NGOs coalesced under the broad umbrella

Coalition for an International Criminal Court (CICC), which was formed in 1995 and comprised about 1,000 organisations, as well as international law experts from around the globe.

Amnesty International, the global human rights organisation, defined the ICC as 'an enormous step forward in the fight against impunity and those responsible for genocide, crimes against humanity and war crimes'.[8] According to Mary Robinson, the former high-profile United Nations Commissioner for Human Rights (UNCHR), 'The Rome Statute is a historic achievement, establishing for the first time a universal framework to end impunity for the most serious crimes under international law.' Robinson further contended that the ICC's Statute 'for the first time ... codifies certain acts as war crimes when committed in an international armed conflict'.[9] Another informed observer summed up these sentiments towards the ICC when stating that 'The statute is the product of years of negotiation between human rights organisations and governments worldwide for an effective international system of investigation, prosecution and trial to deal with the most heinous crimes by individuals.'[10] Welcoming the ICC as 'a giant step forward for mankind', British Foreign Office Minister Peter Hain contended that tyrants and dictators across the world would sleep less soundly as a result of the ratification of the Statute.[11]

For some observers, though, the ICC statute does not go far enough. For one thing, unlike Nuremberg, its remit is not retroactive. Hence, past violators of human rights have effectively been granted immunity from prosecution by the Court. In this sense, the ICC is a court of the future. Also in the spirit of compromise (in effect, watering down its remit), the signatories in Rome agreed to no changes (improvements) to the ICC and its Statute until after a seven-year embedding period.

NOT-SO-SPLENDID ISOLATION: THE USA AND THE ICC

The ICC has not been universally welcomed. Some of the stiffest opposition has come from the USA. For one thing, the USA under President Clinton was reluctant to vote for the Rome Statute. Only in December 2000, at the 'eleventh hour', and more with resignation than enthusiasm, did the Clinton administration sign up for the ICC. Full ratification was, however, another matter and with the onset of the Bush presidency in 2001, the new administration not only shied away from ratification, but even postured about reneging on the USA's December 2000 signature. According to the former USA Ambassador to the UN, Bill Richardson, speaking in August 2001,

> The Bush administration is discussing 'unsigning' the treaty. The administration has already rejected, or expressed reservations about, some half-dozen international agreements; the court appears to be next in line. But to pack up and leave now would send the wrong signal to the world and be a serious mistake.[12]

Moreover, there are the delicate questions of whether a state can legally 'unsign' a treaty that it has not ratified, and whether international law allows a signatory to defeat the purpose of a treaty, even one that it does not intend to ratify. Nevertheless, in May 2002, the Bush administration took the momentous step of officially distancing the USA from the Statute and refusing to be bound by it.

The main concerns of USA opponents to the ICC have centred upon fears of loss of sovereignty and the prospect of seeing USA military personnel or decision-makers being prosecuted, albeit for heinous crimes, by a foreign court. Opponents of the ICC claimed that, if it were to be adopted, it would contravene the guaranteed constitutional rights of American citizens and open up the possibility of 'politically motivated' rulings against the USA. There were fears too concerning the competence of ICC judges and prosecutors, as well as (we recall) the definition of the crime of aggression. In addition, opponents of the ICC maintained that the USA, if it ratified the body, would forfeit the right to protect its national security. For example, it was feared that the USA would need prior approval before any military action took place, or it would run the risk of ICC prosecution. Adam Roberts, Professor of International Relations at Oxford University, voiced strong and critical disappointment over the USA's attitudes towards the ICC: 'The biggest worry is that the US, with almost paranoid concerns about the prosecution of its soldiers, will not ratify the statute. For the ICC to work, US support is vital.'[13]

In the vanguard of American hostility towards the ICC was the veteran right-wing Republican politician and influential Chair of the Senate Foreign Relations Committee, Jesse Helms (North Carolina), who claimed to be 'unalterably opposed'.[14] Helms also co-sponsored a measure aimed at circumventing the ICC. The American Service Members' Protection Act (ASPA) aimed to restrict the USA from co-operating with the ICC and in UN peacekeeping operations, unless the UNSC exempted Americans from the ICC's jurisdiction.[15] ASPA would even jeopardise the USA's aid to states co-operating with the ICC, even if the ultimate goal here were to fight against international terrorism (see below). In fact, the Bush administration went even further in its opposition to the ICC in 2002, by pressurising states to sign up for bilateral agreements with the USA. These so-called 'Article 98 Agreements' declared that signatories would not turn over USA personnel to the ICC if asked to do so by the international community. In return, the signatories could expect continuing support and goodwill from the USA. Unsurprisingly, supporters of the ICC – including the European Union (EU) as a bloc – opposed these agreements as dilutions of the spirit and the letter of the ICC Statute. Moreover, Eastern and Central European states protested that they were now being squeezed unfairly by Washington and Brussels. These states aspired to join *both* the North Atlantic Treaty Organisation (NATO) *and* the EU, but the issue of the bilateral agreements was now seen as an unwanted factor of division between the USA and Europe.

The opposition to the ICC certainly went wider than the Pentagon – concerned about the thousands of American soldiers based across many parts of the globe – and the right wing of the Republican Party. Some of the USA's elected representatives even advocated non-payment of Washington's financial dues to the UN. This bizarre position seemed to be based on the erroneous belief that the ICC was an arm of the UN, rather than an international body in its own right. In effect, the issue of payments to the UN got caught up in the sentiments of hostility towards the ICC; and the debate even overlapped with the reaching of an agreement to alter the system of UN payments that, in fact, reduced the USA's financial contribution. Significantly, this obstructionist and go-it-alone stance was somewhat less conspicuous immediately after 11 September 2001, when the Bush administration, understandably, was keen to build bridges – on a military level.

However, by the spring of 2002, the Bush administration seemed to be hardening its attitude towards the ICC, as illustrated by the distancing of the USA from the Rome Statute in May and the subsequent pressures to achieve Article 98 agreements. According to one view, 'The US has been getting nastier for the past six months and subverting the court with far greater energy and determination.'[16] In response to the USA's approach to the ICC, Amnesty International launched an online petition and campaign for individuals to call upon governments not to enter the impunity (or immunity) agreements being proposed by Washington.[17] The previous month, as the ASPA legislation made its way through the Senate and the House of Representatives, the European Parliament had passed a resolution accusing the USA of undermining the ICC's authority and jeopardising peacekeeping operations. Similar criticisms were heard against the USA in a heated debate at the United Nations Security Council. Without doubt, then, with governments and NGOs across the globe unhappy with the USA's renewed opposition to the ICC, the evolution towards the globalisation of justice was entering a new phase.

11 SEPTEMBER 2001: THE AFTERMATH[18]

On 11 September 2001, suicide bombers hijacked planes and piloted them into the twin towers of the World Trade Center in New York, as well as into the Pentagon in Washington. As is well known, several thousand individuals are estimated to have perished in the attacks. What did these dramatic and terrible events mean for the ICC debate?

In theory, at least, the case for an international criminal court was stronger after 11 September. As Robert G. Patman has argued, an ICC would be able to prosecute terrorists, such as those who masterminded the 11 September atrocities, and make it difficult for them to evade justice. The ICC would also provide indisputable legitimacy and neutrality to the efforts to bring perpetrators of heinous crimes to justice.[19] Again, Dianne Marie Amann, Professor of Law at University of California Davis School of Law contended – clearly as a concerned American – that:

> The attacks of September 11 changed everything. In an instant, we learned that, like it or not, superpower or not, we are part of the rest of the world ... In these last weeks, we have ... learned that international cooperation can be a good thing. That lesson ought to apply to the International Criminal Court ... The court will have jurisdiction over acts that are crimes against humanity, like the attacks of September 11. It could be the key to the fight against terrorism.[20]

A near-immediate response by President Bush and the US authorities to 11 September was to try to build up a coalition to help track down the perpetrators of the crimes. Countries, notably Afghanistan, accused of hiding suspected terrorists – including the prime suspect, Osama bin Laden – were also warned not to obstruct the cause of the coalition. What was striking about the USA's attitude over this period was that the Bush administration moved from a position of increasing isolationism or unilateralism to one of suddenly seeking to build up global alliances – 'you're either with us, or against us' – against terrorism. For, as indicated above, right from the start, the Bush administration had not only shown signs of retreating from the, at best lukewarm, support that the previous administration had demonstrated towards the Rome Statute – with President Clinton 'a reluctant and tardy signatory';[21] but, in addition, Bush had turned his back on the Kyoto Treaty and the Anti-Ballistic Missile (ABM) Treaty, at the same time unilaterally pushing ahead with a new missile defence plan – dubbed 'Star Wars 2' or 'son of Star Wars'. All in all, this was interpreted widely as a 'go-it-alone' strategy from Washington. For instance, according to Andrew Stephen, writing in the *New Statesman*, Bush 'spent the first six months of his presidency insulting most other nations of the world. He tore up the Kyoto Protocol, unilaterally abandoned the ABM Treaty, told the rest of the world he wasn't interested in the proposed international ban on biological weapons and so on.'[22]

At home, the Democrats' Leader in the Senate, Thomas Daschle, accused Bush of a failure of leadership in relation to international agreements: 'Instead of asserting our leadership, we are abdicating it. Instead of shaping international agreements to serve our interests, we have removed ourselves from a position to shape them at all.'[23] Again, Heather Hamilton, of the American Coalition for the ICC (AMICC) linked the negative USA attitude towards the ICC (and ASPA) to the question of coalition-building against terrorism: 'The administration should realize that supporting legislation penalizing countries that join an international law enforcement mechanism is not the way to strengthen international efforts to bring terrorists to justice.'[24] Across the Atlantic, strong criticism of the Bush line came also from Mark Thomas, who accused the USA of operating double standards in urging the world to unite against lawlessness whilst at the same time endeavouring to destroy attempts to create an international rule of law.[25] As regards the ICC, Thomas explained: 'Nearly every major ally of the US and every member of the European Union supports its creation. If it existed today now, it would be the only internationally recognised, purpose-built court in which Osama bin Laden could be prosecuted.'[26]

Mary Robinson, the United Nations High Commissioner for Human Rights (UNCHR) defined the fatal attacks in the USA on 11 September 2001, as crimes against humanity.[27] Tom Hadden, a Professor of Law at Queen's University Belfast and a Northern Ireland Human Rights Commissioner, suggests that this implied that the perpetrators could be tried before an ICC. But the same author also adds a word of caution in this respect: 'It is ironic it was the United States which blocked the specific inclusion of terrorist acts in the statute for [the ICC].'[28] There was still a strong argument, though, for pursuing justice by strengthening the international rule of law. Indeed, an international Hague-type tribunal or an ICC was seen increasingly as the best response to the question of bringing perpetrators to justice for crimes such as those committed on 11 September 2001. The inclusion of Islamic jurists in such courts would strengthen the legitimacy of such bodies.

At an international experts' conference on the ICC, held in the Philippines in October 2001, Chief Justice Hilario G. Davide called the ICC 'the missing link in international justice':

> The fears of terrorism which threaten world peace and stability demonstrate all too clearly the need for, among other things, a world constitution that can immediately respond to the demands of international justice without resorting to war, that is the opposite of peace.[29]

Whilst the Rome Statute did not specifically mention the word 'terrorism', there was a growing sentiment globally that terrorism of the type that committed on 11 September might be classified nonetheless as a crime against humanity. With this in mind, Robertson and Wright, writing in the *Guardian*, suggested that long-term efforts to construct international machinery for fighting international crimes were the best response to 11 September. A new crime against humanity – in the context of the Rome Statute – could be thus described as 'a systematic attack deliberately directed against a civilian population involving acts of multiple murder'.[30] Had the ICC been in existence on 11 September 2001, it would certainly have come into the equation of seeking global justice for the crimes committed in the suicide bombings and in the planning of these atrocities.

The period after 11 September was also notable for various European attempts to come to terms with the situation. For instance, in October 2001 EU governments and parliamentarians began to think more seriously about setting up an international terrorism tribunal, more or less along the same lines as the ICTFY. In the UK, for example, about 70 MPs signed a motion in favour of an international court, including provision for Islamic judges, and operating under the jurisdiction of the UNSC. Ideally, and compared to having a trial held inside the USA for 11 September suspects, such a body would be seen as more acceptable globally, including to Islamic countries.[31] In addition, at the Conference of European Justice Ministers (Council of Europe) in Moscow, 4–5 October 2001, the Ministers called for full support for the ICC as part of the struggle against international terrorism.

To sum up, the reality of the 11 September 2001 atrocities and the weighing up of their consequences have become bound up with questions of global justice and international co-operation and, inevitably therefore, discussion about the role and remit of the ICC has been a feature of the overall debate. This is a debate that is likely to run and run for the foreseeable future.

CONCLUSION

The campaign to establish an ICC is not new. Robertson, again, dates the discussion of an ICC back to 1937, when the League of Nations drew up a draft statute for a court to try international terrorists.[32] Thereafter, the Nuremberg and Tokyo Tribunals were followed up by the passing of a UN reference to 'an international penal tribunal', as the 1948 Genocide Convention was drawn up. However, as the Cold War set in, various fledgling attempts to move the ICC debate forward came to nought. It was not until the 1990s – with the creation of the ex-Yugoslavia and Rwanda Tribunals – that some practical substance was given to the ideas that eventually led to the signing of the 1998 Rome Statute.

Located in The Hague, the ICC will build upon Nuremberg and the ad hoc tribunals of the 1990s – with, for instance, full recognition given to the rights of victims and due regard for the protection of witnesses. At the same time, events in the USA – the Bush presidency, the New York and Washington suicide bombings – have impinged greatly on the discussion about and the progress of the ICC. Moreover, as Hadden suggests, any response to 11 September 2001 should be kept within the general principles of international law and human rights standards:

That is not just because there is an obligation on all states to adhere to international law and human rights. It is also because acting in line with those principles is the only way to ensure effective international co-operation, which in turn is the only way to ensure a lasting protection from international terrorism.[33]

In this context, and that of globalisation, the ICC has a lot to offer. Now that the Rome Statute has been ratified by the required 60 states, the ICC will be the first permanent institution empowered to prosecute individuals for war crimes, crimes against humanity, genocide and (eventually) crimes of aggression. As a permanent court, the ICC will put paid to the necessity of creating limited ad hoc tribunals and, at the same time, there will be important cost savings in moving away from a proliferation of one-off courts. Furthermore, problems and questions of delay and selectivity are more satisfactorily addressed and circumvented with the provision of an ICC, with universal jurisdiction.

Nevertheless, an ICC will not be a panacea for resolving all the heinous crimes in the contemporary world. Moreover, the globalisation of justice cannot simply be equated with the ICC. Indeed, the ICC can be seen as part of a broader fluorescence of human rights initiatives, including truth and reconciliation processes, the postwar attempts to prosecute human rights abusers (such as Nazi war criminals) via national jurisdictions and the creation of human rights instruments such as national human rights courts.[34] But, if it is properly resourced and internationally supported, the ICC will make would-be perpetrators of these crimes think twice, if the prospect of prosecution is a real one. As Robertson again suggests:

> Crimes against humanity will only be deterred when their would-be perpetrators – be they political leaders, field commanders or soldiers and policemen – are given pause by the prospect that they will henceforth have no hiding place: that legal nemesis may some day, somewhere, overtake them. That prospect will only be realistic if there exists an international criminal court.[35]

A lead article from the *Guardian* further summed up the value of the ICC: 'The principle behind the ICC is that the world community should have what any civilised national community has, namely a properly constituted means of dealing with right and wrong.'[36]

A permanent and effective international criminal court, therefore, will be an important step forward in the globalisation of justice. It will hopefully serve as a warning to those states that refuse to pursue perpetrators of serious crimes, that international machinery exists to do so. Moreover, by establishing truth and justice, it will also enable societies and individuals to be better prepared to 'move on', knowing that criminals have been prosecuted and that impunity has not been allowed to prevail. At the same time, it is worth re-emphasising that the provision of an effective and working ICC is a deterrent, a warning to would-be perpetrators of serious crimes that they will be pursued and brought to justice. For all these reasons, an ICC 'with teeth' is to be broadly welcomed.

NOTES

1. Susan George, 'Globalisation and the WTO', *NODE News* (Dublin: Node, September/October 2001), p. 12.
2. Quoted in Barbara Gunnell and David Timms, *After Seattle: Globalisation and its Discontents* (Catalyst: London, 2000).
3. For a discussion of these themes, see Derek Heater, *What is Citizenship?* (Cambridge: Polity, 1999).
4. Geoffrey Robertson, *Crimes Against Humanity: The Struggle for Global Justice* (Harmondsworth: Penguin, 2000), p. 214.
5. Robertson, *Crimes Against Humanity*, p. 215.
6. This and the following section draw heavily upon the sources of Amnesty International, notably the series of information sheets on the ICC: *International Criminal Court: Fact Sheet 1 Introduction to the International Criminal Court; 2 The case for ratification; 3 Prosecuting the crime of genocide; 4 Prosecuting crimes against humanity; 5 Prosecuting war crimes; 6 Ensuring justice for victims; 7 Ensuring justice for women; 8 Ensuring justice for children; 9 Fair trial guarantees; 10 State cooperation with the ICC* (London: Amnesty International, 2000). See also Amnesty International, *Concerns at the eighth session of the preparatory commission* (for the ICC, 24 September to 5 October 2001). Also drawn upon here is the United Nation's web site 'International Criminal Court – Some Questions and Answers' (31 May 2001), <www.un.org/law/icc/statute/iccq&a.htm>; and Robertson, *Crimes Against Humanity*, Ch. 8, 'The Balkan Trials'; and Ch. 9, 'The International Criminal Court', pp. 285–367.
7. Robertson, *Crimes Against Humanity*, pp. 324–5.
8. Amnesty International, *International Criminal Court: Checklist for Effective Implementation* (London: Amnesty International, July 2000).
9. Mary Robinson, 'Rights and Development Now Seen as Going Hand-in-Hand', *Irish Times* (11 December 2000).
10. Dermot Feenan, *Guardian* (9 March 2001).
11. Peter Hain, 'Calling All Dictators', *Guardian* (24 August 2000).
12. Bill Richardson, *New York Times* (21 August 2001).
13. Adam Roberts, 'War Law', *Guardian* (4 April 2001).

14. Quoted in Holger Jensen, 'A Permanent International Criminal Court', United Nations web site <archive.nandotimes.com/ntm/voices13_noframes.html> (31 May 2000).

15. Also see Holger Jensen, 'A Permanent International Criminal Court', note 14.

16. *Observer* (20 September 2002).

17. Amnesty International, *International Criminal Court: US Efforts to Obtain Impunity for Genocide, Crimes Against Humanity and War Crimes* (London: Amnesty International: August 2002), AI Index: IOR 40/025/2002.

18. This section was largely completed in early November 2001, as the USA, in particular, and the wider world, in general, responded to the attacks on the World Trade Center and the Pentagon.

19. Robert G. Patman, 'US Stance Reveals Double Standards: Bush fears an international criminal court would limit US military action in pursuit of national interests', *Canberra Times* (24 October 2001).

20. Dianne Marie Amann, 'A New International Spirit', *San Francisco Chronicles* (12 October 2001) <www.stgate.com/cgi-bin/article.cgi?file=/c/a/2001/10/12/ED20619>.

21. A.C. Grayling, 'The World's Policeman Cannot be Above the Law', *Guardian* (20 August 2001).

22. Andrew Stephen, 'Gee, Have You Heard? There's a World out There', *New Statesman* (8 October 2001), p. 16. Several weeks into the bombing of Afghanistan by the USA-led coalition, there was little sign that alliance-building on a war basis was likely to have a positive spill-over in the sense of persuading the USA to engage more fully with the international community in building a better, ecologically minded world. As Natasha Walter wrote in 'Don't Forget to Save the Planet', *Independent* (1 November 2001):

    Certainly we haven't heard much noise from Bush about wanting to re-engage with the international community on any issue other than waging war ... And despite all the talk that has gone on in the media since 11 September of an end to American isolationism, Bush has shown no signs of wanting America to re-enter the frame on this [the March 2001 Kyoto Protocol] or any other international or humanitarian project ... Wouldn't it be a great sign that the United States was ready to join an international consensus for peace, not just for war, if they decided to re-enter the [Kyoto] negotiations?

23. Thomas Daschle, remarks made at the Woodrow Wilson International Center for Scholars as part of a series called 'A New Century of American Leadership' <www.cicc4@iccnow.org> (9 August 2001).

24. Quoted in the *Coalition for an International Criminal Court (CICC) Newsletter*, 'UK Ratifies ICC Treaty as US Considers anti-ICC Legislation', ICC Update, 23rd edition (October 2001) <www.ICCnow.org>.

25. Mark Thomas, 'One Rule for Americans, One Rule for the Rest', *New Statesman* (15 October 2001), p. 9.

26. Thomas, 'One Rule for Americans', p. 9. A similar point was made by Robert G. Patman (see note 19), a senior lecturer in political studies at the University of Otago, New Zealand:

> What is striking about the period since the appalling crimes against humanity in New York and Washington is that there has been no American attempt to set up or support an international judicial system to ensure that those deemed responsible are brought to trial, despite President George Bush's repeated pledges that 'justice will be done'.

27. Quoted in Tom Hadden, 'Human Rights v. Terrorism', *Fortnight*, No. 399 (October 2001), pp. 11–12.
28. Hadden, 'Human Rights v. Terrorism', p. 11.
29. Quoted in *BusinessWorld* (Philippines) (17 October 2001), and reported on the same day on the web site of the NGO Coalition for an International Criminal Court (CICC) <www.iccnow.org>.
30. Geoffrey Robertson and Robert Wright, 'Bush's Chance to Shape International Norms: Legal way', *Guardian* (14 October 2001).
31. Also see Tom Baldwin, 'EU Considers Tribunal for Terrorist Suspects', *The Times* (30 October 2001).
32. Robertson, *Crimes Against Humanity*, pp. 324–5.
33. Hadden, 'Human Rights v. Terrorism', p. 11.
34. Cf. H. Steiner and P. Alston (eds), *International Human Rights in Context: Law, Politics and Morals* (Oxford: Clarendon Press, 1996).
35. Robertson, *Crimes Against Humanity*, pp. 324–5.
36. *Guardian* (23 August 2001).

The author would like to acknowledge and absolve the following individuals for reading and commenting on the chapter: John Jackson, Dermot Feenan, Maura McCallion, Gerard McCann and Stephen McCloskey.

WEB SITES

Amnesty International	www.amnesty.org
International Commission of Jurists	www.icj.org
International Criminal Justice Resource Centre	www.internationaljustice.org
Justice Without Borders	www.justicewithoutborders.com
Lawyers Committee for Human Rights	www.lchr.org
United Nations index	www.unsystem.org
Human Rights Online Server	hurpeconline.com
Human Rights Without Frontiers	www.hrwf.net/newhrwf
Human Rights Library	heiwww.unige.ch/humanrts
Foreign Policy in Focus	www.foreginpolicy-infocus.org
United Nations human rights site	www.un.org/rights
The Centre for International Human Rights Law	www.rightsinternational.org

4 Women and Development: Examining Gender Issues in Developing Countries

Madeleine Leonard

It is no longer noteworthy to find women included in studies of development. Yet many are surprised to learn that prior to 1975, the United Nations (UN) International Year for Women, less than 1 per cent of standard textbooks referred specifically to women. We have come a long way since then – or have we? The answer depends on what we mean by bringing women into development. Does it mean incorporating women's issues into existing theories and concepts, or transforming traditional approaches to development? The initial response to the neglect of women in development was to 'add women and stir'. Hence, throughout the 1970s, the prevailing assumption was that if women's role in development and economic growth was made more visible then women would no longer be left out of the development process. This initial naivety, ultimately, gave way to more complex arguments concerning the need to incorporate a gender dimension into development studies that not only addressed the concerns of women, but also extended to the relationships between women and men. These relationships form the crux of women's subordinate position in both the developed and developing world. Adopting a gender-aware perspective to development involves examining not only power imbalances between developed and developing countries, but power imbalances between women and men within developed and developing countries.

Examining gender issues in developing countries is no easy task. Women are by no means a unified or homogeneous group. Moreover, they live in countries with diverse historical experiences and levels of development. Within these countries they are likely to be further divided according to class, race and religion among other variables. Indeed, there are just as many factors to divide women as there are to connect them. Despite this heterogeneity, women share some common features wherever they may live. The aim of this chapter is to highlight some of the common features in women's development while reminding the reader at the outset of the enormous variations in women's lives. The chapter commences with a brief historical overview of the neglect of women in development studies and policies. It goes on to outline institutional responses to this omission and argues for the need to incorporate a holistic approach to understanding women's lives. The final section examines how women in developing countries actively engage in processes which dilute and transform their disadvantaged situations.

'MALESTREAM' THEORIES OF DEVELOPMENT

Women and gender relations were largely absent from economic development literature of the 1950s and 1960s. Two main approaches to development characterised this era – modernisation theory and dependency theory – and both ignored the role of women in the process of economic growth and change. Modernisation theory viewed development as an evolutionary, unilinear process of change whereby societies moved through a series of stages towards the final destination of economic development. Each stage transcended the preceding step and once started the process was irreversible. The ultimate goal of this process was to create 'modern men', who could act as rational individuals and entrepreneurs. These 'high achievers' were typically regarded as heads of households capable of stimulating economic growth and development that would trickle down to all family members. Drawing on the work of social theorist Talcott Parsons, modernisation theorists viewed the modern family as a nuclear unit where husbands and wives adopted complementary roles, with the man working primarily outside the household and the woman within the household. This model suited both men and women as modern marriages were seen as democratic and egalitarian. However, Catherine Scott, in *Gender and Development*, suggested that this vision of modernity not only excludes women but ultimately rests on the exclusion of women. Moreover, it presents a largely masculine view of what it is like to be modern.[1]

The dependency perspective focused on the polarisation tendencies of the capitalist mode of production which placed the peripheral countries of the 'developing world' in a relationship of dependency with the core countries of the 'developed world'. Dependency was regarded as a relationship that existed between countries rather than people. Thus, the dependency of the developing world on the developed world supplanted an analysis of the dependency of women on men. As Aidan Foster-Carter succinctly put it, dependency theory viewed women as the satellite that was no-one's metropolis.[2] Dependency theorists focused on gender relationships in the context of the means of production, but ignored relationships between men and women. Moreover, production was elevated at the expense of reproduction, and *exchange* value prioritised while *use* value was marginalised. As Scott suggests, this process rendered the household invisible in dependency theory.

World systems theory expanded the country-level approach of both modernisation and dependency theories to one that looked at capitalism as a global economic system. This system, which emerged in the sixteenth century, gradually evolved into a model of economic production premised on an international division of labour encompassing all nation states.[3] All countries were divided into three broad groups: cores, peripheries and semi-peripheries, with the latter acting as an intermediary zone between cores and peripheries. While world-systems analysts highlighted the role of the household in the world economy, women were drawn into the theory as members of households and, more specifically, as appendages of men in households. According to K.B. Ward, the problems with this approach included its tendency to ignore the possibility that men and women may have divergent interests within the household.[4] Moreover, the theory does not sufficiently acknowledge the relationship between women's formal and informal labour – the links between women's work outside and inside the household. Women were only partially incorporated into the world system theory insofar as their access to formal employment remained related to their access to informal employment and their prominent role in household labour. Women are thereby confronted by a global patriarchy that is underpinned by a system of subordination and domination which predates capitalism. However, under the capitalist economic system the subordination of women has been accelerated, leading some feminists to use the term 'capitalist patriarchy'. This approach highlights the fact that men as well as capital have benefited from women's relegation to the household.

All three approaches to development – modernisation, dependency and world systems – can be criticised for their theorisation of women. In general terms, women are not analysed separately from men as a distinct social group, or are rendered invisible. Conventional development theories are, therefore, unable to provide us with a basic framework which enables us to examine issues affecting women in developing countries.

THE IMPORTANCE OF BOSERUP

The first important challenge to the neglect of women in development theories and policies came from Ester Boserup, writing in *Women's Role in Economic Development* (1970). The book today seems unremarkable, but at the time of its publication it was path-breaking. It was the first time that attention had been paid to the neglect of women in the development process.[5] Boserup outlined the negative impact that colonialism had on women in developing societies, including the allocation of gender roles based on farming and trading premised on the mistaken belief that farmers and traders were men. As a result, women often lost their right to land ownership because of agrarian reforms introduced by European administrators. Modern technology and cultivation methods were made available to men who were considered the ideal sex to understand the workings of machinery. In the process, male productivity and status was enhanced while women's economic activity was undermined and their self-worth diluted. Women were relegated to the subsistence sector of farming and forced to use traditional methods of cultivation. Since official government statistics, especially GNP indicators, tend to ignore subsistence agriculture, then women's work was rendered invisible and they were inaccurately considered economically inactive.

Boserup's solution to the economic marginalisation of women was to incorporate them into the development process. This approach reflected Boserup's academic background, as an economist and as a supporter of modernisation theory. The gender question, as she defined it, was to ensure that the benefits of modernisation were extended to encompass women. Since the main benefits of modernisation were derived from the formal market place then enhancing women's access to formal, paid employment was an important first step in raising their social status in developing countries. Drawing on liberal feminist theory, Boserup advocated education as a solution to enhancing women's position in the formal economy. This individualistic approach to improving women's socio-economic position centred on enhancing the characteristics of individuals rather than situating women within the contexts of their relationship with men. Yet, an examination of women's roles in developed countries suggests that women's roles in the private sphere of the household fundamentally influences public life outside the household. Opening up opportunities in the public sphere without addressing the sexual basis of the division of labour in the private sphere meant that Boserup's approach to enhancing women's status would fall far short of liberating women.

An analysis of gender relations in the developed world suggests that women are still a long way from parity with men. Moreover, it is arguable that the development process itself, in terms of the agricultural and industrial revolutions, actually had a detrimental affect on the social status of women. It required the social upheaval of two world wars and a long political campaign for women to reassert their economic worth. Initially, industrialisation undermined the position of women in society by creating a private sphere designated for women only. In this patriarchal climate, women had limited access to independent sources of livelihood, making them increasingly economically dependent on their male partners. This pattern of gender relations in the developed world, advocated mainly through modernisation approaches to economic development, has been applied to some extent in developing countries under the guise of new development policies. Work in the developing world was largely regarded as a male domain and, consequently, the vital economic value of women's work in the subsistence sector was ignored. As a result, development programmes such as the Green Revolution, in many instances through sheer ignorance, wiped out the bases of these subsistence crops and left women without any independent source of economic production. An emerging debate on the position of women in the developed world led to an increasing focus on the meaning of development and women's role in the process of social change. As Elise Boulding pointed out in 'Integration into what?', there was a mainstream acceptance that development had already been achieved in the developed world with women already integrated into this model of development.[6] Yet women living in the developed world still appeared to hold an inferior position compared to that of men – suggesting that it was something more than development or underdevelopment that accounted for women's subordinate position. This led some feminists to denounce development as 'women's worst enemy', or a 'form of patriarchal colonialism'.[7]

THE INSTITUTIONAL RESPONSE

The theoretical arguments advocated by modernisation theorists fundamentally influenced development planners and practitioners.

Drawing on Boserup's criticisms of women's invisibility in the development process, planners and practitioners attempted to rectify this neglect by establishing a 'Women *in* Development' programme to guide their policies in developing countries. They worked from the assumption that somehow the benefits of modernisation had failed to elevate the social status of women and concluded that drawing women into development, mainly through involvement in income producing activities, would address this failing. The Women *in* Development approach was endorsed by the United Nations throughout the 1970s culminating with the establishment of International Women's Year in 1975 and an international decade for women between 1975 and 1985. Based largely on a liberal feminist approach to gender, the UN advocated enhancing political, employment and educational opportunities for women. However, this focus on incorporating women into the public sphere was not matched by a rigorous investigation of women's work in the private, domestic, sphere. The UN's approach failed to recognise that to fundamentally improve women's socio-economic positions, both the public and private spheres of their lives and work would have to be challenged. The fourth UN Conference on Women held in Beijing in 1995 tackled this issue by presenting women's rights as human rights and challenging, to some extent, the separation of the public and private spheres of women's lives.

Despite advances in the scope of the Women *in* Development perspective, two other approaches went much further in addressing the public versus private divide. The first, Women *and* Development, drew on dependency theory and emerged in the late 1970s in response to criticisms of the Women *in* Development approach. Proponents of this perspective argued that the notion of integrating women into development was a fallacy, and that women had always played a part in the development process. Rather than focusing on development as individual-based change, this approach highlighted the structural causes of development and underdevelopment. Women's work in both the public and private spheres was regarded as central to maintaining international structures of power and inequality. This perspective was forwarded by Third World feminists such as Lourdes Beneria and Gita Sen in 1981, who challenged Boserup's benevolent view of modernisation and the subsequent neglect of the interrelationship between capital accumulation, class formation and the changing status of women.[8] In their view, the liberal feminist approach to enhancing women's development in the way embodied in modernisation solutions was akin to 'treating cancer with bandaid'. The Gender and Development perspective which emerged in the 1980s and drew largely on socialist feminist thinking further developed this approach. The aim was to move beyond 'women in development' or 'women and development' theories to incorporate a gender dimension into the equation by examining the relationships between men and women, and their connection to the development process. Implicit here was the question of male power as an aspect of gender relations. This approach regards women as agents of change rather than passive recipients of development assistance and stresses the importance of women organising from within their own sectors. It also advocated a holistic approach, focusing on all the interrelating aspects of women's everyday lives, including their relationships with men.

GENDER ISSUES IN DEVELOPING COUNTRIES

This holistic Gender and Development approach recognises that development affects women and men differently, and impacts on gender relationships. It involves tackling the social disadvantages of women holistically rather than adopting a piecemeal approach. It thus acknowledges and addresses women's unequal status vis-à-vis men. *The World's Women 2000: Trends and Statistics* highlights the myriad ways in which women are disadvantaged throughout the globe and statistically demonstrates how this impact is more extreme in developing countries. The report documents how continued gender inequalities in economic power sharing, unequal distribution of unremunerated work between women and men, lack of technical and financial support for women's entrepreneurship, unequal access to and control over capital, particularly land and credit, have exacerbated the feminisation of poverty. Moreover, the report indicates that little progress has been made in eradicating illiteracy in some developing countries, aggravating women's inequality at the economic, social and political level. Nearly two-thirds of the world's 876 million illiterates are women.[9] How do we rectify these disadvantages? How do we increase women's access to education and training? How do we ensure that they become property owners? The starting point in addressing these questions is not the public sphere, but the private sphere. It is only through a systematic examination of women's roles in the private sphere and the impact that this has on their participation in the public sphere, that a more valid approach to promoting women's worth in society will be established. Women in all societies remain disproportionately responsible for domestic work and childcare, which is an absolutely vital role in ensuring the reproduction of future generations and for the general well-being and economic development of any country. Yet, despite the importance of this work, it remains undervalued and overlooked in most economic indicators of development. The majority of national accounting systems and household surveys do not include this type of work in their economic measurements – consequently rendering women's work invisible and mistakenly labelling it as unproductive.

In developing societies, women are mainly responsible for subsistence agriculture which is carried out in or near the home. They often grow, harvest and prepare virtually all the food that is consumed by their families. In Africa, women perform between 60 and 80 per cent of all agricultural work, while in Brazil, women are responsible for about two-thirds of agricultural work on small farms and combine this with household production activities. Similar levels of participation in agricultural work has been found in Chile, Peru, Ecuador and Jamaica.[10] Given these statistics it would seem logical for development programmes to be directed at women to enable them to improve their farming methods. Conversely, over the past three decades rural development projects have been directed almost exclusively at men. Research conducted by Z.F. Arat based on a four-country study of projects sponsored by the UN in 1984 – in Rwanda, Democratic Yemen, Indonesia and Haiti – showed that out of a total of 254 projects only 9 exclusively concerned women.[11] Adopting a gender perspective in development means widening definitions of work to incorporate the various roles that women perform. It also means recognising women as active economic agents, particularly in the informal and household sectors of the economy.

The impact of the debt crisis and structural adjustment programmes on the most vulnerable members of societies, including women, has been well publicised in recent years. What is less well acknowledged is the impact that SAPs have on women's working lives. As the real value of wages declines in developing countries and male members of households are squeezed out of the labour market, the onus falls on women, through their subsistence activities and involvement in the informal economy, to implement a series of strategies fundamental to maintaining the survival of the household. If women's unpaid work was properly valued they would emerge in most societies as the major breadwinners given their greater contribution of working hours than men. The unvalued economic contribution of women is such that any reasonable calculation of their labour would lead to a fundamental change in the context in which today's social, economic and political policies are framed.

A gendered perspective on development also means examining more critically the ways in which women are drawn into paid employment. Indeed, the policy of integrating women into the development process has often been restricted to incorporating them into the waged labour force as employees of multinational corporations (MNCs). Developing countries compete against each other to attract inward investment by offering MNCs incentives such as favourable tax laws, free trade zones, lax health and safety standards and a cheap labour force. Moreover, developing countries often exploit women in advertising campaigns targeted at MNCs. Women are often considered by MNCs as a nimble and docile workforce, particularly suited to monotonous unskilled work. Women are thereby regarded as a secondary labour force that will work for lower wage rates than men. This is what attracts MNCs to a female workforce. According to Linda Lim in 'Capitalism, imperialism, and patriarchy', the secondary status of women in developing countries (as in developed nations) results from patriarchal institutions and social relations that continue to uphold the traditional sexual division of labour within the household.[12] Women's natural role is assumed to be a domestic one and female income is considered secondary because the principal breadwinner is seen as male. When women enter paid employment, they are often paid lower wages and experience poorer working conditions than those that pertain for men within the same country. *The World's Women 2000: Trends and Statistics* report outlines how in 27 out of the 39 countries with data available, women's wages were between 20 per cent and 50 per cent lower than those of men.

Employment sectors dominated by women come to be regarded as unskilled or semi-skilled simply because jobs in these sectors are performed by women. This is also true of developed societies. Ethel Crowley's 1997 study of multinationals found that the preferred workforce was female and that jobs were redefined as unskilled or semi-skilled on the sole criterion that they were filled by women.[13] While Lim recognises that women in developing countries may prefer working in MNCs compared to unpaid work in the household, she suggests that such employment only marginally enhances their economic position. It does little to challenge the patriarchal structures which condition such employment. This argument was further developed by Diane Elson and Ruth Pearson in their 1997 account of the relationship between factory work and the sub-ordination of women as a gender.[14] They suggest that factory employment has a multifaceted impact on gender subordination. It tends to intensify gender subordination by preserving and utilising traditional forms of patriarchal power, whereby men rather than women decide where and when to utilise women's labour power. Men as fathers, for example, often send daughters out to work in MNCs, in some cases against their daughters' wishes, although this may be a double-edged sword in that earning a wage may undermine the father's control. However, Elson and Pearson suggest that there is little empirical evidence to indicate that women's wages have any significant impact on their decision-making power in the household. Moreover, working in MNCs in some cases leads to a recomposition and new forms of gender subordination as the management of MNCs (which tends to be male) develop more subtle techniques to control female workers. Companies often cultivate a paternalistic family spirit, by encouraging women to enhance their femininity by taking part in beauty contests or providing lessons in fashion and beauty care. Elson and Pearson conclude that such employment does not provide a 'material basis for politicising the personal because of the way it masses together women not simply as workers but as a gender'.[15] Thus, gender roles established in the family are often transmitted and preserved in the workplace. This too reflects the need to look at the totality of women's lives and how attitudes to the work they perform in the private sphere permeate the operations of the public sphere in ways that lead to the labelling of female employment as unskilled.

Gita Sen uses more recent evidence of gender relations in the workplace to argue that female labour is underpaid and performed in poor working conditions in export-processing zones.[16] Young women are the preferred workforce employed on piece-rates and flexible contracts. Moreover, many countries (particularly in the developing world) have reneged on International Labour Organ-isation (ILO) conventions guaranteeing rights to workers in order to attract foreign investment into export-processing zones. Sen accepts that many young women actively compete to obtain employment in these zones, but suggests that this is due to the magnitude of rural patriarchal dominance in their lives. She argues that existing gender systems continue to oppress women in two separate but linked ways. First, the persistence of the sexual division of labour in the household and the ideologies underpinning and justifying this division, mean that men and women continue to have unequal access to different kinds of resources. Second, women's work in the 'care economy' not only remains unrecognised, but the importance of care in human reproduction continues to be ignored by mainstream development policy-makers.

The evidence illustrates how women's responsibility for housework and care work continues to shape the conditions under which they become available for paid employment.[17] This linkage applies to women in developed and developing countries and also, increasingly, attracts women from all corners of the globe together through migrant labour. Domestic labour is increasingly shared amongst women rather than between women and men. Educated, middle-class women in developed societies with an adequate income often engage migrant women for domestic assistance and in the process reinforce gender stereotypes about both. The gendered division of labour within the household underpins occupational segregation into male and female jobs. Thus, ideologies surrounding domesticity limit the employment options available to women as a group. Promoting a gendered approach to development, therefore, means recognising the resilience of these ideologies and their impact on gender relations in both developed and developing countries.

WOMEN AS ACTIVE AGENTS OF SOCIAL CHANGE

Women, of course, do not passively respond to these wider structural constraints and stereotypical notions of their 'natural' roles in society. Women, individually and collectively, are social actors who often actively aim to surmount the disadvantages that they face within their household, community and wider society. However, women's activism should reflect the broadening context of politics that includes action at local, national and international levels. Women's participation in formal politics remains marginal and falls well behind that of men. Moreover, in the highest echelons of political power, male dominance is even more entrenched. *The World's Women 2000: Trends and Statistics* report states that during the first part of 2000, only nine women were heads of state or government. Only 8 per cent of the world's cabinet ministers are women and women represent just 11 per cent of parliamentarians worldwide. Obviously, women need to increase their presence in formal politics in order to have an effective impact on policy and the implementation of policy. The UN suggests that all countries should strive to reach a minimum target of 30 per cent female representation in national parliaments. However, the under-representation of women in formal politics does not signify that women are politically inactive.

The involvement of women in politics at a local/community level quickly challenges this assertion. Women often become politically active in response to threats to their household or family. For example, women in Argentina formed the Mothers of the Plaza de Mayo non-governmental organisation to demand the return of the children who had disappeared under the military junta in the 1970s. Also, women whose families were drastically affected by the debt-related structural adjustment programmes imposed over the past two decades formed collective community organisations to feed their families. These survival strategies have been viewed by some feminists as little more than women responding to their immediate interests and in the process perpetuating conventional gender roles. However, others have argued that such community-led mobilisation has the potential to raise women's consciousness and enable them to move beyond family concerns to wider issues affecting their lives. Drawing on her work on women's status during the Sandinista revolution in Nicaragua, Molyneaux argued that it is important to distinguish between women's practical interests and their strategic interests.[18] Practical interests arise from specific circumstances and needs, and do not challenge the wider structural constraints that women face in their lives. Strategic gender interests, however, are derived from a feminist consciousness and require collective struggle to transform women's lives. Some feminists argue that while the politicisation of many women arises from the issues of survival and everyday life, others make this transition through exposure to different forms of social, political and economic oppression.[19]

Women's everyday practical issues often translate into strategic interests. Two issues are particularly relevant here, women's lack of control over their own bodies and male violence towards women, and have become transformed from private issues into public concerns demanding national and international action. Naila Kabeer's *Reverse Realities* outlines the various ways in which women are subjected to violence and sexual control in developing societies.[20] In many countries, family honour is linked to the virtue of female members, and sexual harassment and rape are often used in property feuds and disputes to humiliate opponents. This is also a major side effect of war, where the rape of women often accompanies the military defeat of males. Furthermore, women are often unable to remove themselves from violent situations because of their lack of access to income earning opportunities. Lynne Brydon and Sylvia Chant have compiled research on the increase in bride deaths in South Asia. These occur when a girl's parents cannot meet or refuse to meet the dowry payments required by the groom's family. Brides are often murdered by their in-laws or sometimes commit suicide because of systematic physical violence and verbal abuse. Moreover, marriages are often arranged and brides must be virgins. In India, for example, more than 50 per cent of girls aged between 15 and 19 are married.

In the Middle East and North Africa, female circumcision (genital mutilation) is still widely practised. This is performed to protect and control women's chastity both before and after marriage. In its most extreme form, this involves removing the clitoris and surrounding tissue, and then sewing the two parts of the vulva together leaving only a tiny orifice for the passage of urine and menstrual blood. The practice is performed on girls as young as five years and the orifice is widened with a razor or some other sharp implement on a girl's wedding night.[21] The World Health Organisation (WHO) has outlined the side effects of such operations – including haemorrhaging, retention of urine, bacterial infections, infertility and subsequent difficulties in childbirth. *The World's Women 2000: Trends and Statistics* report estimates that 100 million girls have been subjected to genital mutilation. In some African countries, more than half of all women and girls have undergone genital mutilation and its prevalence is not declining. A further 100 million children, mostly girls in Asia, are forced into prostitution. Studies of marriage in Chile, Mexico, Papua New Guinea and the Republic of Korea indicate that two-thirds of married women have experienced domestic violence. Partners or former partners commit more than half of all murders of women in Bangladesh, Brazil, Kenya and Papua New Guinea. Changing national legislation is only part of the solution. Cultural and social values also need to change. Domestic violence, sexual harassment, rape, lack of control and choices over reproduction all serve to limit women's autonomy and perpetuate their low social status. Promoting women's human rights means starting at the basic level of adopting the most fundamental right of all, control over one's body.

In responding to the problems that persist for women in developed and developing countries, the United Nation's 'Women's Decade' has encouraged the proliferation of informal grassroots associations and national movements aimed at improving women's condition and position. Arat states that Kenya alone has over 23,000 women's groups promoting both women's practical and strategic interests.[22] She also highlights the work of the Women's World Bank, established in 1980, to promote credit opportunities for women who lack collateral and are often denied credit through other channels. Another positive development is the emergence of women-oriented NGOs, with Chile alone having 120 NGOs specialising in gender issues.[23] Within the UN, the Division for the Advancement of Women was established in 1988 as a central unit dealing with all issues relating to women, although critics argue that its elevation in status has not been matched by any significant increase in resources or personnel. While, individually, these organisations may appear unconnected and disparate, collectively they represent a rich, diverse movement that has the ability to transform women's lives.

Nonetheless, much remains to be done. In 1979, the United Nations approved the Convention on the Elimination of All Forms of Discrimination Against Women (CEDAW). Forty-one of the member states of the UN have still not signed the Convention, 6 have signed without ratification, and 43 have ratified the Convention with reservations about some of its provisions. In effect, 90 countries have not yet accepted the basic principal of legal equality for women and men. A *Platform for Action* was adopted in 1995 at the fourth World Conference on Women held in Beijing, where twelve critical areas of concern were identified for priority action to achieve the advancement and empowerment of women. This *Platform for Action* forms the basis for further progress towards the achievement of gender equality and development in the twenty-first century. In 2000, a comprehensive review and appraisal of progress made in the implementation of the *Platform for Action* was undertaken by the 23rd special session of the UN's General Assembly. This involved the establishment of a series of development initiatives in relation to gender for the period 2002–06.[24] While these policy developments are laudable, there remains insufficient political will to tackle the root causes of women's unequal relationship to men. Inequalities between men and women continue to persist and major obstacles to achieving gender equality have remained. Nevertheless, there is a growing formal recognition that the empowerment of women and their full participation in all spheres of society is fundamental for the achievement of development. Part of this emphasis is an acknowledgement that men must also be involved in this process and take joint responsibility with women for the promotion of gender equality.

CONCLUSION

Gender refers to women's and men's socially defined characteristics, which are in turn shaped by race, class, religion and culture. Gender relations will, therefore, have different manifestations in different countries and cultures. This chapter has sought to examine some of the ways in which women throughout the world have become interconnected. In particular, women retain an overwhelming responsibility for domestic and care work, and this continues to fundamentally influence the conditions under which they are drawn into formal paid employment outside the household. Political interpretation of the domestic role within societies influences judgements regarding how work is defined and how economic productivity is evaluated and measured. Men continue to exert more power than women and in many instances exercise power over women in ways that go against their interests and the well-being of their families. Bringing women more centrally into development, or expanding the 'benefits' of development to reach women, means addressing these gender relations. Indeed, it is counter-productive to focus on women in isolation of their relations with men. These relationships form the crux of women's subordination, and transforming women's lives means altering these relationships.

Moreover, it is not just the case that women need development but that development needs women. The social status of women has a profound effect on the well-being of households, communities and countries. International agencies have recognised this correlation, but progress in carrying out gender-sensitive programmes remains slow. Gender issues are often treated separately rather than relationally. In a recent review of six World Bank African poverty assessments, Whitehead and Lockwood found that the World Bank incorporated a gender dimension into its assessments by identifying women's specific poverty characteristics rather than the relational implications of poverty for women and men.[25] Yet the relational aspects of poverty are crucial for both understanding the 'feminisation' of poverty and finding ways to eradicate its causes. Thus, to radically change women's lives means recognising the socio-economic interconnections between women and men. Transforming women's lives, ultimately, rests on fundamentally altering the relationships that currently exist between women and men.

NOTES

 1. C.V. Scott, *Gender and Development: Rethinking Modernization and Dependency Theory* (London: Lynne Rienner, 1995).
 2. A. Foster-Carter, *The Sociology of Development* (Ormskirk: Causeway Press, 1985).
 3. I. Wallerstein, *The Capitalist World System* (Cambridge: Cambridge University Press, 1979).
 4. K.B. Ward, 'Reconceptualising World System Theory to Include Women', in P. England (ed.), *Theory on Gender: Feminism on Theory* (New York: Aldine De Gruyter, 1993).
 5. E. Boserup, *Women's Role in Economic Development* (New York: St Martin's Press, 1970).
 6. E. Boulding, 'Integration into What? Reflections on development planning for women', in R. Dauber and M. Cain (eds), *Women and Technological Change in Developing Countries* (Colorado: Westview Press, 1980).
 7. R. Morgan, *Sisterhood is Global: The International Women's Movement Anthology* (New York: Anchor Press, 1984).
 8. L. Beneria and G. Sen, 'Accumulation, Reproduction and Women's Role in Economic Development: Boserup revisited', *Signs*, Vol. 7 (1981), pp. 279–98.
 9. *The World's Women 2000: Trends and Statistics* (New York: United Nations, Department of Economic and Social Affairs, 2000).
10. Inter-American Development Bank, *Women in the Americas: Bridging the Gender Gap* (Washington: Johns Hopkins University Press, 1995), p. 62.
11. Z.F. Arat, 'Women under Layers of Oppression: The (un)changing political economy of gender', in M. Dorraji (ed.), *The Changing Political Economy of the Third World* (London: Rienmer Publishers, 1995).
12. L.Y.C. Lim, 'Capitalism, Imperialism and Patriarchy: The dilemma of third world women workers in multinational factories', in N. Visvanathan, L. Duggan, L. Nisonoff and N. Wiegersma (eds), *The Women, Gender and Development Reader* (London: Zed Books, 1997).
13. E. Crowley, 'Making a Difference?', in A. Byrne and M. Leonard (eds), *Women and Irish Society: A Sociological Reader* (Belfast: Beyond the Pale, 1997).
14. D. Elson and R. Pearson, 'The Subordination of Women and the Internationalization of Factory Production', in Visvanathan et al., *Women, Gender and Development Reader*.
15. Elson and Pearson, 'The Subordination of Women', p. 202.
16. G. Sen, 'Engendering Poverty Alleviation: Challenges and opportunities', *Development and Change*, Vol. 30 (1999), pp. 685–92.

17. M. Leonard, 'Old Wine in New Bottles? Women working inside and outside the household', *Women's Studies International Forum*, Vol. 24, No. 1 (2001), pp. 67–78.

18. M. Molyneaux, 'Mobilisation without Emancipation: Women's interests, state and revolution in Nicaragua', *Feminist Studies*, Vol. 2, No. 3 (1985), pp. 227–54.

19. E. Rooney, 'Women in Party Politics and Local Groups', in Byrne and Leonard, *Women and Irish Society*.

20. N. Kabeer, *Reversed Realities: Gender Hierarchies in Development Thought* (New Delhi: Pauls Press, 1995).

21. L. Brydon and S. Chant, *Women in the Third World* (Aldershot: Edward Elgar, 1989).

22. Z.F. Arat, 'Women under Layers of Oppression'.

23. Inter-American Development Bank, *Women in the Americas: Bridging the Gender Gap*.

24. United Nations General Assembly Resolution S-23/3, 'Further Actions and Initiatives to Implement the Beijing Declaration and Platform for Action' (New York: United Nations, 16 November 2000).

25. A. Whitehead and M. Lockwood, 'Gendering Poverty: A review of six World Bank African policy assessments', *Development and Change*, Vol. 30 (1999), pp. 525–55, p. 527.

WEB SITES

WIDE: Women in Development Education	www.eurosur.org/wide/porteng.htm
Statistics for gender and development	www.ids.ac.uk
Oxfam	www.oxfam.org.uk/policy/gender/lgender.htm
Information on gender and development	www.caa.au/world/gender
Information on gender and aid	globaled.ausaid.gov.au/links/gender.html
Information about aid agencies	www.aidagency.com
Amnesty International	www.amnesty.org
Human Rights Watch	www.hrw.org
UN web site	www.un.org

Part II
Aid and Trade

5 Perspectives on Aid: Benefits, Deficits and Strategies

Maura Leen

Any understanding of aid needs to examine the context of and trends in international development assistance over the past decade. There is also an urgent need to explore some of the challenges facing official donors and non-governmental organisations (NGOs) in ensuring that poverty reduction and participatory development become a hallmark rather than a cliché of development assistance programmes. Given the breadth of debate on aid, any reasonable analysis needs to focus on a few core areas while taking into account the necessity for official aid programmes to form part of a coherent set of government and international policies in support of sustainable development. In particular, there is a need to examine the key strategic policy issue facing official aid agencies and NGOs alike, namely the role of aid in relation to good governance and reform.

This chapter will address all of these issues and will also focus on the challenges facing those engaged in the ongoing humanitarian relief effort that has accounted for a huge share of aid flows over the past decade. It will look ahead to new forms of aid partnership in support of social change, noting that advocacy will play a central role here as distinct from a project-driven approach. Ultimately, such partnerships may well represent the most effective means of tackling poverty and inequality – a shameful legacy of the twentieth century which has followed us into a new millennium.

ASSESSING AID DELIVERY

At the start of the twenty-first century there is a pervading disappointment that development co-operation has not delivered more in terms of a better world for all. Worldwide, the number of poor people continues to increase. While this does not mean that aid has failed, it calls into question issues of quality and effectiveness in the delivery of official overseas development assistance (ODA)[1] by governments and international institutions, as well as the resources provided through non-governmental development organisations

(NGDOs).[2] At the same time, it is equally important to recognise that poverty has fallen more rapidly over the past 50 years than in the previous 500, and there has been a steady improvement in levels of human development. Thus, aid that is properly planned and delivered can contribute and has contributed to these advances in human well-being.

The new millennium and the post-11 September 2001 world is a cogent time to take stock of the state of development co-operation. Indeed, many stakeholders, both official donors and NGOs, are currently assessing their aid efforts in an attempt to devise more effective forms of development assistance. More is known and being learned about the principles and characteristics of 'quality' aid programmes, and a number of key features dominate thinking on aid effectiveness. It is now widely recognised that democratic institutions matter as much as markets. Good governance, both at national and international levels, is seen as essential to any strategy aimed at achieving sustainable development. Good governance deals with not only how states relate to their respective civil societies, but how civil society groups relate to the state and each other. Thus, participation is seen as both part of the process and as an end result, or objective, of development. In terms of the thematic focus of aid programmes, poverty reduction is now the overarching objective of official aid efforts. However, issues of inequality, and the international and domestic policies which facilitate such inequalities, have not been adequately debated.

A common criticism of aid practice – both aid from official donors and aid from NGOs – has been that aid has tended to 'projectise' the development process into individual projects and in so doing has depoliticised the development process. For instance, this 'projectitis' has been deemed to undermine government-to-government (bilateral) aid as developing country ministries have been carved up among donors, with externally funded projects becoming well-resourced islands of excellence in public services which were often crumbling at the seams. Some aid donors have consequently focused on strengthening the national ownership of development policies, and are now investing more resources into direct budget support. Another concern is that aid has been crisis- or emergency-driven, and in some instances it has provided a veil over the lack of political action to tackle the underlying causes of such crises.

There has also been progress in aid policy and practice. For instance, NGOs are building new alliances around advocacy and field-level programmes. The past decade has witnessed a rapid expansion in civil society movements, including NGDOs, in developing countries. Moreover, many developed country NGOs are reflecting more on their core tasks and the added value they offer the development process, while recognising the need for a greater culture of learning. This reflective learning process has been complemented by a growth in the range of research and academic courses on international development. Bilateral donors and multilateral agencies are also taking steps to enhance the co-ordination of their aid efforts, both to address the needs of recipients and to improve aid effectiveness.

A feature of aid policies in recent years has been the increasing alignment between the stated objectives of official aid donors and the NGDO community. Many of the concepts at the centre of current development thinking among official aid donors have been those informing the work of non-governmental agencies over the past 25 years. These include the importance of partnership, local ownership and participation by, and engagement with, civil society in the developing world. In addition, official donors and NGOs are becoming increasingly effective in harmonising and promoting the principles and values informing their actions. These principles have centred largely on concepts of human development, human rights and entitlements. For instance, the UK government's Department for International Development (DFID) has outlined its policy goals and strategies for promoting sustainable development.[3] Most official donors would subscribe to DFID's policies and principles in implementing their aid efforts. These principles include ensuring that aid strategies are:

- People centred
- Led by comprehensive and integrated objectives
- Delivered in the context of national political realities
- Outcome-oriented
- Country-led, nationally owned and participatory
- Informed by a high degree of monitoring and learning
- Fully budgeted
- Capable of incorporating future needs
- Built on existing capacities

As official and non-governmental agencies' aid policies become increasingly aligned, the challenge now is to invest in aid *practice* that reflects such policy innovation.

SOME TRENDS IN AID

In the 1990s, international development co-operation 'flows' were in a state of flux. Aid allocations were volatile and mainly on a downward trend, particularly from the world's richest nations which make up the Organisation for Economic Co-operation and Development's (OECD) Development Assistance Committee (DAC). The Group of Eight (G8) account for 75 per cent of all DAC aid expenditure, with just four of these countries – Japan, the US, France and Germany – accounting for 60 per cent.[4] During the 1990s the DAC decreased its aid flows – US aid was halved during the 1990s while France and Germany cut their aid budgets by about 40 per cent.[5] The steepest fall in global aid occurred over the period 1992–97, which coincided with a number of United Nations (UN) World Summits at which governments, in principle, committed themselves to investing additional resources in tackling the extreme levels of poverty and inequality affecting billions of people worldwide.[6] By 1997, total DAC aid flows stood at $48.4 billion or 0.22 per cent of combined OECD Gross National Product (GNP). Aid contributions increased in both 1998 and 1999 to $52.1 and $56.4 billion respectively or 0.23 per cent and 0.24 per cent of combined GNP. This amounted to just over a third of the 1970 UN target of committing 0.7 per cent of GNP toward overseas development assistance. Yet nearly 40 years ago, in 1964, OECD DAC member nations allocated 0.48 per cent of their combined GNP to overseas aid. The recent, albeit marginal, expansion in aid can be explained, in part, by some dramatic events on the world stage, including the fallout from the Asian financial crisis, the conflict in Kosovo and the resulting emergency, the devastation being wrought by HIV/AIDs, and the UN millennium summit. A number of OECD countries are consequently expanding their aid programmes, including Greece, Ireland, Luxembourg, the UK, Belgium and Canada.

Within aggregate flows, aid to the world's least developed countries has declined considerably,[7] falling from $17 billion to $12 billion between 1990 and 1999, or in per capita terms from $30 to under $20.[8] For sub-Saharan Africa, where the majority of the world's least developed countries are concentrated, it has been estimated that the volume of external resources required to halve the numbers living in poverty by 2015 would need to be more than double their current level. However, many aid donors shifted their focus away from Africa in the 1990s with per capita aid declining from $32 to $19 between 1990 and 1998. Ironically, as aid flows have declined the capacity of the international community to measure the level of resources required to tackle poverty has been enhanced. The 1997 *Human Development Report* estimated that the cost of providing universal basic social services required an additional investment of $40 billion per annum until 2005. The report also noted that a further annual expenditure of $40 billion was needed to reduce the income gap to the minimum level at which people would no longer live in extreme poverty. More recently (2002) the World Bank has estimated that the achievement of the Millennium Development Goals in 2015 would require the allocation of an additional $40 billion to $60 billion per year in aid.

AID AND POLICY COHERENCE

While concerns over inadequate aid flows were a feature of the 1990s and have endured into the twenty-first century, more attention is now being placed on the policies pursued by donors alongside their aid programmes. Donors and recipients alike are questioning whether such policies enhance or undermine the benefits of aid flows. Policy coherence is increasingly viewed as a fundamental principle of official aid programmes at two levels. First, it should permeate all components of official aid programmes, and second, it should be integrated across the policies of all government departments involved in working towards international development objectives. A further major impediment to policy coherence is the delegation of responsibilities for international development co-operation to junior rather than senior government ministers. Moreover, some countries do not have a dedicated minister for development co-operation.

In a retrograde step in the summer of 2002 European Union member states decided to abolish the EU Council of Development Ministers. Yet the pursuit of policy coherence amongst all areas of external policy and international development objectives is highlighted as a EU priority under the 1992 Maastricht Treaty.[9] However, for policy coherence to become a reality at EU level it needs to be institutionalised within the policies of the member states and at EU level. This is far from being the case. At a broader international level, the mechanisms to help ensure policy coherence across the range of government and multilateral agencies remain limited. Particular areas of concern relate to trade, agriculture and international financial policies.

The need for coherence between aid and debt policies is a particularly pertinent example of how policy harmonisation could benefit developing countries. The United Nations Conference on Trade and Development (UNCTAD) has emphasised the need for increased aid and debt relief, as well as market access to the EU and USA, to resource development in sub-Saharan Africa.[10] UNCTAD also noted that there is an urgent need to reduce the debt burden of the poorest countries. It has pointed out that debt relief provided by the Heavily Indebted Poor Countries (HIPC) initiative may be accompanied by reduced aid inflows. UNCTAD research found that 14 of the 17 African countries which reached the decision point for debt relief through HIPC suffered significant reductions in aid flows between 1996 and 1999. The average debt payments for the 22 countries which received some debt relief have been reduced by only 27 per cent. This means that many countries are spending more on debt repayments than on health care. At a regional level, sub-Saharan Africa is spending $13.3 billion per annum on debt repayments, an amount almost equal to the $15 billion per annum which the Global AIDs alliance estimates is required to tackle AIDS. To put this in context, the latter figure is between 1 and 2 per cent of world military expenditure.

STRATEGIC POLICY ISSUES AND AID

Aid, Reform and Good Governance

A number of discernible trends is evident regarding the delivery of development assistance. First, as noted above, is the alarming reduction in the volume of aid going to Africa. A second trend is the tendency of official donors to focus aid on 'high poverty/good policy' countries. Good policy tends to be defined as first generation macroeconomic liberalisation of the kind promoted by the International Monetary Fund (IMF) and the World Bank. In this regard, the World Bank report in 1998, *Assessing Aid: What Works, What Doesn't and Why?* – commonly known as the 'Dollar Report' after one of its authors – has influenced some bilateral donors. The central point in this report is that a reallocation of aid towards those countries deemed to be in the 'high poverty/good policy' bracket would lift 80 million people out of poverty each year compared with the current figure of 30 million per year. The report's authors also point out that where good macroeconomic management and efficient public institutions exist, the success rate for World Bank projects has been 86 per cent, as opposed to 45 per cent when projects are undertaken in the context of weak policies and institutions.[11] Though this argument may appear compelling it is not undisputed. Moreover, any impulse towards 'backing winners' using 'high poverty/good policy' criteria begs the question 'what happens to those countries that do not make the cut'? Of these there are many, including countries with fragile state structures, countries with weak governance and those with bad or corrupt governments.

Official donors could opt to derogate responsibility for aid programmes to these countries to NGOs, who after all work with civil society organisations which are often a competent countervailing power to bad governments. Pursuing [...]tion, however, would deny meaningful support and devel[...]e most disadvantaged people in developing countrie[...]need to invest resources into those countries w[...]nto the 'Dollar' categorisation of 'good [...] penalising poor governance, donors [...]e good governance by investing in i[...]rn-mental and civil society levels.[1...] [...]ively official donors need to develop strate[...]h civil society representatives.

Moreover, performance-based criteria for ai[...]on are not new. Over the past two decades, the World Bank [...]s conducted country policy assessments to inform the allocation of its International Development Association (IDA) resources. IDA loans are provided on highly concessional terms to various low-income countries. At present 20 criteria are used to assess country polices and institutions. These deal with economic management, structural policies, governance, public sector management, institutions, and loan performance.[13] Critics of this process suggest that such criteria operate like a report card, which is applied in all circumstances. Thus, countries that satisfy the criteria become highly dependent on external finance and confront what Abrugre has termed 'a policy monoculture' wherein diversity, dialogue and democratic processes are stifled.[14] The formulation of Poverty Reduction Strategy Papers (PRSPs) by governments, in consultation with their respective civil societies, is one of the conditions for receiving debt relief under HIPC. These PRSPs provide an opportunity for strengthening a key facet of good governance – justice and equity in the distribution of economic resources. However, a key challenge presented by PRSPs is to ensure that the principle of ownership extends into planning and decision-making on macroeconomic policy frameworks as well as on social expenditures. To date, progress in this regard has been disappointing.[15]

Aid in Situations of Weak Governance

Tackling weak governance involves addressing capacity problems in managing ministry portfolios and ensuring effective participation in international negotiations. Equally important is the need to have effective checks and balances at government and civil society levels so that policy issues can be analysed and competently challenged. However, the relationship between government and civil society is an uneasy one with the latter often equated with a political opposition by the former. Even governments deemed by the World Bank and the IMF to be 'good reformers' are often nervous or even hostile to the development of civil society.

An illustration of this hostility was the opposition by African states to the EU–Africa Civil Society Forum which was held in Cairo in April 2000 alongside the inaugural EU–Africa Heads of State Summit. Moreover, because civil society groups receive much of their funding from international NGOs, they are often branded as mouthpieces or advocates doing the bidding of external agents. Somalia provides an interesting example of a failed state. In 1992, about 200 international NGOs supported by official donors were working in Somalia. One decade later, only a few remain with official donor finance difficult to secure. In cases like Somalia, official and NGO donors must consider whether their interventions, or more generally the lack of them, are enhancing or thwarting the prospects for better governance. The Irish aid agency Trócaire is one of the NGOs working in the Gedo province of Somalia. A recent evaluation of its programme found that it made a positive difference to building local governance structures from a grassroots level. Rather than viewing the Somali 'clan' system as a barrier to governance and peace-building efforts, Trócaire used it as a springboard for building up local systems of governance.[16]

Aiding Global Good Governance

Turning to the international scene, good governance must not stop at national borders. The increasing interdependence of the global economy requires appropriate structures for global good governance. For this to happen governments need to strengthen the role of the UN as a convenor and facilitator of policy dialogue and consensus building on global economic, financial and development issues. In addition, enhanced strategic investments by official donors in the UN system, according to the comparative advantage of various UN bodies, could support such a stance. Participation is a core element of good governance and should not stop at the level of nation states. The UN is dependent on the full and participative support of its member states.

In recent years much attention has been placed on the role and operations of IFIs (international financial institutions) such as the IMF, the World Bank and the World Trade Organisation (WTO). African nations have sought major changes within the WTO secretariat to ensure the full and active participation of all member countries. While African countries comprise about 30 per cent of WTO membership they account for only 2 per cent of world trade, while Africa's share of global manufactured exports remains negligible. Many of the African countries that are WTO members do not have a resident mission in Geneva. Africa, therefore, needs to upgrade its negotiating skills, research, financial and human resource capacity in order to participate effectively in WTO negotiations. Strategically placed international aid can play a role in tackling such deficits. In relation to global economic governance and the role of the World Bank and the IMF, NGOs and civil society movements are also advocating change. They are calling for the creation of debt arbitration mechanisms where debtors as well as creditors would have an equal voice, in the context of reform of the IFIs, to make these organisations more open and democratic in their operations.

HUMANITARIANISM UNBOUND: AID IN EMERGENCY AND CONFLICT SITUATIONS

In the 1990s, nine out of ten deaths in conflict situations were of civilians, compared to one out of ten deaths during the First World War. Ninety per cent of disasters occur in the world's poorest countries. Over the past decade NGOs emerged as the primary response mechanism in disaster situations. In the case of the EU, two-thirds of its humanitarian aid is delivered through NGOs. The enhanced role of NGOs was brought about by a number of factors including the end of the Cold War, diminishing confidence in the UN and the extreme nature of the emergencies that occurred. The existence of many weak states has coincided with the increased power and resources of international agencies – particularly NGOs. The role of these agencies in emergency situations has received international recognition with humanitarian agencies winning the Nobel peace prize. Indeed, at the start of the twentieth century the Nobel Prize went to the Red Cross and as the century closed it went to Médecins Sans Frontières (MSF).

While much of the media discussion and analysis of emergencies centres on the work of aid agencies, there has been limited recognition of the coping capacities which those affected by emergencies and disasters use to rebuild their lives and communities. All too often it seems that a disaster is only deemed to have occurred when the media reports on it. Moreover, the media mostly focuses on the immediate aftermath of a disaster, while one of the most important elements in humanitarian relief is in the provision of effective support towards local coping strategies. At this stage the media loses interest. A key challenge facing NGOs is to learn from and professionalise the ways in which they conduct their humanitarian aid operations. Numerous codes, including the NGO Red Cross Code of Conduct (1994), are now in place to guide their work, but the real challenge lies in their full implementation and monitoring. The accepted primacy of NGOs in complex disaster situations has often allowed governments, North and South, to divest themselves of responsibility in reaching political solutions which tackle the root causes of conflict and human rights abuses. The result has been that humanitarian activism has, at times, been used by states to evade their responsibility to guarantee a just and equitable life.[17]

When international assistance is provided in the context of a violent conflict, it becomes a part of that context and, thus, also of the conflict. Although aid agencies seek to be neutral or non-partisan in conflict situations, the impact of their aid can often determine whether a conflict worsens or abates. Aid can reinforce, exacerbate and prolong the conflict or it can help to reduce tensions and strengthen people's capacities to disengage from conflict and work towards peaceful solutions. Often an aid programme does some of both – in some ways worsening the conflict and in others supporting disengagement. In all cases aid given during the conflict cannot remain separate from that conflict. Mary Anderson's analysis of aid, *Do No Harm: How Aid Can Support Peace or War*, begins with the premise that international aid is beneficial in conflict situations. She states, in essence, that the world is a better place because when some people suffer others who are able to, act to lessen that suffering.[18]

The challenge for aid agencies, workers and their supporters is to determine how they can be a positive force without undermining local strengths, promoting dependency or allowing aid to be misused in the pursuit of war. Anderson responds to those critical of international humanitarian aid by suggesting that:

> ... it is a moral and logical fallacy to conclude that because aid can do harm, a decision not to give aid would do no harm. In reality a decision to withhold aid from people in need would have unconscionable negative ramifications.[19]

Anderson points out that aid which is delivered well saves lives, reduces suffering and increases security. In providing aid in conflict situations, agencies should strive to identify connectors and dividers in conflicts, understand the root or proximate causes of conflict and take responsibility at head office and field level for their actions. While NGOs have a responsibility to use whatever influence they wield to build local capacities for peace, dilemmas will always arise in aid provision and dealing with them is a work in progress.

One of the major debates around humanitarian aid is the conditionalities that should be applied for provision. Information has emerged based on past practice on how aid has sometimes fuelled conflicts and been commandeered by warring factions. In seeking to avoid such outcomes by awarding or denying aid flows, what competencies do aid agencies possess? How do they anticipate the outcomes, the future, or the impact of their actions? And whose rights to humanitarian relief will dominate? DFID has been developing guidelines for peace and conflict impact assessment in an attempt to address these central questions. Such work serves to help humanitarians in assessing the potential impact of their interventions on the political landscape.

AIDING NEW FORMS OF PARTNERSHIP FOR SOCIAL ACTION

For many progressive NGOs and civil society organisations, social action – people's capacity to organise together for a common, social goal – lies at the heart of their understanding of development. Deborah Eade in *Development and Social Action* notes that 'popular mobilisation, whether to defend existing rights that are under threat, or to protest against the denial of these rights, is seen to be just as critical to the development process as economic growth – if not more so'.[20] Eade also points out that the forces which oppress and divide contemporary societies are stronger, more widespread and more diverse than they have ever been, but that the potential to generate international solidarity across borders and frontiers for a rights-based approach to development has never been greater.

In working towards this goal, global alliances such as the international campaign to ban landmines and the Jubilee 2000/Drop the Debt movements are important. Indeed, in many developed countries, political party affiliations are falling while membership of special interest and campaign groups has been constantly rising.[21] Moreover, the constituencies that global alliances can draw upon may be broader than previously envisaged. A survey commissioned in advance of the UK (2001) general election by 29 UK development charities, campaign groups and churches, under the umbrella Global View 2001, found that political parties and journalists underestimated public attitudes to international development issues. Of those aged between 16 and 44, 92 per cent wanted politicians to address international issues, including the environment, HIV/AIDS, global poverty and Third World debt. Six out of ten voters said they would be more likely to vote if international issues were featured on the political agenda. In the youngest age group (16–17), the HIV/AIDS crisis in the developing world was deemed to be a more important political priority than asylum policy in the UK, or concerns surrounding domestic transport systems. Alan Fowler argues that civil society partnerships should focus on the organisational level so as to tackle the structural causes of injustice. He noted that the 'structural nature of poverty is not particularly amenable to change using what aid has mainly had to offer – time bound programmes and projects'.[22] Instead, it needs to be challenged through organisational alliances, with projects as the vehicle rather than the end or basis of relationships.

Anderson's analysis also reflects this approach when she comments that 'international aid is fundamentally about relationships'.[23] One of the criticisms of NGDO aid relationships, noted by Fowler, is that they display a careless application of the partnership principle. Authentic partnerships require a joint commitment to long-term interaction, shared responsibility towards achieving common goals, reciprocal obligations, equality, mutuality and a balancing of power in relationships. Aid agencies, therefore, need to honestly assess the realities they confront and learn from them rather than obliquely applying the term 'partnership' to a vast and disparate array of aid relationships.[24] Eade has also noted that North–South NGO partnerships necessitate a high level of mutual accountability. In paraphrasing an analytical framework proposed by English parliamentarian and lifelong campaigner, Tony Benn, she poses the following questions to aid agencies:

- Whom do you represent?
- Where do you get your money from?
- To whom are you formally accountable?
- To whom are you morally accountable?
- How can we get rid of you?[25]

Likewise, Hauck and Land's analysis of partnership relations suggests that genuine partnership provides a framework for building greater equality, for identifying shared development objectives and for accommodating both developed countries' accountability requirements and their ownership needs. They note that:

> Those who champion the partnership concept see it as reflecting a deliberate policy choice which seeks to establish new roles and relationships between North and South that challenge structural inequalities and the inculcated mind-set of giver and taker in aid relationships. Partnership, in this sense, becomes a development objective and is closely linked to notions of capacity development, ownership and participation which see the current distribution of roles and relationships between North and South as undermining sustainable development.[26]

The challenge for aid agencies, both official and NGDOs, in the coming years will be to devise new forms of partnership for development. For aid to fundamentally address global socio-economic inequalities, it must be genuinely transformative. It must challenge unjust structures, and the aid sector itself must be open to challenge, criticism and change. While progress has been made in terms of arriving at a common understanding that tackling poverty is the primary goal of development co-operation, there is little evidence to suggest that there is a shared understanding regarding the structural changes needed to achieve this goal. Moving in this direction will be a key challenge in our globalised and polarised world.

NOTES

1. ODA covers grants or loans to countries and territories on part one of the Development Assistance Committee (DAC) list of aid recipients – developing countries which are supported by the official sector with the promotion of economic development and welfare as their main objective. This includes concessional financial flows, that is, loans with a grant element of at least 25 per cent. In addition to financial flows, technical co-operation is included in aid but loans and credits for military purposes are excluded.

2. There is no universally accepted definition of NGDOs (non-governmental development organisations). The terms 'NGDO' and 'NGO' (non-governmental organisation) are used interchangeably in this text. Alan Fowler defines them as third-party serving, non-profit based, legally constituted non-state organisations, directly or indirectly reliant on the system of international aid (Alan Fowler, 'Beyond Partnership: Getting real about NGO relationships in the aid system', *IDS Bulletin* (Sussex: IDS, 2000), pp. 1–13). In most cases they function as intermediaries to promote poverty eradication, sustainable development, social justice and lasting improvements in the circumstances of poor and excluded groups. In some cases they focus on advocacy work for policy reform. In other cases they do both.

3. Department for International Development, *Strategies for Sustainable Development* (East Kilbride: DFID, September 2000). Also see 'Governance and the Role of Civil Society: A Dochas discussion paper', presented at the Aid Forum, 16 November 2001. Dochas is the national platform of Irish Development NGOs.

4. The G8 comprises the US, UK, Italy, Canada, Japan, Germany, Russia and France.

5. Development Assistance Committee (DAC), Development Co-operation 2000 Report, *Efforts and Policies of the Members of the DAC, International Development* (Paris: OECD, 2001).

6. These summits included the Rio Earth Summit (1992), the World Summit on Social Development (1995) and the World Conference on Women (the 'Beijing Conference' 1995).

7. To be classified as a least developed country (LDC), countries must fall below thresholds established by the UN for income (US$765 per capita in 1995), economic diversification and social development. See the DAC Journal, *Development Co-operation*, 1999 Report, *Efforts and Policies of the Members of the DAC, International Development* (Paris: OECD, 2000). Of these 49 LDC countries, 35 are in sub-Saharan Africa.

8. Rubens Ricupero, Cham Prasidh and Maria Livanos Cattaui, 'World's Poorest Nations are Increasingly Marginalised', *Financial Times* (9 May 2001). See also Arthur van Diesen, *The Quality of Aid: Towards an Agenda for More Effective International Development Co-operation – A Synthesis Report on Three Case Studies of British and EC Aid* (London: Christian Aid, April 2000), p. 15.

9. Maura Leen, 'Irish and EU Development Co-operation Policies: Priorities for Ireland's presidency', *Development Review Journal* (Dublin: Trócaire,

1995), pp. 83–100. Maura Leen and Bob van Dillen, 'EU and Developing Country Relations beyond 2000: Priorities for policy action', *Development Review Journal* (Dublin: Trócaire, 2000), pp. 27–48.

10. UNCTAD Report, *Trade and Development Report: Reforming the International Financial Architecture* (New York: UNCTAD, 2000).

11. World Bank Report, *Assessing Aid: What Works, What Doesn't and Why?* (New York: World Bank, 1998). Following the 'Dollar Report', another World Bank study, *Aid and Reform in Africa* (New York: 2001), noted that if aid donors believe that they have a limited impact on policy development, the rational way to allocate aid would be based on the observed quality of poor countries policies. The study's authors point out that such an approach is also the best way to ensure that aid has a positive effect on policy. The authors explore the composition of aid and its importance, noting that technical assistance and policy dialogue is vital in the pre-reform period. With rapid reform under way, policy dialogue and financial flows are clearly important but conditional loans can also be helpful. At a later stage, conditionality is less useful as it diminishes national ownership though external finance remains important. However, the authors, in referring to conditionality, refer to those conditions which are consistent with the government's own priorities. (David Dollar and Ian Pritchett, 'Overview', *Assessing Aid: What Works, What Doesn't and Why?*, A World Bank Policy Research Report (Oxford: Oxford University Press, 1998), pp. 1–27.)

12. See Tony Fahey and Mary Sutton, 'An Abundance of Aid', *Trócaire Development Review 2000* (Dublin: Trócaire, 2000), pp. 17–25.

13. Fahey and Sutton, 'An Abundance of Aid', pp. 20–5. Also see the DAC Journal *Development Co-operation*, Vol. l, No. 1 (2000). Particularly, the chapter on 'Assessing Aid Effectiveness and Performance: An overview of approaches', pp. 127–46. Also see van Diesen, *The Quality of Aid*.

14. 'Who Governs Low-Income Countries? An interview with Charles Abugre on the PRS initiative', *News and Notices for IMF and World Bank Watchers*, Vol. 2, No. 3 (Fall 2000).

15. Kathy Selvaggio, *From Debt to Poverty Eradication: What Role for Poverty Reduction Strategies?* (International Co-operation for Development and Solidarity (CIDSE) *Caritas Internationalis*, June 2001). Also see J.P. Cling, M. Razafindrakoto and F. Roubaud, 'The PRSP Initiative: Old wine in new bottles', Annual Bank Conference on Development Economics Europe (Oslo: June 2002). This can be found at <www.world bank.org/abcde>.

16. Kathleen Fahy, 'Post-Governance Somalia beyond 2000: Prospects for a Nation without a State', *Trócaire Development Review* (Dublin: Trócaire, 1999), pp. 81–104.

17. Alex de Waal, 'Humanitarianism Unbound: The context of the call for military intervention in Africa, NGO agendas', *Trócaire Development Review* (Dublin: Trócaire, 1995), pp. 29–46.

18. Mary Anderson, *Do No Harm: How Aid Can Support Peace or War* (London: Lynne Rienner, 1999).

19. Anderson, *Do No Harm*, p. 2.

20. Deborah Eade (ed.), *Development and Social Action* (London: Oxfam, 1999).

21. See the *Human Development Report 2002: Deepening Democracy and Development* (New York: United Nations Development Programme/Oxford University Press, 2002).

22. Fowler, 'Beyond Partnership', pp. 1–13. Also Alan Fowler (ed.), *Questioning Partnership, the Reality of Aid and NGO Relations*, Vol. 31, No.3 (July 2000).

23. Fowler, 'Beyond Partnership', pp. 1–13.

24. See Alan Fowler, 'NGO Futures: Beyond aid. NGDO values and the fourth position', *Third World Quarterly, Journal of Emerging Areas*, Vol. 21, No. 4 (2000), pp. 589–603.

25. Deborah Eade (ed.), *Development and Patronage, Development in Practice Readers* (Oxford: Oxfam, 1997), pp. 4–6. Also see Deborah Eade and Ernst Ligteringen (eds), *Development in Practice Readers: Debating Development* (Oxford: Oxfam, 2001).

26. V. Hauck and T. Land, *From Beyond the Partnership Rhetoric: Reviewing Experiences and Policy Considerations for Implementing 'Genuine' Partnerships in North–South Co-operation*, ECPDM discussion paper No. 20 (Maastricht: ECDPM, 2000), p. 2.

WEB SITES

Overseas Development Institute	www.odi.org.u
Development Finance	www.fao.org/ag/ags/agsm/dfn.htm
UNESCO	unescostat.unesco.org
Global Development Finance	www.worldbank.org/prospects
OECD Development Indicators	www.oecd.org/dac/indicators/index.htm
Trócaire	www.trocaire.org
Oxfam	www.oxfam.org.uk
Save the Children	www.savethechildren.org.uk
Information about aid agencies	www.aidagency.com
The People-Centered Development Forum	iisd1.iisd.ca/pcdf

6 Is Trade an Agent of Development?

Denis O'Hearn

Economists have always found trade to be an important agent of development. Not trade generally, of course, but the 'right kind' of trade. Ironically, the right kind of trade always seems to result in the poorer regions not trading in goods that compete with the most profitable products from richer regions. Moreover, they always seem to produce commodities that the richer regions either need or desire in exchange for products that the richer regions produce and control. Yet, despite this apparent inequity, economic theory has always produced mechanisms whereby regions that follow their prescribed policies should expect to achieve economic development and modernity. They also produce analyses that explain the continuing poverty of certain regions by their failure to follow the right macroeconomic policies, primarily policies of *free trade*.

ECONOMIC THEORY, TRADE AND DEVELOPMENT

The earliest arguments to this effect were the Ricardian models of *comparative advantage*. These were static models which simply proposed that each country or region should focus production on commodities it could produce most cheaply, and then trade with other regions for items its people needed or desired. The classic example was where two regions (say, Britain and Portugal) produced two goods (cloth and wine, representing clothing and nourishment). Both countries could produce both goods. But, since Portugal could produce wine more cheaply while Britain was especially efficient in producing cloth, both countries would be better off if Portugal produced only wine and Britain only cloth, and then each traded for what they did not produce. Significantly, Ricardo argued that specialisation was advantageous even if Britain could produce *both* wine and cloth more cheaply, but the differential was greater in cloth.

There were three basic problems with this model of comparative advantage. The first was that it was static. There was no conception that in the long run regions might be advantaged by developing

111

alternative skills or productive capabilities, even if they were presently at a comparative disadvantage in these areas of production. Thus, the conception of comparative advantage is ahistorical. Portugal could enhance its economy over the long term if it enhanced its production of cloth for trade instead of just concentrating on its current competitive advantage in wine. The more recent concept of competitive advantage suggests how a country or region might *develop* its abilities to compete in certain products, especially those that are most desired in the world economy, technologically advanced and, therefore, most profitable for those regions that dominate in their production.[1] Historically, we know that this was the basis of wealth generation and developed industries in West European countries.[2]

A second problem with comparative advantage was that, like most economic models, it had no conception of distribution. A region might trade for a basket of goods with a higher market value than it could produce domestically. But would this necessarily mean that its population is better off for having done so? To the contrary, the kind of political regime that is necessary to exploit a region's 'comparative advantage' may also be one that creates inequality and benefits a prosperous elite at the expense of the majority. Economics is not primarily concerned with this problem. When economists claim that a trading regime enhances a region's 'welfare' they are not referring to the social well-being of the majority in the region but to an abstract conception of overall 'welfare' with the prerequisite that resources must be allocated in an 'efficient' manner.

The third and perhaps most damaging problem with comparative advantage was that it failed to recognise the possibility of *unequal terms of trade*, in other words, certain regions might actually *exploit* other regions through trade. Specific products – for example, tropical resources and agricultural produce – might command prices that are far lower and, thus, disadvantageous compared to others (such as manufactured goods). Raul Prebisch and Hans Singer developed an analysis of international trade in 1950 that proclaimed a structural tendency for the terms of trade of developing countries to deteriorate in their dealings with industrial countries.[3] In other words, countries of the South in trading with those of the North receive less than the full value for their primary goods, in exchange for overvalued manufactured products. Prebisch and Singer (and subsequent social scientists) empirically demonstrated that this was the model governing world trade during the twentieth century. And, analytically, they explained the basis of 'unequal terms of trade' by reference to differing conditions of demand for primary and manufactured products, the differential amounts of technology incorporated in the two sets of products, and the different conditions of labour (productive organisation and incomes) in the Northern and Southern hemispheres.

Accepting the thesis of unequal terms of trade leads us to conclude that the dynamic consequences of free trade policies based on comparative advantage, are the accumulation of wealth in developed regions and greater poverty in developing regions. Thus, trade would be an agent of development for the richer industrialised regions, but an agent of *underdevelopment* for the poorer less industrialised regions of the world. Therefore, to reprise the earlier example, if Portugal continued to produce and trade only wine, while Britain *manufactured* and traded in cloth, unequal terms of trade would ensure that Portugal became poorer and Britain became richer. Moreover, if we bring global power into our analysis of trade, we can see that Britain or, later, the United States of America, might use their global power to *ensure* that countries of the South continued to produce those products that commanded lower prices and lower profits. They might also use state power to assist transnational corporations (TNCs) to monopolise the most profitable products which are, generally, the most hi-tech industries (and, more recently, services).

The simple model of comparative advantage has, more recently, been developed by another model that replicates its outcomes – the maximum free movement of goods and money, and the regional production of local resources without government interference – but which has a more dynamic character. The Heckscher-Ohlin (H-O) model argues that each region's advantage arises from its relative factor endowments, that is that a country should produce and trade in those products for which it is best endowed. Thus, countries with relatively abundant labour (countries of the South) should produce labour-intensive products while those with relatively more capital and technology (the North) should produce more technology-intensive products.

While H-O was superior to the Ricardian model because it explained comparative advantage on the basis of differential endowments, it still suffered from a failure to recognise the historical pattern by which a country became 'endowed' with one factor of production or another. Mexico was not 'naturally' endowed with surplus labour, just as the US was not 'endowed' with high technology. These conditions were developed over time through certain political and economic strategies. For now, it is sufficient to point out the apparent problem with H-O, which is that a country like Mexico is confronted with two different development paths. The first, preferred and prescribed by orthodox economists of the North, is to produce and trade labour-intensive products until such time as its relative factor endowments change and it moves into more capital-intensive lines of production. But if one accepted the possibility of unequal terms of trade, this path might lead Mexico into an underdevelopment trap, where it would perpetually trade undervalued labour-intensive goods for overvalued Northern products. Alternatively, Mexico could pursue a different development path (which, incidentally, was the historical path of the United States and Western Europe) by trying to *create* a different competitive advantage in higher-technology (thus, more profitable) modes of production.

For orthodox economists and economic policymakers, then, it was necessary to demonstrate that there was a dynamic process whereby *free trade could become an agent of development* (by facilitating convergence between the richer and the poorer countries). It fell to Paul Samuelson to revive the connection between comparative advantage, free trade, and convergence between poorer and richer regions. Samuelson further developed the H-O model to 'demonstrate' (according to the orthodox parameters of his model) that specialisation and trade according to comparative advantage would naturally lead to convergence between the labour-intensive (poorer) and capital-intensive (richer) countries. *So long as there was free trade*, the North would export its relatively abundant capital to Mexico to mix with that country's cheap labour. Mexican labour would consequently become scarcer and the cost of labour would rise. In other words, free trade alone is an agent of convergence in incomes, factory prices and commodity prices between richer and poorer regions. One of the most important political aspects of Samuelson's analysis was the view that labour did not have to migrate in order for global incomes to equalise. It was sufficient for capital and goods to move freely. Maximum free trade would ensure global development and convergence without the need for large-scale movements of populations (a cynic might observe that this was quite convenient, since Southern people of colour were now replacing white Europeans as the major migrants into industrialised Northern countries).[4]

POLICY APPROACHES

The orthodox economic approach is closely tied to the policy of free trade. Most current policy positions, from the US right wing to European social democrats, clearly favour free trade and are vehemently opposed to protecting local markets against imports as an agent of development. The usual policy argument is that increased exports generate resources for developmental purposes, as well as the foreign exchange, to avoid foreign governmental debt. Thus, in theory it is not trade generally but *exports* that are the engine of growth and development. This model is often described as *export-led development* (ELD). It is argued that economic policy-makers should strive to maximise export growth and the best way to achieve this is through free trade.

There are, however, economists and social activists who, for developmental purposes, promote trade policies other than free trade. The traditional policy in this regard is *import-substitution indus-trialisation* (ISI). The argument here is that countries can upgrade their economic activities (in other words develop new *competitive advantages*) by protecting certain products like basic manufactures and then machinery, until local producers are competitive enough to survive without protection. Another way to put it is that *infant industries* need protection from being competed out of business by mature firms from other countries, and trade policy (barriers to imports) is the most effective way to do this. A common argument against such protectionism is that there are no mechanisms to guarantee that protected infant industries will sufficiently mature to become competitive. Indeed, they are more likely to continue relying on protection for their profitability instead of innovating and becoming more efficient. For example, if there is political corruption in a country, local businessmen are likely to use their resources to ensure that politicians maintain trade protection for their industries.

Moreover, it may be possible to become competitive in a few lines of basic industries, during a period called *easy industrialisation*. But then it is much harder to *deepen* industrial development into more technically sophisticated lines such as machinery or hi-tech products. If a country finds itself unable to deepen and produce resources that are necessary for basic manufacturing purposes (for example, to produce machinery to make cloth and not just to produce clothing), it will have to continue importing these necessary products and eventually incur trade deficits. This will, in turn, stop development dead in its tracks.

For some time, the arguments against ISI held sway within economics and in wider policy circles. More recently, however, the rapid growth of the East Asian economies has opened up a revived interest in some forms of trade protectionism for development. The refined protectionist argument is that countries should *strategically* or *selectively protect* certain key products, in a policy environment that encourages the producers of those products to eventually move into export. The Japanese car industry, for example, began by making cars for a tightly protected internal market. This market was not large enough for the car industry to become a major impetus toward sustained industrial growth, but the protective policies sustained the industry long enough for Japanese cars to become competitive. Then Japanese car-makers entered the global market with widely recognised successful consequences. Similar arguments have been made about the success of the South Korean electronics industry. The key point here is that protection is not sufficient to sustain industry in itself. A *developmental state* must also have a kit bag of economic incentives and sanctions that will guide local industries towards efficiency and export-orientation. Thus, the period since the 1970s saw the revival of interest in policies of *protection for export*.

SOCIOLOGICAL APPROACHES

The sociology of development, as opposed to orthodox development economics, bases its analysis of trade and development largely on empirical observations of actual cases of 'successful developers' (like the recent East Asian states mentioned above or late-nineteenth-century European states) and less successful ones (too numerous to mention). Rather than base its analysis on abstract models, this approach begins by observing and analysing actual political-economic institutions and actors. Thus, sociologists are more likely than economists to assume that capitalist markets are and will inevitably be controlled and distorted by states and corporations – the major agents of economic power.

Moreover, as corporations have enhanced their wealth and power, and attained global reach, their ability to influence and manipulate markets has become more profound. States, too, attained global reach and began to organise *inter-state institutions* like the World Bank and the International Monetary Fund (IMF). It was no accident that the British state sponsored its leading manufacturers by protecting trade in machinery during the so-called classical era of free trade in the nineteenth century. More recently, the ultimate institutional sponsor of free trade – the World Trade Organisation (WTO) – has made it a priority to protect *intellectual property*. In doing so, it protects the most profitable products of the world's large TNCs from the competitive environment of free trade, since their products are based on 'intellectual property'. Even if this were not the case, however, a strong argument could be made that 'free trade' is not really 'free' because such a high proportion of products that are traded across international borders are actually exported by one subsidiary of a TNC to another. As far back as the 1970s, a fifth of US exports and a third of imports comprised intra-firm trade, that is, exports of one subsidiary to another within a single company.[5] Intra-firm trade has undoubtedly risen during the 1990s and into the twenty-first century along with new forms of agglomerated investment that emerged during that time.

The importance of this manipulation of trade is the degree to which, as the world-systems approach argues, international inequality is the product of a worldwide division of labour, where certain (core) regions produce the most hi-tech, high-profit products while other (peripheral) regions produce the most labour-intensive and lowest-profit products. This unequal division of labour expresses itself in two ways. First, that certain poor regions largely specialise in primary products that command lower relative prices in international trade. Second, that the world economy is made up of a series of *commodity chains*, where the lower-profit stages of production (extraction, basic assembly) are concentrated in poorer peripheral regions while the higher-profit stages of production (research, product development, hi-tech production) are concentrated in richer industrialised regions. The increasing complexity of this division of labour causes the increased movement of goods between different modes of these commodity chains in international trade.[6] Various parts of a car or computer may be produced in Malaysia, Mexico, South Africa, Britain and Ireland for final consumption in Germany or the United States, with each stage of production involving the importing of parts and resources, and exporting of semi-fabricates and final products.

The extent to which large corporations control this trade form hardly designates it as 'free' in the classical sense. It is more comparable to a cross-border version of central planning, although the planning board is a corporate board of directors rather than an arm of the state. The prices at which a computer or pharmaceutical TNC sells parts or chemicals from one subsidiary to another are not determined by 'the global market', but rather by corporate accountants whose business is not 'efficiency' but increasing profit margins in areas such as tax avoidance and the protection of technology.

PATHS OF DEVELOPMENT

Students of imperialism have analysed the development of the worldwide division of labour through successive stages of colonialism.[7] They have attempted to support the view that the interests of the core regions, whether in mercantilism or industrialism, have helped to mould, reproduce and reshape this division of labour and its constituent commodity chains. The extent to which regions are incorporated into this global regime of production and trade is crucial to their development possibilities and determines how trade impacts on their development. There are three broad regional developmental outcomes arising from commodity chains, although these may change over time or may be combined in a given region. For the most *peripheral* regions, the main outcome is marginalisation into the restricted production of primary goods, which are traded at terms that are insufficient to draw the region out of poverty. For the most advantaged *core* regions, a large proportion of local production is in products that incorporate large amounts of technology and 'intellectual property' so that exports are profitable and trade becomes an engine of (further) development. Regions at a stage of development between the core and periphery have sufficiently profitable activities, in intermediate modes of global commodity chains leading to export, to enable them to maintain incomes substantially better than the marginalised primary exporters. Yet few of these regions ever catch up with the hi-tech exporters in the core regions.

A region's location in the three broad productive and trading positions – which world-systems analysis has named as the *core* (richest regions), *periphery* (poorest regions), and *semi-periphery* (intermediate) – is not a matter of chance or 'endowment', but one of historical development. Some critical analysts would go so far as to propose that regions can be 'locked in' to historical paths that either enable them to achieve further prosperity or make it more difficult for them to achieve upward mobility in the global divisions of labour.[8] Empirical analysis has shown that there is relatively little movement between these regional positions, although mobility may appear fluid because of the attention given to upwardly mobile cases such as Western Europe, North America and, most recently, East Asia.[9]

The most marginal historical path to development is that of *export monoculture*, where local farmers of a region become producers of a single crop for export. Some regions of West Africa, for example, are concentrated in the production of peanuts or cocoa for export. Central American regions are highly dependent on the production and trade in coffee beans. From the ahistorical point of view of orthodox economics, this is a 'natural' state of being where such regions are endowed with these products and have not yet developed their productive capabilities beyond a comparative advantage in such crops or extractive raw materials. Yet historical analysis shows that this is hardly a 'natural' state of affairs but the result of how the region was incorporated into the world economy. McMichael, for example, in *Development and Social Change*, shows how a colonial division of labour was forced on such regions, breaking down their indigenous manufacturing industries and forcing the reduction of local production to export monoculture.[10] However, irrespective of how export monocultures were created, their salient feature remains the creation of a negative path dependency, where overdependence on exports of a crop actually impedes the region's development. Farmers in a country like Guatemala can be offered reduced prices for their coffee beans even as the North American luxury coffee chains roast and sell them at record rates of profit. It becomes extremely difficult, if not impossible, for the region to break out of its poverty trap and restricted pattern of trade to the point that it may be plunged – as with the recent example of sub-Saharan Africa – further into poverty. Surely, this is an example of where trade is an *agent of underdevelopment*.

The second historical path, that of the industrialised core, is in many ways the opposite of export monoculture. In this case, trade is almost certainly an agent of development (although these are the regions where it is least needed). In historical terms, perhaps the most interesting question about these regions is how they achieved such a position where trade became an engine of development. In other words, why are exports 'developing' rather than 'under-developing'? The transition of the major world powers to such a situation – e.g., the *hegemonic* states of Holland, Britain and the US – may be generally explained by how they combined their overwhelming military power with new forms of economic organisation and means of sourcing raw materials to achieve global domination.[11] But this is perhaps the least interesting historical path for other regions that simply want to achieve a higher degree of development. For such regions, more interesting cases include the small European states that achieved upward mobility during the latter half of the nineteenth century, and the East Asian states (and possibly Ireland) which appeared to combine trade and development in the last decades of the twentieth century.

The Scandinavian states provide some good case studies of upward growth within small regions.[12] These small European countries, having been compelled to integrate into the world market, realised the gap that had opened up between them and the industrialised European core after the industrial revolution. But, instead of continuing to adapt to an externally imposed division of labour, they developed the international competitiveness of their domestic infant industries. In particular, countries like Denmark encouraged broad-based agricultural revolutions and then used the gains from agricultural productivity to raise the average incomes of all of their economic sectors. This created a sufficiently robust internal market that was strong enough and once protected against imports from the more powerful European countries, able to sustain domestic industrial products, especially with the specialised processing of local agricultural produce. While countries like Denmark 'succeeded' in industrialising through the use of strategic trade protectionism, other countries that accepted their narrow role of primary goods exporters to the rich European core (Ireland, Portugal, Spain, Romania) were further peripheralised and failed to industrialise.

Similarly, during the recent development of East Asian countries like Japan, South Korea and Taiwan, according to analysts like So and Chiu, states did not follow neo-liberal policies of free trade and free enterprise, but instead had 'a strategic role to play in taming international and domestic market forces and harnessing them to national ends'.[13] For example, the South Korean state violated free trade principles by extending subsidised credit and foreign exchange to its corporations as long as they met targets for introducing new technologies and expanding exports. They also protected these companies against imports in local markets with the proviso that they made satisfactory progress toward becoming strong exporters. Likewise, Taiwan violated free trade prescriptions by protecting its key sectors from imports until its firms were able to compete in export markets. Despite neo-liberal assertions that economic growth requires free enterprise and free trade, the experiences of East Asian economies appear to validate an alternative strategically protectionist approach.

The examples of Western Europe in the nineteenth century and East Asia in the twentieth appear to contradict the economic orthodoxy that favours free trade. They suggest that development is more likely to be achieved through strategic policies that include the protection of local economies. Free trade is an agent of further development only *after* a country or region has made the initial shift into competitive advantage in high profit industrial products. Therefore, a country benefits from free trade after it has achieved upward mobility in the global division of labour from peripheral modes of production to core production and export.

But there is a recent third example that many experts believe to be a prototype of the benefits of free trade in the new globalised economy. Ireland is widely argued to illustrate the fact that free trade *is* an agent of development because it became one of the most liberalised countries in the world while developing one of the most rapidly expanding economies during the 1990s and into the twenty-first century. At the end of the 1980s, the Irish economy was stagnant, unemployment was at a record high not exceeded anywhere in the European Union except possibly Spain, and the state was one of the most indebted in the world. By 1994, however, the southern Irish economy began to boom with GDP growth rates rising to 5.8 per cent and remaining at least as high since. Southern Irish per capita national income, which had been barely 60 per cent of the EU average in 1988, reached the EU average a decade later. Southern Irish rates of growth were so high in the 1990s, at least by EU standards, that a 1994 article in Morgan Stanley's *Euroletter* asked, only partly in jest, whether Ireland was now a 'celtic tiger', aping the high-growth economies of East Asia.[14] However, the sources of Irish growth are still debated. Most economists credit Irish economic success to neo-liberal policies of free trade, fiscal controls, social partnership agreements that ensured pay restraint and flexible labour, the accumulation of highly educated human capital, exchange rate stability, and a generally favourable macroeconomic environment. In this liberal environment, some economists argued, trade (especially exports) clearly became an agent of economic growth.

There are, however, good reasons for disputing the neo-liberal interpretation of Ireland's economic growth (and the model it produced) not least the very particular circumstances pertaining to the Irish experience. It grew rapidly during the 1990s for several unique reasons that enabled it to attract a historically high proportion of US-based TNC investments into Europe. Just as the Single European Market opened up in the early 1990s, the USA was going through a record period of economic expansion. After severe cutbacks in foreign investment during the 1980s, the USA began to reinvest in Europe, particularly with a view to getting its exports into the new EU 'big market'. Ireland was the ideal bridgehead from which to launch these new investments. It had an English-speaking workforce prepared to accept low wages and work flexibly because unemployment rates were so high. The unemployed included engineers who were trained to work in the information technology (IT) companies that were the backbone of US investments. Moreover, the Irish government was not only committed to liberal policies like free trade and free enterprise, but also willing to offer huge incentives to any company that would locate in Ireland. These incentives included government grants and, most crucially, a corporate tax rate that was by far the lowest in the EU (10 per cent, compared to 30–40 per cent elsewhere). When the Irish state attracted the computer giant Intel to Ireland in 1991, several major IT firms followed it into Ireland over the next few years.

It was this inflow of foreign investments that shifted value-added profits into Ireland to exploit its low tax rates and underpinned its subsequent rapid growth. The dominant overseas perception of Ireland's economy was that free trade had encouraged rapid export growth, and thus became an agent of development. But this unique set of circumstances could hardly be repeated in developing countries. This argument is supported by the fact that Ireland's economic growth was so rapid in the 1990s because its population was very low (3–3.5 million) and, therefore, capturing 20 per cent of US investments in Europe could have a significant effect on economic growth. US investments alone directly accounted for 50 per cent of Irish growth in the 1990s, and an even greater share in the late 1990s and early 2000s. Britain, comparatively, captured *twice as much* of the US investment in Europe but had a population 20 times greater. Far from this resulting in rapid growth, Britain simply sank further down the European league table of economic prosperity.

CONCLUSION

Whether exports are an agent of development or growth is highly dependent on the specific circumstances of a country. Historically, it appears that free trade is *not* an agent of development, rather, trade is an economic instrument, like many others, that must be carefully managed if a country is to achieve economic growth. In most historical cases, the policies that led to development were the antithesis of the free trade policies that are being prescribed today by the world's leading international economic institutions.

NOTES

1. M.E. Porter, *The Competitive Advantage of Nations* (New York: Free Press, 1990).
2. D. Senghaas, *The European Experience* (Leamington Spa: Berg, 1985).
3. See Hans Singer and Patricia Gray, 'Trade Policy and Growth of Developing Countries', *World Development*, Vol. 16, No. 3 (1988), pp. 395–403.
4. C. Edwards, *The Fragmented World: Competing Perspectives on Trade, Money and Crisis* (London: Methuen, 1985).
5. R. Jenkins, *Transnational Corporations and Uneven Development* (London: Methuen, 1987), p. 115.
6. G. Gereffi and M. Korzeniewicz (eds), *Commodity Chains and Global Capitalism* (Westport, Conn.: Praeger, 1994).
7. H. Magdoff, *The Age of Imperialism* (New York: Monthly Review, 1969). Also see I. Wallerstein, *Historical Capitalism* (London: Verso, 1983).
8. W.B. Arthur, 'Self-reinforcing Mechanisms in Economics', in P. Anderson, K. Arrow and D. Pines (eds), *The Economy as an Evolving Complex System* (Santa Fe: Santa Fe Institute, 1988). Also see J. Haydu, 'Making Use of the Past: Time periods as cases to compare and as sequences of problem solving', *American Journal of Sociology*, Vol. 104, No. 2 (1998), pp. 339–71; and D. O'Hearn, *The Atlantic Economy: Britain, the US and Ireland* (Manchester: Manchester University Press, 2001), pp. 1–11.
9. G. Arrighi, G. and J. Drangel, 'Stratification of the World-Economy: An explanation of the semiperipheral zone', *Review*, Vol. 10, No. 1 (1986), pp. 9–74.
10. P. McMichael, *Development and Social Change: A Global Perspective* (Thousand Oaks, Calif.: Pine Forge Press, 1996), pp. 18–19. Also see J. Madeley, *Hungry for Trade: How the Poor Pay for Free Trade* (London: Zed Books, 2000), pp. 42–56.
11. See G. Arrighi, *The Long Twentieth Century* (London: Verso, 1994).
12. Senghaas, *The European Experience*.
13. A. So and S. Chiu, *East Asia and the World Economy* (Thousand Oaks, Calif.: Sage, 1995), p. 12.
14. K. Gardiner, 'The Irish Economy: A Celtic tiger?', *Ireland: Challenging for Promotion*, Morgan Stanley *Euroletter* (1 August 1994), pp. 9–21.

WEB SITES

WTO	www.wto.org
GATT	www.ciesin.org
International Trade Centre	www.intracen.org
UK Department of Trade and Industry	www.dti.gov.uk/ worldtrade/intro.htm
Magazine of the International Trade Centre	www.tradeforum.org
McMaster History of Economic Thought	www.socsci.mcmaster.ca/ ~econ/ugcm/3ll3
History of Economic Thought	cepa.newschool.edu/het
Third World Network	www.twnside.org
World Development Movement	www.wdm.org.uk

7 Building a Global Security Environment

Purnaka L. de Silva[1]

In the decade prior to 11 September 2001 there were over 100 armed conflicts taking place in over 70 different locations around the globe. The proliferation of conflicts that have arisen out of these older domestic disputes have been exacerbated by the inflow and use of conventional weaponry, particularly small arms, light weapons, ammunition and explosives. Indeed, of the 24 largest conflicts in the year 2000, 17 had origins that predated 1989.[2] Land mines and Improvised Explosive Devices (IEDs) are other conventional weapons systems that continue to maim thousands of non-combatant civilians each year in countries like Cambodia and Mozambique, even after the conflicts for which they were imported have long ended. Indeed, only a small minority of the contemporary armed conflicts worldwide involve the deployment of high-technology weaponry. While weapons of mass destruction – nuclear, chemical and biological – continue to take centre stage in debates and policy making surrounding disarmament in the international arena, small arms and light weapons have accounted for the majority of armed conflict–related deaths, disabilities and injuries. The post-Second World War statistics on the kill rate of conventional weapons is quite staggering. As Andrew Pierre points out: 'Over the past fifty years an estimated 159 wars have claimed over 25,000,000 lives … [therefore] … We should be acutely aware that conventional weapons do all of the killing in today's world.'[3] Pierre cogently argues that the proliferation of conventional arms is of immediate global concern and has specified several factors that provide a backdrop to the debate around global security and conventional arms usage.[4]

CONVENTIONAL WEAPONS AND METHODS OF CONFLICT

Conventional arms remain the central bulwark on which the operations of state military *and* insurgent forces are built and are, therefore, the first choice of weapons in any armed conflict. Moreover, the deterrence protocol with respect to the use of nuclear, chemical and biological weapons has effectively prevented states from using them on the battlefield. For example, even though the Iraqi armed forces are reported to have used chemical and/or biological weapons against opponents of the Ba'athist regime, like the 'Marsh Arabs' and the Kurds, there was a marked reluctance to use such weapons during the invasion of Kuwait. Also, the increasing sophistication and lethalness of conventional arms have made them more attractive to state and non-state combatants alike. A military–technical revolution has led to the development of smart, computer-driven weapons systems with a high single-salvo kill probability and extended ranges of delivery with greater accuracy. For example, cruise missiles and conventional artillery have the capacity to detect and identify long-range targets through hi-tech sensors aided by the development of command, control, communication and intelligence technology.

In effect, new military technologies are eroding the traditional distinction between conventional arms and weapons of mass destruction. Some of the new generation of conventional weapons systems have a dual use which can ensure medium or mass destruction. The enhanced power and accuracy of current conventional weaponry can make their deployment as devastating as tactical nuclear weapons. High-technology conventional weapons are becoming more widely available and are rapidly appearing in the arsenals of an increasing number of countries. This technology includes advanced combat aircraft, electronic warfare technology, long-range and more accurate missiles, smart munitions and quiet submarines. For example, in the 2001–02 war in Afghanistan, in which over 22,000 bombs were dropped within its first four months, the United States (US) tested the new so-called 'Daisycutter' with its capacity to obliterate a square kilometre within seconds. The effects can be similar to that of a small nuclear explosion.

The trade in conventional arms is widespread and voluminous. Overcapacity is one of the main reasons for this trend, where the export of arms is seen as *the* solution to the industry's problems and is pursued fiercely among competing nations with an increasing willingness to sell even the most destructive weapons to often volatile regimes. Also, arms sales are often secured through the use of inducements including technology transfer and offset agreements, barters and bribes (which are even tax-deductible in Western Europe). However, the consequences of increased arms sales include disreputable and oppressive regimes acquiring excessive levels of conventional arms which can often destabilise a region (e.g. the Persian Gulf and the Middle East). According to the US Department of Defense, the audited worldwide aggregate demand for the importation of conventional weapons and delivery systems by region from 1994 to 2000, saw the Middle East and East Asia account for 30 per cent each, or 60 per cent in total of global arms sales.[5] The Middle East is a highly volatile region, especially in light of the regional ramifications of the Israeli–Palestinian conflict and the 'war on terror' implemented by Ariel Sharon, the Israeli premier. East Asia is another volatile region with potential flashpoint situations that could spill over onto the global stage, such as Taiwan–China and North–South Korea, and the contested control of the Spratley and Paracel Islands. In these circumstances, the export of weaponry to such regions is both irresponsible and counter-productive, as arms proliferation will serve only to fuel conflicts. It is illogical to assume that conventional weapons parity among hostile or warring nations is a 'guarantee of stability', though it provides a convenient premise for major arms exporting countries like the US, Britain, France, Russia and China to maintain sales to regions in conflict. In effect, the arms trade is extremely lucrative for manufacturers and suppliers, and is often justified on the grounds that the weapons industry creates jobs and investment.

The arms trade debilitates socio-economic development in the regions affected by conflict. The purchase of conventional arms drains resources needed to ameliorate unacceptable social and economic conditions. Within the developing world, military expenditure is substantially greater than the combined public expenditure on health and education. There is a growing consensus among development NGOs that development assistance should be made conditional to limitations on the military spending of aid recipients. Among some developed nations, the financial burden of acquiring advanced arms technologies has increased public debt, thus contributing to a fiscal imbalance. There is also a significant correlation, particularly in countries subjected to authoritarian regimes, between the acquisition of arms and human rights abuses. Oppressive regimes often engage armed forces in an internal policing role resulting in the repression of ethnic and religious minorities.

Weapons exported to the developing world by developed countries have frequently been used to suppress dissident domestic groups and movements. For example, Indonesia's former president, General Suharto, was a Western-supported dictator of the world's fourth largest country from 1965–98. Operating under a thin veneer of democracy, Suharto exercised power with a strong military hand that included widespread internal repression of trade unions, opposition political movements, students, the media and religious groups. Suharto's power was largely unchallenged by Western governments for three decades because Indonesia was a major importer of arms from countries that included Britain and the United States. Despite widespread evidence produced by human rights organisations and NGOs that Suharto was using imported weaponry for the means of internal repression, Western arms exports to Indonesia continued unabated. Even Suharto's sanctioning of genocide in East Timor (where 200,000 people, almost one-third of the population, were killed from 1975–2000) failed to bring an immediate halt to the supply of arms to Jakarta. Suharto ultimately agreed to hand over power to his deputy, B.J. Habibie, in May 1998 following internal unrest and economic collapse. The handover was significantly facilitated by the military which still retained its influence over political events in Indonesia and continues to be widely condemned for human rights abuses throughout the archipelago. Suharto's period in power provided clear evidence of the destructive effect that arms exports from developed countries to oppressive regimes can have for civilian populations in the developing world.[6]

A discernible trend at the beginning of the twenty-first century has been the fast-growing, widespread use of small arms, light weapons, ammunition and explosives in armed conflicts throughout the developing world. These weapons are easily obtained and most commonly used, often exclusively and in large quantities, in ethnic conflicts and internal disputes. According to one UN study, light armaments have been responsible for 90 per cent of the casualties and deaths in recent wars, often illicitly trafficked in black markets, which are especially difficult to control and monitor.[7]

REGIONAL CONFLICTS

The growth of both national and internal terrorism is a compelling reason for governments to be concerned about the availability of light weapons and explosives in illicit world markets. For example, in Peshawar in the troubled north-west frontier province of Pakistan, weapons used during the Afghan civil war are freely available and their use has acted as a catalyst for destabilising Pakistani domestic politics following the 1999 military coup led by General Pervez Musharraf. Small arms and light weapons are also manufactured in

Peshawar which considerably adds to the turmoil in the region. Afghan war surplus includes US-made Stinger shoulder-held anti-aircraft missiles, which were widely dispensed by US agencies to the Mujahideen during their conflict with occupying Russian forces in the 1980s. The alleged involvement of the Pakistani Inter-Services Intelligence (ISI) agency in the Taliban regime's rise to power in Afghanistan has further exacerbated the situation and destabilised the whole central and South Asia region, particularly in bordering countries such as Tajikistan and Kashmir that are vulnerable to infiltration by armed Islamic militants. Although the American-led coalition war in Afghanistan in 2001–02 deposed the fundamentalist Taliban regime, it also sharpened regional hostilities and increased tensions in Afghanistan's neighbouring countries. Moreover, the US/British intervention in Afghanistan dramatically increased the number of refugees in the region and exacerbated poverty levels in an already underdeveloped society. As in other conflict scenarios civilians suffered the highest death toll.

Arming a region where there has been pre-existing tensions and conflict, whether through the transfer of arms from outside powers or the local manufacturing of weapons, may seriously aggravate civil or sectarian tensions and spur an arms race toward conflict. The Middle East (and the Persian Gulf) over the last five decades and East Asia in the 1990s are cases in point. Hi-tech aircraft and naval radar sales by US president George W. Bush to Taiwan are creating further tensions with China. Compelling evidence from the Cold War era suggests that contributing to an arms race creates regional instability, thereby ensuring that any ensuing war is even more violent and destructive. Regional conflicts can potentially draw major arms-supplying nations into the conflict – in this case the US and Europe.

Competition between arms manufacturers can also aggravate international political tensions. Economic competitiveness for new markets among arms-producing countries, particularly those suffering the effects of overproduction, is to be expected and is in most cases manageable without leading to major political disagreement. Nevertheless, political disputes may result from disagreements about particular arms transfers in the context of critical international security considerations. For example, Chinese missile sales to the Democratic People's Republic of Korea, Iran and Pakistan, as well as USA sales to Taiwan have been a source of tension between Washington and Beijing. Conventional arms sales by cash-strapped nations from the former Soviet controlled Eastern bloc to maverick states and insurgent forces are another serious problem. For example, the *Guardian* reported on 29 April 2002 that Iraq purchased an arms shipment from the Czech Republic costing Baghdad $800,000. The arms were exported under licences for Syria and Yemen and included anti-aircraft missiles and long-range missile guidance systems. These semi-legal sales cannot be easily stemmed, especially when the USA, Britain and France are among the largest arms-exporting states, thereby setting a less than desirable example for other weapons-producing states or those with a post-Cold War surplus. For multilateral restraint to become a reality, major arms exporters like the USA, Britain, France, China and Russia must take the lead in setting a global standard of conventional arms control and in monitoring the end use of exports.

THE QUESTION OF PROLIFERATION

Pierre's *Cascade of Arms* refers to both the legal and illicit trade in hi-tech conventional weapons and delivery systems, as well as small arms, light weapons, ammunition and explosives.[8] He specifically highlights the hi-tech end use of conventional weapons and delivery systems, which is relevant to a broader discussion on conventional arms control. Pierre suggests that the potential casualties resulting from the use of hi-tech conventional weapons would be very high. Although similar to weapons of mass destruction, hi-tech conventional weapons have a far greater killing potential than small arms, light weapons, ammunition and explosives, and therefore must be subject to specific disarmament strategies and international treaties as part of a more robust structure of deterrence. This initiative would introduce a more effective and manageable means of limiting the trade in light weapons. The main focus of the debate needs to be on conventional weapons that have caused the greatest number of casualties in recent armed conflicts worldwide. The trade in conventional weapons, therefore, needs to be addressed as a matter of urgency given the ongoing toll of casualties, and should be central to a disarmament agenda. Moreover, a more comprehensive structure of deterrence in relation to weapons proliferation (for example, of weapons of mass destruction and all types of conventional weapons) is required to make the more volatile regions of the world more secure and peaceful.

The type of conflict management advocated by NGOs involves the control or regulation of the legal trade in conventional weapons and the development of new strategies to combat the illicit trade in these arms. The debate on the arms trade should be informed by the situation on the ground in many deeply divided societies and the vulnerability of the non-combatant civilian population in conflict situations – specifically women, children and the elderly. The targets in contemporary armed conflicts are mostly people and property – homes, infrastructure and sites of production or livelihood – and this results in mass refugee flows (across recognised international borders) and internally displaced persons (IDPs – within national borders). The response from the international community to these human catastrophes by way of humanitarian assistance and peace-keeping operations – such as those in Cambodia, East Timor, the Balkans and the Congo – pales in comparison with an estimated annual global expenditure of US$750 billion on conventional weapons. This situation is often exacerbated by the fact that humanitarian assistance and peacekeeping operations are delivered in a climate of political indifference and dithering by international leaders and their civil servants – the genocide in Rwanda and Bosnia-Herzegovina being two recent examples.

The major arms-producing nations need to shoulder greater responsibility in making available necessary resources for humanitarian assistance and peacekeeping operations to alleviate the suffering of victims of conflict. Immediate steps also need to be taken in the area of disarmament in tandem with more long-term initiatives. Arms control measures should include countering the fast growth and widespread use of conventional weapons in armed conflicts in the developing world. Similarly, new innovative strategies are required to reduce the availability and transfer of such weapons. There is a particular need to target illicit black market trafficking in arms and to enforce the decommissioning of weapon stockpiles as a strategic measure to short-circuit overcapacity. These measures could be part of a code of conduct for multilateral restraint which would necessarily entail the co-operative scaling down of defence industries in the face of post-Cold War overcapacity in arms production. Disarmament in the form of the decommissioning of weapons stockpiles, demobilisation and reintegration of ex-combatants into society dovetails into the final phase of peacekeeping operations and helps create conditions for stability and sustainable peace.

A longer-term and more difficult strategy is to create the necessary global, regional and national conditions for peaceful co-existence that would limit the need for national governments or their political opposition to resort to conflict. A central pillar of this strategy for creating a global security environment is to question the Clause-witzian logic (where evolving needs should be supplied) underlying modern weapons proliferation and to undermine the reliance on weapons as the first means of recourse for defusing politicised conflicts. Peaceful coexistence involves eliminating the reliance on technologies, such as armaments, which tend to destabilise a country or region. In addition, a robust structure of deterrence is required to dissuade states and insurgent forces from using conventional weapons, particularly against civilian targets. This measure would also target authoritarian regimes where there is a significant correlation between the acquisition of arms and human rights abuses.

Global security could also be enhanced by redirecting resources and finances expended on arms into poverty alleviation and human development. Demilitarisation would potentially minimise the option of resorting to armed conflict in national and international disputes, and enable countries in the developing and developed worlds to significantly increase public expenditure on housing, health, education and overhead infrastructural investment, thereby, improving the quality of life of their citizenry. Reducing the defence burdens on states would ease their public-debt problem and assist them in overturning their fiscal imbalances. Furthermore, large arms exporters such as the USA, Britain, France, China and Russia, should be obliged to take the lead in setting the demilitarisation agenda by introducing a global standard of conventional arms control so that multilateral restraint can become a reality.

GLOBAL SECURITY AND DEVELOPMENT: REQUIRED RESPONSES

The post-Cold War surge in internal disputes and civil conflicts has underlined the need to encourage disarmament as part of a broader human rights and humanitarian agenda. In his millennium report, *We the Peoples*, the Secretary-General of the United Nations, Kofi Annan, noted that:

The death toll from small arms dwarfs that of all other weapons systems – and in most years greatly exceeds the toll of the atomic bombs that devastated Hiroshima and Nagasaki. In terms of the carnage they cause, small arms, indeed, could well be described as 'weapons of mass destruction'. Yet there is still no global non-proliferation regime to limit their spread, as there is for chemical, biological and nuclear weapons. Small arms proliferation is not merely a security issue; it is also an issue of human rights and development. The proliferation of small arms sustains and exacerbates armed conflicts.[9]

In other words, building a secure global environment through disarmament is beneficial for human development and the protection of human rights as enshrined in the United Nations Declaration of Human Rights.

Legal and illicit arms trading practices, and political and military opposition to reform hamper the creation of a secure environment. Measures that could surmount these impediments include the establishment of an international institution for restraining conventional arms sales to monitor and, ultimately, control weapon flows. There is also a lack of coherence in policy making in relation to the legal and illicit trade in conventional weapons as opposed, for example, to nuclear non-proliferation agreements which have halved the number of stockpiled weapons since 1982.[10] Controlling or regulating arms sales necessitates: eradicating the dangerous and destabilising transfers of conventional weapons to conflict regions and deeply divided societies; limiting excessive spending on arms by poor countries; scaling down armaments production within developed countries; and ensuring that weapons are not exported to regimes that violate human rights. The ideal situation is the co-operative scaling down of defence industries in the full acknowledgement of the dangers of overcapacity in arms production. This means the facilitation of institutional structures which can monitor and enforce disarmament and develop counter-measures to conventional weapons proliferation.

These counter-measures designed to regulate arms production would need to involve:

- Securing compliance with disarmament treaties
- Preventing the arming and re-arming of the world's military forces through multilateral restraint
- Addressing the issue of weapons overproduction and the decommissioning of weapon stockpiles
- Reducing threat and conserving resources
- Dealing with rogue states and arms dealers involved in the illicit trade of conventional weapons
- Co-ordinating international responses to arms proliferation

- Devolving more effective and coercive powers to international arms-control agencies
- Integrating disarmament more comprehensively into the larger UN agenda and, thereby, ensuring that all offices and agencies in the UN system recognise how disarmament can advance the broader principles and purposes of the Charter

A concrete example of how this process could work is the Co-ordinating Action on Small Arms (CASA) mechanism which was set up by the United Nations Department for Disarmament Affairs (UNDDA) as an instrument for consultation, information exchange and priority setting among numerous UN departments and agencies concerned with the issue of conventional weapons. Similar co-operation exists between the United Nations Development Programme (UNDP), United Nations Mine Action Service (UNMAS) and the Office for Drug Control and Crime Prevention (ODCCP).

These UN bodies require strong legal enforcement powers to regulate the multibillion-dollar armaments industries responsible for the development and growth of a worldwide trade in weapons. However, political leaders and governments are also culpable in facilitating the growth of the arms trade by politically approving the sale, purchase and delivery of weapons systems. Given the power of the actors involved in the arms trade and their vested interests, disarmament is a difficult but extremely necessary endeavour especially in terms of societal advancement and the development and security of civilian populations. Disarmament is both a short-term and a long-term process. In the short term, a constructive agenda must be established with the capacity to deal with the threat posed by the proliferation and use of conventional weapons. Over the long term, a secure global environment, and the structures needed to achieve this aim, must be established to mainstream disarmament.

A positive move in this direction was indicated by Kofi Annan, when he stated that 'member States [of the UN] must act to increase transparency in arms transfers if we are to make any progress. I would also urge that they support regional disarmament measures, like the moratorium on the importing, exporting or manufacturing of light weapons in West Africa.'[11] There are other concrete measures in this direction that have the potential of being replicated in those developing countries suffering the negative effects of armed conflict. For example, the UNDDA, working together with the UNDP, has reported significant success in its 'Weapons for Development' initiative in Albania, where arms have been exchanged for different forms of development assistance.

CONCLUSION

An integral part of a strategy towards mainstreaming disarmament is incorporated within the pedagogy of *disarmament education*, where the aim is to encourage universities, research institutions and think-tanks to promote disarmament as a major field of study involving teaching and research. Such a process could be extended from metropolitan centres to developing countries and, particularly, to deeply divided societies. Such an approach would require serious financial and intellectual investment from the world's academic and research institutions in terms of financial support for curriculum development along with dedicated staff, infrastructure and research facilities. It would also need serious efforts from all concerned to overcome the difficulties that could arise from the resistance of business universities to new initiatives and curricula. From academics to policy makers, development needs to embrace innovation that would ensure that a concerted effort is made towards long-term disarmament. Sustained global efforts in promoting disarmament education would eventually feed into greater commitments on the part of future generations of world leaders, legislators and civil servants towards disarmament, non-proliferation and the creation of a genuinely secure global environment. As Amnesty International states in its report linking arms sales to human rights:

> The failure of governments from seven of the Group of Eight (G8) largest economies – the USA, the Russian Federation, France, the United Kingdom (UK), Germany, Italy and Canada – to regulate arms transfers is contributing to grave human rights abuses in developing countries and the destruction of millions of lives, particularly in Africa.[12]

In an increasingly unstable world there is a necessity to build primarily for a sustainable peace.

NOTES

1. Special thanks to Jayantha Dhanapala, Under-Secretary-General of the United Nations Department for Disarmament Affairs (UNDDA) and David Jackman of the Quaker United Nations Office (QUNO) for their helpful comments on contemporary issues of disarmament. Preparatory

Committee discussions for the UN Conference on the 'Illicit Trade in
Small Arms and Light Weapons', which was held at UN headquarters in
New York, 19–30 March 2001, have been useful in the writing of this
chapter. Thanks to Ayça Ariyörük, a UNU intern, who provided
assistance in gathering background reference material. For detailed
statistics on armed conflict across the world visit <www.peace.uu.se>.
Also see United Nations, *Report of Governmental Experts on Small Arms*
(A/52/298) (New York: United Nations, 27 August 1997); and United
States Department of Defense, *World-Wide Conventional Arms Trade
(1994–2000): A Forecast and Analysis* (Washington: Center for Defense
Information, December 1994).

2. Peter Wallensteen and Margareta Sollenberg, 'Armed Conflict,
1989–2000', *Journal of Peace Research*, Vol. 38, No. 5 (2001), p. 629–33.
The UN uses the following definition of small arms, light weapons,
ammunition and explosives: '...small arms includes revolvers and self-
loading pistols, rifles and carbines, sub-machine guns, assault rifles and
light machine guns; light weapons includes heavy machine guns, hand-
held under-barrel and mounted grenade launchers, portable anti-aircraft
guns, portable anti-tank guns, recoilless rifles (sometimes mounted),
portable launchers of anti-aircraft missile systems (sometimes mounted)
and mortars of less than 100 mm; ammunition and explosives includes
cartridges (rounds) from small arms, shells and missiles for light
weapons, mobile containers with missiles or shells for single-action anti-
aircraft and anti-tank systems, anti-personnel and anti-tank hand
grenades, landmines and explosives.' *Report of Governmental Experts on
Small Arms*, A/52/298 (New York: United Nations, 27 August 1997). Also
see Stockholm International Peace Research Institute, *SIPRI Yearbook
2000* (Stockholm: SIPRI, 2000).

3. Andrew Pierre (ed.), *Cascade of Arms: Managing Conventional Weapons
Proliferation* (Washington, DC: Brookings Institution Press and
Cambridge, Mass.: The World Peace Foundation, 1997), pp. 1–2. For
additional statistics see Ruth Leger Sivard, *World Military and Social
Expenditures 1996* (Washington, DC: 1996), pp. 18–19. On the theories
of war see Caleb Carr (ed.), *The Book of War: SunTzu The Art of War and
Karl von Clausewitz On War* (New York: The Modern Library, 2000).

4. Pierre, *Cascade of Arms*, pp. 1–6.

5. United States Department of Defense, *World-Wide Conventional Arms
Trade (1994–2000): A Forecast and Analysis* (Washington: Center for
Defense Information, December 1994), p. 15.

6. For a full account of Suharto's Indonesia, see Paul Hainsworth and
Stephen McCloskey (eds), *The East Timor Question: The Struggle for
Independence from Indonesia* (London and New York: I.B. Tauris, 2000).

7. Swadesh Rana, *Small Arms and Intra-State Conflict* (Geneva: United
Nations Institute for Disarmament Research (UNIDIR) Research Paper
No. 34, 1995), p. v.

8. Pierre, *Cascade of Arms*, pp. 5–6. Also Rana, *Small Arms and Intra-State
Conflict*, p. v. Also see The International Action Network on Small Arms,
Founding Document (London: IANSA, 1999).

9. Kofi Annan, *We the Peoples* (New York: United Nations Millennium Report, 2000), p. 52; to view the full document see <www.un.org/millennium/sg/report/full>.
10. Annan, *We the Peoples*, p. 50.
11. Annan, *We the Peoples*, p. 52. Many of these ideas evolved from seminars held during the international conference on 'Building The Future Today: World Peace' organised by the International Association of University Presidents (IAUP), UN Commission for Disarmament Education, Conflict Resolution and Peace, held at Universidad La Salle, Mexico City, 1–4 April 2001. Also Graham Kennedy (ed.), *The Planetary Interest: A New Concept for the Global Age* (London: University of London Press, 1999).
12. Amnesty International, 'G8: Failing to stop the terror trade', press release (London: AI, 24 June 2002).

WEB SITES

Amnesty International	www.amnesty.org
Campaign Against the Arms Trade	www.caat.org.uk
Institute for Media, Peace and Security (UN)	www.mediapeace.org
European Platform for Conflict Prevention and Transformation	www.euconflict.org
United Nations offices	www.unsystem.org
Department of Peace and Conflict Research, Uppsala University	www.pcr.uu.se
European University Centre for Peace Studies	www.aspr.ac.at
International Campaign to Ban Landmines	www.icbl.org
Peace 2000 NGO	www.peace.is/forum/index.asp
United Nations Institute for Disarmament Research	www.unog.ch/unidir

Part III
Debt and Poverty

8 Debt: Cancellation by Instalments

Jean Somers

One of the key economic issues over the last two decades for developing countries has been the debt crisis. This crisis has contributed to a development slowdown for many regions, and in some cases has led to the reversal of hard-won social and economic improvements. It has also resulted in the establishment of one of the most successful global development movements of the last century, the Jubilee 2000 campaign. This chapter outlines the background to the debt crisis, the approaches taken by creditors to address it and the response from campaigners for debt cancellation. It concludes by discussing the current debt initiatives and the way in which developing regions are responding to shifting patterns of international development and the related debates.

A SNAPSHOT OF THE CRISIS

Developing country debt increased dramatically from $68 billion in 1970 to $658 billion in 1980, and rising to $2.4 trillion in 2001. This represented an approximate increase of 3,500 per cent over this timespan.[1] Debt repayments by developing countries in 2001 amounted to $381.9 billion[2] and can be contrasted with the $53.7 billion received in aid.[3] Countries eligible for the Heavily Indebted Poor Countries (HIPC) Initiative – designed by creditor countries to reduce the debt burden in the world's poorest countries – have had to direct more than 20 per cent of public funds to debt payment. Forty-two countries with per capita income below $760 have national debts which have been deemed unsustainable by the International Monetary Fund (IMF) and the World Bank, and have been defined as Heavily Indebted Poor Countries.

The current definition of 'unsustainable debt' is where the ratio of debt to exports is 150 per cent or more. For example, there are six African countries which spend more than a third of their national budgets on servicing debt and less than a tenth on basic social services.[4] In 1997 the United Nations *Human Development Report* spelt out the implications of the debt system:

> Relieved of their annual debt repayments, the severely indebted countries could use the funds for investments that in Africa alone would save the lives of about 21 million children by 2000 and provide 90 million girls and women with access to basic education.[5]

The origins of the debt crisis can be traced, at least partly, to the predominant development model of the post-war decades, in which developing countries were encouraged by the 'developed' North to engage in rapid modernisation and industrialisation. In effect, developing countries were being told to 'catch up' with the developed economies. The required pathway for such a model of redevelopment demanded large-scale infrastructural development projects, for example, highway systems, dams, and industrial plants. It also necessitated finance – raised through either increased taxes or borrowing. For developing countries trying to aspire to this model of development, borrowing was to become an important avenue of generating finance because of a lack of internal resources and capital.

The quadrupling of oil prices by the Organisation of Petroleum Exporting Countries (OPEC) in 1973, provided an enormous pool of new wealth and resources, mostly deposited in Western banks by the oil-producing states. Western governments encouraged banks to lend this money to stimulate trade in the face of a feared world economic recession. Consequently, developing countries deepened their public borrowing requirements to cover their increased oil costs and sustain development. There was a prevailing myth at the time that sovereign states, irrespective of their regional status, could not go bankrupt, so potential new 'customers' were risk free. While some loans were used productively, others were misdirected into inappropriate forms of expenditure such as weaponry, or siphoned off by corrupt regimes. A number of developments at the end of the 1970s turned this financial recycling process into a crisis, most notably an increase in global interest rates caused by the US Federal Reserve as it tried to combat rising US inflation through tight monetary policy. As commodity prices plummeted, the effect of rising global interest rates reduced demand in the West for the exports (mainly primary commodities – coffee, cotton, copper, bananas) of developing countries. The debtor countries found themselves in a bind because their interest payments had risen and foreign exchange earnings had fallen. Both factors were outside the control of developing countries and the debtors soon found it hard to meet their rising debt servicing requirements.

The debt crisis erupted in August 1982 when Mexico declared that it was unable to continue to service its loans. This resulted in panic across the financial markets – they feared that a default by such a major creditor could result in a meltdown of the international financial system. The loan portfolios of many banks were over-exposed to the threat of default by the debtor nations to the point where defaults could result in the collapse of many of these financial institutions. This potential scenario fixated finance ministries and boardrooms in the West and was countered by international action, led by the G7 (the seven richest countries in the world – the US, Japan, Germany, Britain, France, Canada, Italy – were joined by Russia from 1998 with the new grouping being referred to as the G8) and the IMF, in the form of new loans to ensure the continued servicing of debts.

In the 1980s, Latin American countries, while owing the bulk of commercial debt, were also important markets for industrialised country exports. At this stage the crisis was misdiagnosed as a temporary problem from which countries could resolve to repay their debts if given more time. However, as the 1980s progressed it became increasingly clear that the huge outflow of debt payments from the developing world, together with the stringent cuts imposed by economic adjustment programmes, had pushed indebted countries into deeper recession. The debt crisis resulted in Southern countries becoming net exporters of capital to the North. The net transfer of funds from the South between 1980 and 1986 totalled almost $650 billion, with more than half of that total representing interest payments alone.[6] In the same period there were popular protests throughout the developing world, sometimes called 'IMF riots', against the effects of the adjustment programmes introduced in response to the crisis. The largest protests were organised in Peru, Jamaica, Argentina, Ecuador, Bolivia, Chile, Brazil, the Dominican Republic, Haiti, Guatemala, El Salvador and Mexico. Riots in Venezuela in 1989 were particularly violent leaving hundreds of protesters dead.

The 1989 'Brady Plan' was the first initiative to recognise that debt reduction was necessary, and was named after its proposer, the US Treasury Secretary Nicholas F. Brady. The Plan was partly a response to the destabilising riots in Venezuela – seen by the USA as being in their 'backyard' – and offered creditors the opportunity to exchange their commercial debt for new 'Brady' bonds that carried a guarantee of repayment backed by the US treasury. The bonds were offered in a number of forms that aimed to offer some debt reduction by carrying lower interest rates or a lower value than existing debt repayment rates. However, the Brady Plan did not significantly affect the debt burden. By 1994, the overall debt of countries with Brady Plans had been reduced by only 6 per cent although it did contribute to restoring a level of investor confidence.[7] Private capital returned to Latin America with net inflows of new capital rising from about $8 billion per annum in the late 1980s to an annual average of $60 billion from 1992 to 1994.[8] Thus the trend, set during the 1980s when more capital was flowing out of Latin America in debt repayments than was flowing in as new capital, was reversed. This financial upturn in Latin America, however, was based largely on speculative rather than on productive investment. Described as 'hot money', the financial returns on this investment could flow out of the economy very quickly and precipitate major financial crises. This happened in Mexico in 1994 and Asia in 1997–98. Despite pronouncements that the Latin American debt crisis has been resolved, many countries continue to teeter on the brink. For example, in 2000 there was much concern over the capacity of Brazil to meet its debt payments and Ecuador deferred repayments on its Brady bonds – the first country to take this course of action. The Argentine economy collapsed completely in 2001.

MANAGERS OF THE DEBT CRISIS

The IMF and the World Bank have a twofold involvement in the debt crisis; as creditors, and as authors of the conditions on which countries receive further loans and debt relief. Working closely together, these organisations were the architects of countless stabilisation and structural adjustment programmes throughout the 1980s and 1990s. The IMF was set up in 1944 to ensure the international financial stability necessary to enhance global trade. It was originally established to provide countries with short-term loans to cover temporary balance-of-payments problems that arose when import costs exceeded export earnings. The IMF is funded by its 182 members, whose contributions are based on the size of their economies. Voting rights are indexed to financial contributions, which ensure that the richer states have a de facto veto over policies. The IMF makes loans on concessional terms (0.5 per cent interest rate) to low-income countries and offers loans to other countries at market interest rates.

The World Bank was established as a complementary organisation to the IMF with the aim of providing long-term funding for development projects. It provides loans to developing and transitional countries and, while initially favouring support for major infrastructural development projects – dams, electrification, major roads – in recent years its lending for the social sector has risen. The Bank's role in structural adjustment lending programmes evolved out of the debt crisis. The Bank has a variety of lending arms – including the International Bank for Reconstruction and Development (IBRD), which lends at commercial interest rates to middle-income countries (countries with a GNP per capita between $761 and $9,360) and funded by raising loans on the financial markets. The International Development Association (IDA) lends on concessional terms, with a 0.75 per cent service charge and repayment periods of up to 40 years. The IDA is funded through donations from member countries and like the IBRD lends to governments, whereas the Bank's third wing, the International Finance Co-operation (IFC), lends to the private sector.

In the 1980s and 1990s, the IMF and the World Bank designed a development model based on 'structural adjustment'. From the start of the debt crisis, the IMF and the World Bank required that debtors place structural adjustment programmes at the heart of all debt management plans. The argument was that this would make countries economically viable and they would be able to repay their debts. Although the term 'adjustment' suggests minor technical changes, it in fact represented an ideological battering ram aimed at economic revolution and typically involved two phases, stabilisation and adjustment. The former aimed to stabilise the macroeconomy by reducing inflation and cutting balance-of-payments deficits. The latter aimed to restructure the economy to allow a greater role for the private sector in resource allocation and production, and to roll back the role of the state in the economy. It also promoted foreign trade as a key to economic development. A typical adjustment programme will contain some of the following policies:

- Remove price controls
- Restrain wages
- Cut public expenditure
- Privatise state enterprises and marketing boards

- Eliminate trade barriers
- Promote exports
- Encourage foreign investment

The theory behind adjustment – neoclassical economics – is centred on the belief that the market is the most efficient mechanism to allocate resources. This theory of economic development views government intervention in the economy as causing distortions, inefficiency and corruption. It also represents a break with the post-Second World War development model, which recommended state intervention in order to rectify the failures of the private sector to promote economic development. Politically, structural adjustment has been at the centre of one of the most heated debates on South–North relations since the eruption of the debt crisis, with controversy raging over the impact of a range of adjustment policies. A number of these will be discussed in the following section.

DEBATING ADJUSTMENT

Contesting Social Impact

The most significant debate between debt campaigners and the international financial institutions has been over the social impact of adjustment, largely measured through trends in social spending as key indicators. Social indicators for the Heavily Indebted Poor Countries (HIPCs) are particularly revealing. Compared to rich countries, social indicators for HIPC nations show that:

- Life expectancy is 25 years lower
- Less than 40 per cent of the population are literate
- Women are 30 times more likely to die in childbirth
- Children are 10 times less likely to live to the age of five[9]

These indices suggest that spending on health and education are the key to human development. *Increasing access* to health and education was one of the central elements in the World Bank's strategy for reducing poverty outlined in their *World Development Report 1990*. However, a subsequent World Bank study found that per capita social spending fell in 60 per cent of countries implementing adjustment programmes.[10]

The IMF has consistently denied the negative social impact of their programmes, claiming that between 1986 and 1997 health and education spending increased by 4 per cent per annum in real per capita terms in countries following Enhanced Structural Adjustment Facility (ESAF) programmes.[11] Oxfam deconstructed the averages and found in a study of 16 countries in sub-Saharan Africa implementing IMF programmes that 12 had cut public spending in education, while there had been a small increase in health spending. Several countries, including Mali, Tanzania, Zambia and Zimbabwe, suffered significant cuts in health spending under IMF programmes.[12] These are countries with large numbers of their populations living with HIV/AIDS. Moreover, in Zambia life expectancy has dropped from 54 years in 1990 to 40 years in 1998.[13] While the conflict over the social impact of adjustment continues, it is now moving on to focus on the correlation between poverty, economic growth and trade liberalisation policies which form part of adjustment.

Exporting Out of Debt

Structural adjustment programmes promote export-led economic development and the removal of trade barriers. In developing countries this has resulted in the prioritisation of cash crops for export over subsistence (food) crops, and consequently there have been negative effects on food security and nutrition levels. It can also result in a redistribution of income within the household from women to men. Men generally take responsibility for cash crops while women grow food crops to feed the household. The potentially contradictory outcome of prioritising cash crop production is illustrated by evidence from Kenya, where family incomes increased through greater export revenues, but women and children's nutritional status declined because fewer subsistence foods were produced. Women's share of the family income was consequently reduced.[14] The impact of export-led growth on women as farmers and carers is one element in a broader critique provided by feminist social scientists of the impact on gender relationships caused by such adjustment programmes.

External pressures to increase exports have also resulted in countries depleting their reserve natural resources to a level which is unsustainable and dangerous for the environment. For example, Côte d'Ivoire, the world's leading producer of cocoa, has been implementing IMF programmes for 20 years. Under adjustment, cocoa output has increased by 44 per cent. The Friends of the Earth has related this production to high levels of deforestation in the country.[15] The debate on export-led growth in adjustment programmes is becoming integrated into the wider discussion on trade liberalisation sparked off by the popular mobilisation against globalisation which started at the 1999 World Trade Organisation (WTO) meeting in Seattle.

Growth and Investment

Structural adjustment programmes aim to enable countries to economically grow out of their debt problem. Progress on this front has not been encouraging, which is a fact that the IMF/World Bank, academics and debt campaigners largely agree on, even if they dispute the social costs of adjustment. The IMF's review of ESAF found that improvements in growth in countries that implemented ESAF programmes have been marginal.[16] Furthermore, where growth has occurred, for example in Uganda, there are doubts surrounding its sustainability because growth is coupled with low investment. While the IMF claims that the approval of adjustment programmes serves as a catalyst for encouraging inflows of Foreign Direct Investment (FDI) into the borrowing countries' economies, an external review of the IMF's Enhanced Structural Adjustment Facility did not find the evidence to support this assertion.[17] The World Bank has also recognised that the recovery of growth in adjusting countries has been disappointing. The *World Development Report 2000*, states that '... growth in the developing world has been disappointing, with the typical country registering negligible growth', although it claims that substantial progress has been made implementing adjustment policies.[18] The debate on growth has now deepened to include qualitative methods of assessing impact. The concept of 'pro-poor growth', i.e. growth which is substantially generated in the sectors where poor people are concentrated, is challenging the IMF/World Bank 'trickle down' theory of growth.[19]

A NEW PHASE OF ADJUSTMENT?

The international financial institutions continue to claim that on balance their programmes are working and that in any event there is no alternative. The framework for the debate on debt has however been reshaped by changes introduced in 1999 in how adjustment programmes are developed. Low-income countries must now develop Poverty Reduction Strategy Papers (PRSPs) in order to be eligible for debt reduction and for concessional loans from the IMF and the World Bank. The stated aim of this new approach is to place poverty reduction at the centre of adjustment and to link debt reduction to the eradication of poverty. PRSPs cover all aspects of social and economic policy, and must be developed with the participation of civil society groups. According to the IMF and the World Bank:

> A poverty reduction strategy should ensure consistency between a country's macroeconomic, structural and social policies and the goals of poverty reduction and social development, and be produced in a way that involves transparency and broad based participation in the choice of goals, the formulation of policies and the monitoring of implementation.[20]

IMF and World Bank programmes in low-income countries should now be based on nationally developed strategies rather than those previously designed in the institutions' Washington offices. In line with this development, the IMF renamed its highly unpopular ESAF programme with the friendlier title 'Poverty Reduction and Growth Facility' (PRGF). The new programme suggests that the conditions which countries have to fulfil in order to become eligible for debt reduction and fresh loans will be set by the country itself. However, PRSPs must be submitted to the IMF and the World Bank for their endorsement.

The new PRSPs were introduced because of the breakdown in adjustment programmes – up to 75 per cent in the case of IMF programmes in low-income countries – together with the growing recognition over the 1990s that programmes could not be imposed. These factors led to a greater focus on the concept of programme 'ownership'. Another significant factor was pressure from debt campaigners to de-link debt cancellation from adjustment programmes, stressing that Northern creditors should not impose conditions on democratically elected Southern governments. How the PRSP process has worked in practice will be examined below.

IMF AND WORLD BANK: HARSHEST CREDITORS

The Latin American debt problem dominated the 1980s until the introduction of the Brady Plan and the easing of fears for the survival of commercial bank creditors. The focus during the 1990s consequently shifted to low-income countries which were clearly unable to repay their debt. From 1988, about two-thirds of the increase in low-income countries' debt stock arose from the accumulation of interest and arrears.[21] Their debt was mainly owed to official sources, including the IMF and the World Bank. As part of the refinancing process undertaken by the indebted nations, they borrowed increasing amounts of finance from both the IMF and the World Bank. These bodies were preferential creditors, which meant that their debt servicing had to be prioritised – arrears to them could result in the loss of further loans or hinder aid from bilateral or multilateral bodies. Multilateral bodies – the IMF, the World Bank and a number of regional development banks – accounted for half the debt service payments of low-income countries by the mid-1990s, although they only held a quarter of their debt stock. While, in numerous Paris Club initiatives, various debt relief measures were undertaken to reduce the burden of bilateral debt, the IMF and the World Bank refused to participate in any debt relief schemes.[22] The latter claimed the need to protect their credit ratings or protested that they were unable to afford such schemes, in spite of their substantial reserves.

THE HEAVILY INDEBTED POOR COUNTRIES' INITIATIVE: THE THEORY

The focus of debt campaigning during the first half of the 1990s was the cancellation of multilateral debt. This campaign culminated in the introduction of the Heavily Indebted Poor Countries (HIPC) Initiative in l996 through a joint World Bank/IMF strategy. HIPC proposed that all creditors – multilateral, bilateral and commercial – were to play a part in reducing debt to 'sustainable' levels. Sustainability was defined as debt which could be repaid without compromising growth, running up arrears on old debt or requiring the rescheduling of loans. The main indicator used to define an unsustainable debt was a debt-to-revenue ratio that was higher than the 250 per cent threshold set by the World Bank. The Bank and the Fund identified a total of 42 countries eligible for entry into the HIPC process. However, shortcomings identified by debt campaigners included the following:

- The lengthy time-frame for debt cancellation. Countries had to implement six years of structural adjustment programmes to become eligible for debt relief.
- The link between adjustment and debt relief was controversial – adjustment was seen by campaigners as part of the debt problem.

- The debt sustainability targets themselves were felt to be too high and irrelevant. A more meaningful indicator would be the percentage of government revenue spent on repaying debt. Tanzania, for example, had been paying 27 per cent of government revenue on debt payments.
- Too few countries were deemed eligible for HIPC; states such as Ecuador, Haiti and Nigeria, for example, which had severe debt burdens, were excluded.

Whilst the inclusion of multilateral debt in this initiative marked an important breakthrough for some observers, for others HIPC was a cruel hoax that would increase the IMF and the World Bank's stranglehold on developing-world economies by further strengthening the role of adjustment programmes.

HIPC: The Practice

At the launch of HIPC, the World Bank's President, James Wolfensohn, stated that the initiative was good news for the world's poor. HIPC's record in the four years after its adoption, however, did not fulfil that promise. By the end of 1999, only four countries had completed the HIPC process – Uganda, Mozambique, Guyana and Bolivia. In addition to substantial delays, HIPC also failed to reduce national debts in any constructive way. Many low-income countries were only able to service a proportion of their debt – for example, Mozambique and Tanzania were servicing about 40 per cent of their debt during the late 1990s.[23] Even partial debt repayment placed impossible strains on the social, economic and physical infrastructures of such countries. This pressure would only be relieved if the total debt of low-income countries was cancelled, particularly as HIPC was largely cancelling debt which countries were unable to service anyway.

JUBILEE 2000: A NEW DAWN

Within twelve months of its launch in 1996, HIPC was under pressure from the Jubilee 2000 campaign, which was growing in strength in five continents. While the focus of HIPC was the cancellation of 'unsustainable' debt (based on economic and financial criteria), Jubilee's call was for the cancellation of 'unpayable' debt (based on human and ethical criteria) before the end of the millennium. Jubilee 2000 questioned the morality of the debt, highlighting a number of factors which cast doubt on its legitimacy. Firstly, there was 'Cold War lending' to oppressive regimes. In international law, debt is deemed 'odious' where loans are used to oppress the people of a country rather than benefit them, and it can be argued that subsequent governments should not be liable for repayment of such loans. An estimated one-fifth of original lending went to dictators.[24] Secondly, there was lending for failed projects or programmes, for which creditors shared the responsibility. For example, the External Review of ESAF criticised the 1991 IMF programme in Zambia, where liberalising the financial markets before achieving stabilisation led to avoidable inflation with heavy social costs. Between 1991 and 1993, public expenditure in Zambia halved as a share of GDP.[25] A third factor which cast doubt on the morality of the debt was lending at usurious interest rates. In the mid-1970s, median interest rates averaged 1.6 per cent. By the early 1980s, interest rates had increased to an average of 11 per cent.[26] Fourthly, Jubilee drew attention to the decline in the terms of trade suffered by heavily indebted countries. It highlighted the fact that if Africa's export prices had kept pace with import prices since 1980, their debts would have been paid one-and-a-half times over.[27] The above factors led Southern Jubilee campaigners to ask 'Who owes what to whom?', and to adopt the slogan 'Don't owe, won't pay'.

Jubilee 2000 focused its campaign efforts on the G8, arguing that this body dominates the main forums where decisions are made about debt – the IMF, the World Bank and the Paris Club. The first overt challenge came at the 1998 G8 meeting in Birmingham, when 70,000 Jubilee activists surrounded the city centre. At the time, debt was not on the summit agenda because the G8 held that it was being addressed through HIPC. The level of public mobilisation and media coverage challenged this notion and effectively brought the debt question into public focus. From early 1999, it became clear that the Cologne Summit in 1999, which was to receive millions of Jubilee petition signatures from around the world, would become the 'Debt Summit'. With much fanfare, the Cologne Debt Deal was announced, promising $100 billion in debt cancellation, or the equivalent of roughly half the debt owed by HIPCs. As much of this finance was already promised through the Paris Club or HIPC, the Cologne Deal boiled down to some improvements to HIPC. The IMF and the World Bank were called upon to place HIPC within an 'enhanced poverty framework'. This received a mixed response, with some campaigners focusing on the enhanced debt reduction as evidence of a breakthrough. Others, particularly Southern Jubilee groups, argued it was still a creditors agenda with adjustment central to the scheme. They also feared that it would enhance the role of the IMF by giving it an explicit role in poverty reduction – an area where it has no expertise.

ASSESSING THE COLOGNE DEAL

In responding to the Cologne Deal, the IMF and the World Bank introduced the 'Enhanced HIPC' in September 1999. This increased the debt reduction on offer mainly by lowering the debt-to-export target to 150 per cent. Subsequently, all G8 countries have promised 100 per cent cancellation of bilateral debt owed to them by HIPC countries, but this was still linked to countries following the HIPC initiative. The major innovation of Cologne was the introduction of a mechanism to link debt reduction to poverty reduction – a requirement to produce Poverty Reduction Strategy Papers (PRSP) with the participation of civil society as a further condition for receiving debt relief. Extra finance released through HIPC must be used to fund the country's PRSP, which in turn has to be implemented for a year before debt reduction is granted and subsequently revised thereafter every three years. In theory, the PRSP appeared to respond to the criticisms directed by campaigning groups at the IMF and the World Bank during the 1990s, namely that debt reduction is required for poverty reduction; that IMF stabilisation and World Bank adjustment programmes undoubtedly have a negative social impact; and the political point that countries should 'own' their social and economic policies, rather than have them imposed by outside bodies, e.g. IMF, World Bank and donor governments, in the form of adjustment programmes. A closer examination of the 'new deal', together with the evidence of its implementation to date, provides a less positive picture.

Firstly, there remains the unresolved issue of the link between debt reduction and poverty reduction. In spite of HIPC's 'enhanced poverty reduction framework', the initiative still does not take the resources needed for poverty reduction into account when assessing how much debt reduction a country should receive. Conversely, progress on poverty reduction is a condition for receiving debt reduction, and debt sustainability is still defined largely in terms of debt-to-export ratios. Although there appeared to be significant progress in 2000, with 22 countries receiving notification of how much debt reduction they would receive after fulfilling specified conditions, in many cases it is likely that the reduction will not be significant. The European Network on Debt and Development (EURODAD), the Brussels-based lobby agency, in an open letter to national governments, the IMF and the World Bank, estimated that:

> The HIPC initiative has managed to reduce total debt servicing of the HIPCs by just over 3 per cent since 1996. When current debt reduction promised has been delivered, HIPC debt servicing will be reduced on average by a third. Many will still spend more on debt servicing than on either health or education.[28]

Secondly, in theory poverty reduction will be central to all IMF and World Bank programmes in 72 low-income countries, as these programmes will be based on the countries' participatory Poverty Reduction Strategy Papers. Debt campaigners and civil society groups in Southern countries remain sceptical as to whether the PRSP approach represents a sea change or not. Among the key questions raised by these groups have been: Will the IMF ease off on its stringent lending conditions, for example, by allowing countries to set their own inflation and budget deficit targets consistent with their poverty reduction targets? Also, will the World Bank endorse PRSPs in which some public companies are not privatised but made more competitive – where the consensus within the country is that particular sectors need some protection rather than being opened up immediately to the international market?

According to EURODAD, which has been closely monitoring the implementation of PRSPs, poverty reduction is not being placed at the centre of adjustment programmes. Civil society groups report that a dual process is taking place, with social issues being discussed in the context of the PRSP, with some public participation, while macroeconomic issues are discussed in the context of the IMF's Poverty Reduction and Growth Facility, which is still negotiated largely behind closed doors (in a manner suspiciously similar to the old ESAF programmes).[29] A review of the PRSP by the IMF and the World Bank found that the core macroeconomic and structural elements of PRSPs were broadly similar to previous IMF and World Bank programmes. There was little evidence that alternative policy options were discussed.[30]

The fact that PRSPs have to be submitted to the IMF and the World Bank for endorsement leaves a large question mark over the extent to which a real shift to country ownership has taken place. For example, Tanzania's Social and Economic Trust has argued that the

PRSP is a country-*led* rather than a country-*owned* strategy.[31] The international financial institutions argue that if they are to finance part of these programmes they have a responsibility to their shareholders to ensure they are viable. This may seem a reasonable position, but the right to endorse or reject a PRSP offers the IMF and the World Bank a far greater overseeing role than before, which enables them to assess a country's overall development plan. This has raised the fear that the PRSP is a device established merely to legitimise adjustment.

CONCLUSION

This chapter has covered the history of the debt crisis and the international response from creditor groups and civil society groups, and ends with an overview of the current state of play on debt and adjustment policies together with contemporary debates. Where to now? In spite of Jubilee 2000, arguably the most successful global campaign of the last century, the debt problem has followed us into the twenty-first century. This reflects the extremely undemocratic nature of the institutions which police the global economy. The claim of the international financial institutions and the G8 that there is no alternative to current free-market policies was seemingly strengthened by the fall of communism at the end of the 1980s. It is too soon to assess whether this ideological hegemony will hold in the face of the new confidence among global civil society groups and organisations which formed the Jubilee 2000 campaign and the growing, more loosely formed, movement against the current model of globalisation. The IMF, the World Bank and the G8 have tried to disarm this opposition by adopting their language – for example, poverty reduction is now the declared central aim of the IMF and World Bank adjustment programmes and these programmes are to be 'owned' by the countries implementing them. They have attempted to blur the lines of conflict, claiming that anti-debt campaigners and the international financial institutions are 'working together' for a solution to the debt problem. This issue is set to continue.

NOTES

1. World Bank, *Global Development Finance, Analysis and Summary Tables* (New York: World Bank, 2000), p. 222. Also see M.P. Todaro, *Economic Development* (Harlow: Longman, 2000); Catherine Caulfield, *Masters of Illusion: The World Bank and the Poverty of Nations* (New York: Henry Holt

and Company, 1996); UNCTAD, *The Least Developed Countries 2000 Report* (New York and Geneva: UN, 2000).

2. World Bank, *Global Development Finance*, p. 222.
3. Judith Randel, Tony German, Deborah Ewing (eds), *Reality of Aid* (Manila: IBON Foundation, 2002), p. 145.
4. World Bank, *World Development Report, Attacking Poverty* (New York: World Bank, 2000), p. 82. Also see IMF, 'Debt Initiative for the Heavily Indebted Poor Countries (HIPCs)' (2000), Fact Sheet, <www.imf.org/external/np/hipc/hipc.htm>.
5. UNDP, *Human Development Report* (New York: UNDP, 1997), p. 93.
6. George Ann Potter, *Deeper than Debt: Economic Globalisation and the Poor* (London: Latin American Bureau, 2000), p. 14. Also see Duncan Green, *Silent Revolution: The Rise of Market Economics in Latin America* (London: Cassell, 1995); Peadar Kirby, 'The Social Impact of Economic Liberalisation: Evidence from Latin America', *Trócaire Development Review* (2000).
7. Duncan Green, *Silent Revolution: The Rise of Market Economics in Latin America*, p. 69.
8. Potter, *Deeper than Debt*, p. 15.
9. Oxfam International, *Education Now: Break the Cycle of Poverty* (Oxford: Oxfam International, 1999), p. 1.
10. World Bank, *Social Dimensions of Adjustment: World Bank Experience 1980–1993* (New York: World Bank, 1996), p. 85.
11. IMF, *IMF Survey* (New York: IMF, March 1999), p. 79. The Enhanced Structural Adjustment Facility (the IMF's lending programme to low-income countries) was introduced in 1987. ESAF made loans on concessional terms – 0.5 per cent interest rate, 10 years repayment period with a 5-year grace period. ESAF was renamed the Poverty Reduction and Growth Facility (PRGF) in 1999.
12. Oxfam International, *The IMF: Wrong Diagnosis, Wrong Medicine* (Oxford: Oxfam, 1999), p. 18.
13. UNDP, *Human Development Report 1992* (New York: UNDP, 1992), p. 128; *Human Development Report 2000* (New York: UNDP, 2000), p. 160.
14. Oxfam, *Trade Liberalisation: At What Price?* (Oxford: Oxfam, 1996), p. 22.
15. Friends of the Earth, *The IMF: Selling the Environment Short* (Washington: FOE, March 2000), p. 5.
16. IMF, *The ESAF at Ten Years: Economic Adjustment and Reform in Low Income Countries: Summary Report* (New York: IMF, 1997), p. 37.
17. IMF, 'External Evaluation of the ESAF' (New York: IMF, 1998), p. 32.
18. World Bank, *World Development Report: Attacking Poverty*, p. 64.
19. Debt and Development Coalition, *Growth Who Benefits: Perspectives from Zambia and Ireland* (Dublin: Debt and Development Coalition/Jubilee 2000, December 2000).
20. IMF and International Development Association, *Poverty Reduction Strategy Papers: Operational Issues* (New York: IMF/World Development Bank, December 1999), p. 8. <www.imf.org/external/np/pdr/prsp/poverty1.htm>.
21. Kevin Watkins, *The Oxfam Poverty Report* (Oxford: Oxfam, 1995), p. 179.

22. EURODAD, *World Credit Tables, Creditors' Claims on Debtors Exposed* (Brussels: EURODAD, 1996), p. 15. Set up in 1956, the Paris Club is a forum which meets under the auspices of the French Ministry of Finance. It deals with bilateral debt (government to government) and debt arising from loans. EU states became the harshest creditors of low income countries.

23. UK Jubilee 2000, *Basic Data on 92 Poorest Countries*, <www.jubilee2000uk.org>.

24. Joe Hanlon, *Dictators and Debt* (London: Jubilee 2000 Coalition UK, November 1998), p. 1.

25. IMF, *External Evaluation of the ESAF*, pp. 96–101. Also see Graham Bird, 'A Suitable Case for Treatment: Understanding the ongoing debate about the IMF', *Third World Quarterly*, Vol. 22, No. 5 (2001), pp. 823–48.

26. Potter, *Deeper than Debt*, p. 12.

27. Potter, *Deeper than Debt*, p. 6.

28. EURODAD, *An Open Letter to National Governments and IMF and World Bank* (Brussels: EURODAD, December 2000). Also see Graham Bird, 'IMF Programs: Do they work? Can they be made to work better?', *World Development*, Vol. 30, No. 3 (2002), pp. 355–73; John Pender, 'From "Structural Adjustment" to "Comprehensive Development Framework": Conditionality transformed?', *Third World Quarterly*, Vol. 22, No. 3 (2001), pp. 397–411.

29. EURODAD, 'Panel on PRS: Some cross-country lessons so far' (Brussels: Presentation to World Bank Seminar, 4 December 2000).

30. IMF and International Development Association, 'Review of the Poverty Reduction Strategy Paper (PRSP) Approach: Early experience with interim PRSPs and full PRSPs' (26 March 2002). <www.worldbank.org/poverty/strategies/review/earlyexp.pdf>.

31. Debt and Development, 'Tanzania: Caught in the HIPC maze' (Dublin: DDCI/Jubilee Ireland, December 2000).

WEB SITES

Information on Jubilee 2000 and Drop the Debt	www.jubilee2000uk.org
Third World Network	www.twnside.org.sg/econ_3.htm
Oxfam papers on Third World debt	www.oxfam.org.uk/policy/papers/okinawa/debt.htm
Debt and Development Coalition	www.debt_ireland.org
Development finance	www.fao.org/ag/ags/agsm/dfn.htm
Econonomic and social development	www.jiscmail.ac.uk/lists/econ-soc-devt.html
Global development finance	www.worldbank.org/prospects
OECD development indicators	www.oecd.org/dac/indicators/index.htm

9   Child Poverty and Development

Paula Rodgers and Eimear Flanagan

'Children enjoy the unenviable privilege of being invisible; except for rare cases, children simply do not exist.'[1] The statistics covering the plight of the world's poorest children are a stark reminder of how inadequate the current Western-sponsored models of global development are. Today's global population includes 613 million children under the age of five. There are 1.7 billion children and adolescents between the ages of 5 and 19. Fifty per cent of the world's poor are now children and as populations grow there will be more children living in poverty than ever before. Children under the age of 15 make up 40 per cent of the population of the world's poorest countries. There are at least 600 million of these children living in absolute poverty of which 183 million children under 5 years of age weigh less than they should for their age – an indicator of poverty and malnourishment. If current trends continue there will be 8.5 million child deaths in 2015, with a disproportionate number of these children living in sub-Saharan African countries.[2]

Despite these horrifying statistics, children remain largely invisible as members of society. They are often regarded as being 'owned' by parents, receiving rights only as family members rather than as individuals. Any improvement in their living conditions and personal development is more likely to result from programmes or policies aimed at their family unit rather than specifically targeting them as individuals. The low social and economic status consistent with child poverty often consigns children to a vulnerable existence characterised by a lack of opportunity to influence their future. In societies particularly afflicted by poverty, children and the elderly are most at risk from hunger and social marginalisation. While childhood should be characterised by personal growth, education and the time to play, many children carry a burden of responsibility far beyond their years.

This chapter will begin by analysing the key statistics on child poverty in both local and global contexts. The concept of child poverty will be unpacked, with a particular focus on its consequences for children's health, education, working status and gender inequality. The key issues affecting children today will be explored in the context of globalisation and the rapid economic changes of the past decade. This chapter will go on to offer a rights-based approach to child development as a means to understanding and improving the situation of children worldwide, drawing on the complexities of implementing the United Nations Convention on the Rights of the Child. A central theme throughout the chapter will be the importance of involving children in the development process, and this will be exemplified in case studies of children's participation at local and global levels.

CONTRASTING THE NORTHERN AND SOUTHERN HEMISPHERES

Poverty exists across the globe, but while children in the North may not be as materially poor as their counterparts in the South, they share a lack of access to services, and of full inclusion and participation in society. In an increasingly interconnected global market, economic policies in the North and South are converging. Developed and developing countries are becoming more interdependent through international trade, the activities of transnational corporations, and capital and labour exchanges between countries and continents. The consequences of these global economic forces on children are becoming markedly similar throughout the world, as evidenced in an increasing poverty gap between rich and poor across the globe.[3] The *World Bank Development Report 1999–2000* illustrates the fact that the number of children living in poverty is growing, regardless of whether they are living in developed or developing countries. The report indicates that the quality of life for the majority of children is deteriorating regardless of their geographical context.[4] Moreover children's own experiences of poverty highlight specific issues such as health and education that are important to them and can offer insights into the impact of policies and expenditure. For example, children in the North and South are expressing concern over threats to the family unit from a range of social and economic sources. Children also share a common concern that poverty denies them the right to fulfil their fullest potential as global citizens.

> Studies from the few countries with the data necessary to track children through to later life confirm that there is a very strong association between low income in childhood and a whole range

of later outcomes. Children from poor households are much more likely to have low educational achievement, to become teenage parents, to serve a prison sentence and to have less success in the labour market.[5]

Whether in Africa, Europe, the USA or Latin America, it is children who are exposed to the greatest risk of living in poverty than any other section of society, and the social constraints of poverty are likely to persist into adulthood. However, childhood offers a unique opportunity to develop and lay the foundations for a full life. Indeed, the future of all societies depend on their capacity to offer children self-esteem and self-worth to effect their full participation in civil society. The alternative is an adulthood of deprivation, lack of dignity and choice. Furthermore, children suffer most from macro-economic policies aimed at 'reforming' welfare services or 'adjusting' post-communist and developing societies toward the global market. The rationalisation of the global market system over the past decade has resulted in massive cuts in health and education, which in turn have impacted directly on children's welfare. As such, there is a direct correlation between policy making and child poverty.

CHILD POVERTY IN DEVELOPED COUNTRIES

The persistence of child poverty in rich countries undermines both equality of opportunity and commonality of values. It therefore confronts the industrialised world with a test both of its ideals and of its capacity to resolve many of its most intractable social problems.[6]

One in every six of the developed world's children is living in poverty. Developed countries are defined in this context as the 29 members of the Organisation for Economic Co-operation and Development (OECD) – the countries that collectively produce two-thirds of the world's goods and services. The majority of OECD members combine economic growth with an increasing poverty gap between those who are benefiting from increased material wealth and those whose lives remain untouched and unimproved by this financial prosperity. Britain and Ireland offer prime examples of developed countries that have experienced macroeconomic development and yet remain subject to high levels of poverty and social exclusion at a micro-level.

The Irish economy has recently been growing at an annual rate of 8–12 per cent which has positioned it as one of the most globalised economies in the world. Its growth has been lauded by the United States as an example of a new-order economy. Unemployment rates have fallen and wages have risen but the incomes of those without jobs and of the low paid have not kept pace with average incomes, thereby increasing rates of relative poverty. Moreover, Ireland also has the highest proportion of children (aged under 18 years) within the EU, representing approximately 29 per cent of the population, compared to the EU average of 21 per cent.[7] Despite the fact that economic performance has improved, vast numbers of children continue to live in poverty. A quarter of Irish children live in households receiving below half the average income, leaving the country with one of the highest child poverty rates in the European Union. By 2000, many EU member countries had child poverty rates which were half the Irish rate or below which suggests that rapid economic growth is no guarantor of child welfare and development.[8] There is a comprehensive Children's Strategy in the South of Ireland which outlines specific anti-poverty objectives. It states:

> Child poverty must be a major concern and it will continue to be a key priority for government. In view of its multifaceted nature, tackling poverty requires a range of supports and interventions ... Our strong economic position provides us with the capacity to tackle child poverty. The success of the National Anti-Poverty Strategy needs to be built on and re-orientated under this Strategy towards a more direct focus on children.[9]

The situation is no less alarming for British children. A fifth of Britain's children lived in poverty in the 1990s, a rate twice that of France and five times higher than Norway or Sweden. While child poverty has remained stable or has marginally increased in most developed nations over the last 20 years, it has tripled in Britain. The British children's charity, National Children's Home (NCH) 'Action for Children', claims that child poverty in Britain has trebled over the last 30 years with 4.3 million children currently living in poverty.[10]

Infant mortality rates, a prime indicator of poverty, average six deaths per thousand under the age of one in developed countries. The average for the least developed countries is 107 per thousand with this figure dramatically higher in the countries worst affected by poverty, such as Sierra Leone, where in 1998, 182 children died per thousand live births.[11] A recent report, *Poverty and Social Inclusion in Britain*, concluded that by the end of 1999, one in six people considered themselves to be living in 'absolute poverty' as defined by the UN.[12] It stated that between 4 million and 10 million people could not afford one or more of: adequate housing, clothing, food, or financial security. Poverty commentators in Britain have consistently been warning that the scale of the problem is immense and getting worse. A Child Poverty Action Group (CPAG) report in 2001 thus concluded its analysis of progress to date on tackling child poverty in Britain: 'Is there an end in sight for child poverty? Our society has the resources: we need only to maintain and strengthen the political will.'[13]

THE FREE MARKET

The dominance of the free market economic model in governing global trading exchanges has had a direct effect on children worldwide through drastic spending cuts in health, social housing and education. Some countries have been hit harder than others. For example, in sub-Saharan Africa between a quarter and a third of national budgets are now devoted to servicing national debts, with expenditure on basic social services often amounting to less than half of this.[14] Economic policies such as structural adjustment programmes (SAPs) imposed by the International Monetary Fund (IMF), debt relief schemes, and World Trade Organisation (WTO) rules have a direct influence on the daily realities of the poorest and most vulnerable people. Statistics, including those provided by the World Bank and the United Nations, suggest that the model of development advocated by free market economists fails to make the crucial link between balance sheet economics, poverty and the needless and preventable premature deaths of some 35,000 children daily.

In February 2001, an international conference in London brought together the heads of the international development, policy and financial institutions, UNICEF, UNDP and the OECD, with government ministers from developing and developed countries and representatives of NGOs and faith groups, to address the issue of child poverty. In preparation for the conference, the development agency Save the Children co-ordinated a group of NGOs and faith groups to produce a paper outlining a series of anti-poverty proposals. The paper underpinned the core conviction that there could be no 'child-neutral' economic policies, and that this core principle should inform all debate on development and public sector reform. Governments around the world were urged to become more child focused, and to take into account issues impacting on children's lives. Save the Children advocated the potential and importance of investing in the future of children. The agency also stressed the importance of developing strategies for poverty reduction that took cognisance of the voices and experiences of young people, with a view to developing macroeconomic and fiscal policies that result in better outcomes for children.

THE ROLE OF TRANSNATIONAL CORPORATIONS

The last 20 years has witnessed the continued economic growth of powerful transnational corporations (TNCs) – international corporations that operate across different countries. Children come into contact with these corporations as employees or consumers, but mostly with limited welfare or protection. TNCs have enormous influence and power over today's society, and during intense periods of economic growth the global pattern of their activity has been to avoid responsibilities to children or the disadvantaged in general. TNCs operate across a range of trading areas, from textiles and pharmaceuticals to arms industries, and have diverse and sometimes exploitative relationships with children. Millions of children directly contribute to their profits, by providing cheap, unregulated and unprotected labour, or as consumers of the commodities. Yet TNCs continue to operate with a large degree of social and economic impunity, particularly in regard to their treatment of children and children's rights in general. Speaking about the lives of three particular children from India, Uganda and Afghanistan, J.P. Joyce, in *Taking Children Seriously*, stated that:

> ... unchecked forces of globalisation can have a profound and often harmful effect on individual young people. Unfettered capitalism, the growing divide between rich and poor, and the proliferation of conflicts have scarred the development and happiness of all three at some stage in their lives.[15]

Child poverty is further exacerbated by conflict and an arms industry which depends on conflict for growth. Around the world conflict and violence is an increasing characteristic of a number of children's lives. Since 1990, more than 2 million children have been killed and more than 6 million injured or disabled in armed conflicts.

Moreover, an estimated 20 million children have been forced to flee their homes because of war.[16] Even more disturbing is the fact that at least 300,000 children are currently participating in armed conflicts around the world as child soldiers, and there are many more thousands being actively recruited into armed forces.[17] It is usually the most vulnerable children who find themselves entrapped in conflicts, with those children who are child labourers in times of peace being most likely to become child soldiers in times of war. 'They forced me to learn how to fight the enemy in a war I didn't understand. We were constantly beaten, just to keep us in a state of terror.' (Emilio, aged 14, Guatemala)[18]

The impact of poverty and conflict on the health of children is visible both in comparisons between North and South, and within each country. Poor children are more likely to be prone to illness, to be malnourished, to live in poor environmental conditions, and never to reach their mental and physical potential. Each year, 12 million children under five years of age die from easily preventable diseases, caused largely by polluted drinking water and inadequate sanitation. Every minute of every day, nine children die from the effects of lack of sufficient food.[19] While conditions are much more extreme in developing countries, there is widespread acceptance of the links between poverty and ill health in developed countries also, with many governments acknowledging this fact by initiating a process of change.[20] It is generally agreed in the North that 'the long term implication for health, is an additional reason for tackling poverty and social exclusion when the child is young'.[21]

While there have been advances in health care in recent years in many countries, improvements in health and increases in life expectancy have not been equally distributed throughout the world. While rates of infant mortality have fallen, babies born to parents in unskilled and manual social classes continue to be at higher risk. Infant mortality rates could be as much as 50–60 per cent higher among the economically excluded classes within a country than among the professional classes. Children in poorer families are also more likely to experience illnesses such as respiratory infections, and are more at risk of accidents and injuries.[22] As with access to education, health care is unevenly provided, with particular groups of children and young people more at risk than others. These include young people in the care system, orphaned children and children from ethnic minority groups. Indeed, in Britain and Ireland the death rates for Traveller children aged under 10 years are ten times those for non-Traveller children.[23]

Lack of good quality educational opportunities is another significant aspect of child poverty. There is a clearly defined and accepted link between poverty levels and low educational achievement, in both the developed and developing countries. Children from disadvantaged homes face greater barriers to achieving their potential at school, with children from poorer communities more likely to be suspended or excluded from school. For example, school exclusions have been increasing across the UK, rising dramatically in the 1990s. Permanent exclusion rates in general have increased by 400 per cent between 1990 and 2000, and are correlated to the increasing market function of the schooling system.[24] There continues to be concern about the educational attainment of specific groups of children – such as children from ethnic minority families, children in contact with juvenile justice systems and children in care.

Educational provision for children in developing countries is of particular concern. Education is chronically under-resourced in most developing countries, resulting in large class sizes, teacher shortages and a chronic lack of teaching materials. In many African countries it is not unusual to find a class containing in excess of 120 children of various ages, with just one teacher and virtually no other resources. This should be seen in the context of the 130 million children of primary-school age in developing countries who do not attend school. In addition to the millions of children who do not attend school, many others start school but do not complete their education.[25]

While the world of economics may seem far removed from what goes on in classrooms around the world, the impact of economic pressures is increasingly encroaching on educational provision. The implementation of World Bank and IMF SAPs has led to severe reductions in the educational budgets of developing countries and the enrolment numbers in schools.[26] 'African countries with SAPs had a 30 per cent decrease in access to first grade compared with countries without SAPs ... As enrolment decreases the gender gap has widened in primary goals.'[27]

CHILD LABOUR

Hundreds of millions of children are working worldwide, often in dangerous and exploitative conditions. They are engaged in a range of employment areas from domestic work to manufacturing industry

– at the worst end of the scale children are trafficked between countries as part of a growing trade in child sex workers.[28] The nature of child work varies across the world, as do the causes and consequences of their employment. Surveys conducted in eight countries by the International Labour Organisation (ILO) in the 1990s found that a quarter of children aged between 5 and 14 years were engaged in economic activity. Asia accounts for 61 per cent of working children, Africa 32 per cent and Latin America 7 per cent. Most child workers are engaged in agriculture, while others are forced to work in the manufacturing, trade and entertainment sectors.[29]

Although we normally associate child labour with developing countries, research has shown that employment is also a dominant part of children's lives in the developed world.[30] While not employed in hazardous or exploitative industries common to working children in the Third World, there are many children who work in the First World to supplement family income. An overview of studies of children working in the UK, *Children and Work in the UK*, suggested that by the age of 16, between 63 and 77 per cent of children have a job, as have 15–26 per cent of 11-year-olds. Research carried out by the Child Poverty Action Group and Save the Children revealed that far from working for 'pin money' many British children were making a substantial and important contribution to family income.[31] It would appear, then, that while the geographical context differs considerably and experiences are varied, child employment is a worldwide phenomenon. While the types of jobs, working conditions and wage levels may differ from one society to another, wherever children work they are generally paid less well than adults and have less power and fewer rights than adults to change adverse and unfair working conditions. The whole area of children's working patterns is a complex, multidimensional issue which operates at various levels, and is affected by geography, gender, economic context and cultural variation. However, to tackle the unfair treatment of child workers and develop working practices which are monitored, regulated and protective of children while also recognising a child's right to engage in paid employment, policy agents such as the United Nations and the European Union need to advocate the full participation of children in policy discussions and developments. Children's participation should form the foundation of any strategy.

Excluding working children from the development of employment policies and practices serves only to fuel a debate which is dominated by adult opinion and adult views on how the world should operate, and most importantly on where children are located within that world, and will result in action which is detrimental and harmful to children. For example, the developed world's attempt to ban child labour outright without consulting working children has often resulted in children being driven into even more harmful and dangerous jobs, and being put more at risk than they had been previously.[32] Firing children without consultation, without offering alternative sources of livelihood for them and their families, and without helping them obtain good quality education could amount to a breach of the rights of the child.[33]

GENDER DISCRIMINATION

> In Nepal, girls have a very hard life, especially girls who are not in school. They work 18 hours a day. They have no time for play and recreation. We have discrimination from birth. In our country parents' preference is for sons, not girls. Girls are less educated than boys. They haven't any choices or freedoms compared with boys.[34]

In developing countries girls receive less food, health care and access to education than boys. Access to education provides a dramatic example of the discrimination suffered by girls. Girls represent two-thirds of the world's 130 million children and most go without access to education at either primary or secondary level.[35] An international conference in 2000 on the education of girls concluded that educating girls is probably the single most important vehicle towards development and economic progress.[36] The need to address this has become all the more urgent because the discrimination faced by women is intergenerational in its impact. It makes good development sense to invest in the education of girls due to the fact that as girls grow up they reinvest in the development of their families – their children are more likely to survive and be healthier. The gender gap has been found to have a negative impact on social and economic growth in developing countries, with studies showing that the 'narrower the gender gap in education, the higher a country's GNP per capita and the longer the male life expectancy. A smaller gender gap also lowers the infant mortality rate and the total fertility rate.'[37]

The factors underpinning the disadvantages faced by women include the division of labour within the household, which plays a huge role in deciding if girls attend school. Girls often marry at an early age and it is normally expected that they will remain within the family home. Thus, when resources are low within the family and decisions have to be made regarding which children should attend school, it is often the case that the boys will be selected above their sisters. As one girl, Zarifa from India, states:

> About 20 or 30 children pass their exams every year – but only about six of them are girls. The rest of them are boys. Girls fail more because of the heavy workload at home, so we have less time to study. And because of the social set-up here people criticise the girls if they see a boy working in the house or in the fields. They expect the girls to work and the boys to study, so in a way we are forced to work.[38]

This is often a very practical decision, because in such gender-stratified societies the return on family investment for a child's education is much more obvious if a boy goes to school rather than a girl. Less value is placed on the education of girls by many parents who consider it more important for a girl to learn how to do household chores and expect that a girl will grow up, get married and remain as the main household carer.

CHILDREN'S RIGHTS

Given the social and economic inequalities faced by children in developed and developing countries, it is clear that more concrete steps should be taken to ensure that children are treated as equals in society. A recent Save the Children report on children's rights argued that society as a whole is damaged by the neglect of children, who are being viewed as just another special interest group.[39] The report claimed that what happens to children is a major determinant of what happens to society. Essentially, development processes that ignore and thereby damage children will never work. The report draws comparisons between the situation of children today and the situation of women 20 or 30 years ago. Previously, development planners overlooked the different roles of women and men in society, and as a result policies and interventions failed because they were targeted at the wrong people. But with increased understanding and the collection of a body of evidence on the role of women in society, combined with intensive lobbying, there has been a major shift among those concerned with development and social policy in their understanding of the position of women in economic and social change. Consequently, good policy making or planning cannot be undertaken without an awareness of gender issues and the participation of women as equal partners. Similarly, children's rights campaigners now want to get to a situation where children's status is seen as a yardstick against which we measure progress in development, and where children are consulted and involved in the formulation of policies that affect them. Anything less would fail both children and society as a whole.

Previously, the specific human rights of children were assumed to be met within the broader human rights framework. However, those NGOs working with children across the world knew from their experience that the rights of children were largely invisible within the broader human rights agenda. As Graca Machel, United Nations expert on the impact of armed conflict on children and long-time children's rights activist, stated: 'Children's rights are human rights. This may sound like a statement of the obvious. Yet for millions of children around the world, this one simple undeniable fact is being overlooked time and time again.'[40] The almost universal ratification of the United Nations Convention on the Rights of the Child (UNCRC) has meant that the importance of children's rights as a set of principles and minimum standards has been at least acknowledged, irrespective of local beliefs and values. The UNCRC applies to all children, regardless of where or under what circumstances they live. 'In rich and poor countries, regardless of children's personal status or situation, it provides internationally agreed, minimum standards to ensure the child's well-being.'[41]

The UNCRC was unanimously adopted by the UN General Assembly on 20 November 1989. Since then it has been signed by all but two of the world's governments – it is the most widely ratified human rights treaty in history and is a comprehensive statement of children's rights, combining economic, social and cultural rights with political and civil rights. Children are regarded by the Convention as full human beings who should have access to a comprehensive set of rights and who could play a key role in the protection and development of these rights. The Convention empowers children to be viewed as equal stakeholders in society, with the right to be involved and included in how we run our communities, locally and globally. Referring to the impact of the UNCRC, the *Children's Rights* report claimed that:

There is no place for discrimination against children nor for their exploitation and abuse. No child should live in poverty ... This vision has yet to be realised in any country in the world, rich or poor. It challenges all societies to make greater efforts on behalf of – but also, increasingly, with – their children. It expects greater achievement from richer societies with their greater resources but it also expects them to support, through their aid and development policies, poorer countries less able or struggling to achieve full respect for children's rights.[42]

Article 12 of the UNCRC states that children have the right to have a say in decisions affecting their lives, and to be consulted and to participate in policy making. Governments are duty-bound to look in more detail at the *right to participation*. It is now enshrined in international law that children should be consulted about decisions that affect their lives. The UNCRC is one of the most remarkable and significant documents to bring children's rights centre stage. Article 12 of the Convention states:

> State Parties shall assure to the child who is capable of forming his or her own views the right to express these views freely in all matters affecting the child, the view of the child being given due weight in accordance with the age and maturity of the child.

For various reasons, society has historically deemed children and young people as not having the capacity to meaningfully contribute to the future. Children and young people are more often seen as a problem than as part of a solution. As a result young people can feel that they are on the margins of society and, consequently, that they are alienated and excluded. The outcome of these feelings of alienation can be life-defeating and dangerous, as young people may disengage from any sense of ownership of their community or society. Instead they become apathetic or even actively antagonistic towards the societal structures and processes which they believe have nothing to offer them.[43]

The reluctance to accept children and young people as full partners in society is common across the world. Current debates have presented children as out of control, a menace to society and generally in need of firm discipline.[44] Adults claim that until children learn the value of responsibility they should not receive rights as individuals. However, the reality is that many children adopt adult responsibilities while still being children, in both developed and developing countries. For example, young people who grow up in the public care system in developed countries may be living independently from the age of 16 and, thereby, develop skills in negotiating a complex benefit system to the point that they are no longer dependent on anyone.[45] As outlined above, many children in the developing world have significant responsibilities within families, providing much necessary family income.

Children are not encouraged to participate, or make their opinions known, in the various settings in which they find themselves – school, home, public forums or local community. As agreed throughout the children's lobby, if young people are to identify with the communities in which they live and the institutions which govern them, then efforts must be made to engage them in discussions and partnerships. Young people are often seen as problems and not *partners,* and this causes dissatisfaction and alienation. As Henderson states:

> Achieving such a partnership will require agencies and policy makers to consider children's future with a mixture of vision and modesty: they need to see the scope for releasing the energy and goodwill which exists among children and adults in communities, and they need to listen more attentively to the voices of children themselves – how they feel they can participate, what the neighbourhood means to them.[46]

Society is currently paying a heavy price for not involving children and young people in the policy and practice of development. It is crucial that the voices of vulnerable children and young people are heard and, most importantly, that the structures are created to facilitate the full participation of children in policy development that reflects the reality of their lives. Young people have an important contribution to make and have expert knowledge of what services and policies would improve their lives. They are the experts at being young and, most importantly, they can offer solutions which adults would not necessarily think of.

MODELS OF CHILD PARTICIPATION

The Real Deal initiative in Britain was an attempt to consult with young people with experiences of disadvantage. It looked at the issues that affected them, and sought to find ways of presenting these views directly to policy and decision makers. Ten groups of young people from around the UK were recruited to this initiative through existing projects run by Save the Children and the Centre-point London homeless charity.[47] Each group engaged in a series of discussions and activities over a period of six months in 1998. The idea was to generate ideas and proposals which could inform the government's policy agenda. The workshops culminated in a visit to Downing Street, where the young people presented their shared views on issues which impacted on them to government ministers and policy makers. The most striking aspect of these workshops was the way in which the ten groups of young people had very similar views and opinions on the issues they sought to raise in their presentations to ministers. The exercise also demonstrated to government the importance of engaging with marginalised young people and illustrated a model of how this could be achieved.

It has also been encouraging to find evidence that countries in transition have been taking a lead in bringing children and young people to the centre of political structures. For example, Slovenia has established a national children's parliament which has proved an invaluable vehicle for communication between politicians and young people. In 1992, more than 200 children from 20 different regions of South Africa met together for a six-day summit and developed the Children's Charter of South Africa. The charter reflected children's demands to be placed at the heart of the political agenda at that time. As one 15-year-old participant stated:

> The summit couldn't have come at a more appropriate time than now. Political bodies are presently busy planning for South Africa and a new constitution. We want a part of that constitution to belong to the future leaders of South Africa, which is us. The Children's Charter will secure our place and we will be recognised as human beings, the young people of South Africa.[48]

Initiatives to involve children in policy making have taken place in other countries, such as Zimbabwe and Senegal, where children's parliaments have been established at regional and national levels. These parliaments have been disseminating information on the UNCRC and have been contributing to the reporting procedures of their governments.[49] In India's Rajasthan region, a children's parliament is headed by a 13-year-old Prime Minister, Laxmi Devi. In this parliament, the adults take a back seat to the child MPs, who are aged between 11 and 14. The child MPs, voted into office by other children, have the power to help govern their schools, push for practical improvements in their villages and ensure that children can participate in every aspect of village life. While initially feeling threatened by the prospect of derogating responsibilities to children, the adults have come to accept the benefits of youth participation. Laxmi's influence included heading a 10-strong cabinet, whose portfolios ranged from finance and education through to water resources and women's development.

Many children's rights NGOs are working at local and global levels to protect working children in ways that both protect their rights and recognise that family poverty is one of the main causes of their involvement in such work. One way of helping is to enable children to become their own advocates in public forums. For example, an initiative by Save the Children in 1997 saw an international group of working children being brought to the International Labour Organisation conference on child labour in Oslo. During the proceedings some adults voiced an opinion that child labour should be banned and that all children should be in school instead of working. The argument ignored the reality of children's lives in poor countries, where child labour is common and often necessary as a means of supplementing family income. Child delegates expressed their desire for education but in a way that would be flexible enough to allow them to work as well. Representatives of working children's organisations wanted to make similar points and on the last day of the conference a young Malian girl made a powerful presentation, speaking directly from her own experiences and that of many other children.[50] The experience of working children's organisations is perhaps one of the most prominent examples of children who are living in extremely poor and difficult circumstances and, yet, demanding an input into the policy debates that affect their lives. Working children's organisations have recently started to make their voices heard in international child labour debates, representing working children from around the world.[51]

As a result of increasing recognition of the importance of children in policy making a number of working children living in villages on the West Coast of India are now experiencing real participation in their communities. Working children in five villages are officially involved with local governments in identifying problems, planning solutions and acting on them. Children have been elected to sit on a parallel form of local government run by village children, and have been given the opportunity to participate equally in the micro-planning of their communities.

> Children are reshaping their villages and redesigning services and amenities to be more child friendly. They are slowly but very surely building an inclusive and participative village environment. They have contributed to the planning of schools and relocated public distribution outlets closer to their homes. These children are setting new parameters for development and are changing structures that require them to work.[52]

CONCLUSION

Despite being the social group most vulnerable to poverty, children are too often invisible from textbooks on development. It is wrongly assumed that when we talk about the causes of, and solutions to, global poverty for adults that children will inevitably benefit from such strategies. This assumption is based on the premise that what benefits adults will also benefit children. However, poverty can have very different consequences for children and adults. Children's needs, interests and perspectives must be placed at the centre of global social and economic policy making, alongside and on an equal footing with those of adults. Without placing children centre stage in policy development we will witness an increasing number of marginalised young people who believe they have no stake in society and who lack a meaningful way to contribute to a prosperous and just future. The debate over children's participation in society is perhaps best summed up by a comment by one rights activist working in India:

> The time has come for us to build a partnership with children, to begin to listen to them and to allow them to take our hand and lead us in finding solutions that are good for them and contribute to a sustainable model of development for our countries. We must fight this battle together, hand in hand.[53]

NOTES

1. G.B. Sgritta and A. Saporiti, *Childhood as a Social Phenomenon*, Eurosocial Report 36/2 (Vienna: European Centre for Social Welfare Policy and Research, 1990), p. 4.
2. World Health Organisation, *The World Health Report* (Geneva: World Health Organisation, 1989); B. Bell, R. Brett, R. Marcus and S. Muscroft,

Children's Rights: Reality or Rhetoric (London: Save the Children, 2000); Save the Children, *International Action Against Child Poverty: Meeting the 2015 Targets* (London: Save the Children, 2001).

3. UNDP, *Human Development Report 1999* (New York and Oxford: Oxford University Press, 1999).

4. World Bank, *The World Bank Development Report 1999/2000* (Washington: World Bank, 1999); UNICEF, Innocenti Research Centre, *Child Poverty in Rich Nations*, No. 1 (Florence: UNICEF, 2000); A. Sen, *Mortality as an Indicator of Economic Success or Failure*, International Development Centre (Florence: UNICEF, 1995).

5. UNICEF, *Child Poverty*, p. 9.

6. UNICEF, *Child Poverty*, p. 1.

7. Central Statistics Office, *Census of Population* (Dublin: The Stationery Office, 1996).

8. B. Nolan, *Child Poverty in Ireland* (Dublin: Combat Poverty Agency, 2000).

9. Irish Government, *The National Children's Strategy: Our Children – Their Lives* (Dublin: The Stationery Office, 2000), p. 64.

10. J. McCluskey, *Factfile 2000: Facts and Figures Facing Britain's Children* (Kent: NCH Action for Children, 1999).

11. UNICEF, *State of the World's Children* (New York: UNICEF, 2000).

12. D. Gordon, I. Adelman, K. Ashworth, J. Bradshaw, R. Levitas, S. Middleton, C. Pantazis, D. Patsios, S. Payne, P. Townsend and J. Williams, *Poverty and Social Exclusion in Britain* (York: Joseph Rowntree Foundation, 2000).

13. G. Fimister (ed.), *An End in Sight: Child Poverty in the UK* (London: CPAG, 2001).

14. World Bank, *Global Economic Prospects* (Washington: World Bank, 1988).

15. J.P. Joyce, *Taking Children Seriously* (London: Save the Children, 2001), p. 27.

16. Joyce, *Taking Children Seriously*, p. 27.

17. See the discussion in Bell et al., *Children's Rights*.

18. Bell et al., *Children's Rights*, p. 41.

19. Save the Children, *What's Up With the World?* (London: Save the Children, 2001).

20. British Government, Department of Health and Social Security, *Inequalities in Health* (London: HMSO, 1980).

21. Bell et al., *Children's Rights*, p. 41.

22. Fimister, *An End in Sight*.

23. See P. Noonan, 'Pathologisation and Resistance: Travellers, nomadism and the state', in P. Hainsworth (ed.), *Divided Society* (London: Pluto Press, 1998), pp. 152–83.

24. Social Exclusion Unit, *Truancy and School Exclusion* (London: SEU, 1998). Also see McCluskey, *Factfile 2000*.

25. See UNICEF, *State of the World's Children*.

26. C. Heward and S. Bunwaree (eds), *Gender, Education and Development: Beyond Access To Empowerment* (London: Zed Books, 1999).

27. Heward and Bunwaree, *Gender, Education and Development*, p. 21.

28. International Labour Organisation, *Child Labour: What is to be Done?* (Geneva: ILO, 1996).
29. R. Ebdon, *Working Children's Future* (London: Save the Children, 2000).
30. B. Pettit (ed.), *Children and Work in the UK: Reassessing the Issues* (London: Save the Children/Child Poverty Action Group, 1998).
31. S. Middleton, J. Shropshire and N. Croden, in B. Pettit (ed.), *Children and Work in the UK: Reassessing the Issues*, pp. 41–59. Also, see S. Hobbs, S. Lindsay and J. McKechnie, 'The Extent of Child Employment in Britain', *British Journal of Education and Work*, Vol. 9 (1996), pp. 5–18.
32. N. Reddy, 'Child Work in India: Lessons for the Developed and Developing World', in S. McCloskey (ed.), *No Time to Play: Local and Global Perspectives on Child Employment* (Belfast: One World Centre, 1997), pp. 29–47.
33. Save the Children, *Big Business, Small Hands: Responsible Approaches to Child Labour* (London: Save the Children, 2000).
34. G. Landsdown, M. Gidney and L. Woll, *Children's Rights: Equal Rights? Diversity, Difference and the Issue of Discrimination* (London: Save the Children, 2000), p. 36.
35. UNICEF, *Facts and Figures* (New York: UNICEF, 1998).
36. Landsdown et al., *Children's Rights: Equal Rights?*
37. Heward and Bunwaree, *Gender, Education and Development*, p. 155.
38. Save the Children, *One in Four* (London: Save the Children, 2001).
39. B. Bell, A. Chetley, M. Edwards, N. MacDonald and A. Penrose, *Towards a Children's Agenda: New Challenges for Social Development* (London: Save the Children, 1995).
40. Bell et al., *Children's Rights*, p. 1.
41. B. Bell and A. Penrose, 'From Policy Towards Practice', in C. Cuninghame (ed.), *Realising Children's Rights* (London: Save the Children, 1999), p. 60. Also pp. 58–66.
42. Bell et al., *Children's Rights*, p. 17.
43. G. Mulgan and M. Wilkinson, *Freedom's Children* (London: Demos, 1995).
44. B. Franklin, *The Handbook of Children's Rights* (London: Routledge, 1995).
45. A. West, 'Citizenship, Children and Young People', *Youth and Policy*, No. 55 (1997), pp. 69–74.
46. P. Henderson, *Children and Communities* (London: Pluto Press, 1995).
47. Centrepoint, Demos, Save the Children, *The Real Deal* (London: Demos, 1999).
48. Bell et al., *Towards a Children's Agenda*, p. 61.
49. S. Ruxton, *Implementing Children's Rights* (London: Save the Children, 1998).
50. Save the Children, *Working for Change in Education* (London: Save the Children, 2000).
51. A. Swift, *Working Children Get Organised: An Introduction to Working Children's Organisations* (London: International Save the Children Alliance, 1999).
52. Reddy, 'Child Work in India', p. 45.
53. Reddy, 'Child Work in India', p. 46.

WEB SITES

Save the Children	www.savethechildren.org.uk
Children's Law Centre	www.childrenslawcentre.org
Child Poverty Action Group	www.cpag.org.uk
Children Now	www.childrennow.org
Joint Council on International Children's Services	www.jcics.org
Nelson Mandela Children's Fund	www.mandela-children.org

10 Education as an Agent of Social Change

Stephen McCloskey

The past decade has been characterised as a period of accelerated globalisation that has enhanced interdependence between societies in social, economic and political terms. The current era of globalisation has been distinguished from previous periods of economic development by innovations in information technology, the flow of commodities, capital and people across national borders, and global integration of governance and culture. Globalisation, however, has also spawned the increasing dominance of the private sector in global commodity markets – most starkly evidenced in the wealth and influence of transnational corporations (TNCs) – which in turn has undermined the capacity of national governments to regulate trade. While the benefits of globalisation have been immense – greater integration of cultures and societies, unprecedented means of global communication, and increased profits – they have come at a high human cost. The social and economic inequalities that plagued the last century have persisted into the new millennium. According to the United Nations (UN), 1.2 billion people live on less than a dollar a day and 2.4 billion people lack basic sanitation – statistics that represent an indictment of global financial and governmental structures and seriously question the path to development underpinned by globalisation.[1]

The post-Cold War era has witnessed a widening poverty gap between developed and developing countries, to the extent that by the late 1990s one-fifth of the world's population, living in the highest income countries, controlled 86 per cent of the world's Gross Domestic Product (GDP) – while the bottom fifth controlled just 1 per cent.[2] These socio-economic inequalities represent a major challenge to education both in enabling learners to understand the globalisation process and in addressing its impact on the world's poor. As Lynn Davies puts it:

In terms of health, 35,000 children die every day from perfectly avoidable causes. 8,000 children will have died just today because of diarrhoea. We can treat diarrhoea with safe drinking water, sugar and salt – we have the technical capacity, but not the political will ... so what is education doing about the right to life?[3]

This chapter will examine the theory and practice of development education, a distinctive and radical model of learning designed to raise awareness of development issues in local and global contexts. Development education encompasses an active, participative approach to learning that is intended to effect action toward social change. I will, therefore, consider the response of development education to the renewed and accelerated process of globalisation. The chapter will also assess the contribution of development education in the formal and non-formal education sectors and discuss the challenge of effectively measuring the impact of this work. I will outline the policy environment in which development practitioners operate and examine the contribution of development education to the concept of education for sustainable development (ESD). The chapter will begin by focusing on some definitions of development education before considering the educational philosophy of Paulo Freire, which provides the theoretical base of contemporary practice.

DEFINING DEVELOPMENT EDUCATION

Defining development education can be problematical as it involves capturing the range of components that comprise this broad and far-reaching pedagogical process. For example, do we focus on methodology (active, participative learning), the social and economic issues it addresses (trade, aid, conflict, etc.), the skills it engenders in learners (tolerance, respect, cultural awareness), the outcomes it intends (social justice and equality), the social relations it examines (between rich and poor, developing and developed countries), the educational sectors in which it operates (adults, schools, youth groups), or the tools it employs (resources, training, information technology)? This problem is compounded by the various labels applied by educators to the methodology, content and process encompassed by development education. Alternatives include global education, education for sustainable development, development studies and development awareness. In fact, some proponents of development education oppose the use of definitions by arguing that they can be counter-productive in limiting its terms of reference or relating it to a particular point in history when it is a fluid, non-static process.

While accepting the limitations of definitions, they can at least point to the main parameters of development education activity and offer some guidance as to its aims. A commonly used definition is that framed by the UN, which states that development education is:

> ... concerned with issues of human rights, dignity, self-reliance and social justice in both developed and developing countries. It is concerned with the causes of underdevelopment and the promotion of an understanding of what is involved in development, of how countries go about undertaking development, and of the reasons for and ways of achieving a new international economic and social order.[4]

The definition of the Development Education Association (DEA)[5] echoes that of the UN but goes further in suggesting how the objectives of development education can be achieved by encompassing the following:

- Enabling people to understand the links between their own lives and those of people throughout the world
- Increasing understanding of the global economic, social, political and environmental forces which shape our lives
- Developing the skills, attitudes and values which enable people to work together to bring about change and to take control of their lives
- Working to achieve a more just and sustainable world in which power and resources are equitably shared[6]

From both definitions we can discern the need to enhance our understanding about development, address poverty-related issues, promote social justice and bring about change. The UN emphasises the role of countries in the development process, whereas the DEA focuses on 'people' as agents of change and suggests the importance of individual action and responsibility. The common themes that permeate most definitions of development education include:

- The need to encourage action as an outcome of the educational process

- The local-global axis of education involving both an under-standing of development issues and our interdependence with other societies
- The development of new skills – values, attitudes, critical awareness, knowledge and understanding – that will underpin individual action
- The use of participative, active learning methodologies
- Education as a visioning exercise toward social transformation
- Social justice, inclusion and equality
- Informing practice with a developing world perspective

The methodologies and outcomes promoted by development education have been largely derived from the philosophical thought of Paulo Freire. His work has been a mainspring for development education practice since its emergence in the early 1970s, combined with that of missionary groups and religious orders that have worked in developing countries.

THE THEORY OF DEVELOPMENT EDUCATION

The philosophical thought on which development education practice is based is central to its method and ideals. The seminal development education text is Paulo Freire's *Pedagogy of the Oppressed*, which was initially lauded for its contribution to the illiteracy problem in Latin America. Indeed, Freire was the General Co-ordinator of the National Plan for Adult Literacy in his native Brazil, but his educational philosophy had a methodology and social analysis targeted at all socially oppressed peoples. What dis-tinguished Freire's discourse on education from existing models was its assertion that learners could engage in a process of social transformation from oppression to liberation. Freire's radical philosophy struck a chord with dispossessed people throughout Latin America where educational access was limited and poverty endemic. Almost three decades after the publication of *Pedagogy of the Oppressed*, Freire's work still resonates in societies where educa-tional provision is a casualty of neo-liberalism. However, Freire recognised the capacity of the educational process to attain something more than the eradication of illiteracy. His work frowned upon the dominant didactic model of education where students were mere receptacles of information delivered by the teacher. Freire advocated an active learning approach to education through which students could engender a critical consciousness that would inform their future actions. He proposed that teachers should work with students 'in acts of cognition, not transferrals of information'.[7]

Freire's pedagogy also facilitates a process of problem solving whereby the students and teacher engage in dialogue and reflection that draws on their own experiences and 'strives for the emergence of consciousness and critical intervention in reality'.[8] Freire's 'banking theory', whereby the teacher deposits information in the mind of the student as an incontestable, indelible truth, represented a negation of education 'as a process of enquiry'.[9] The main benefit in approaching education as a process of dialogue is in enhancing the capacity of the learner to develop values such as respect and tolerance for the views of others. Education, therefore, should involve the development of new skills that equip the learner to actively engage in society to effect change. Thus, the anti-globalisation protest movement that emerged in the 1990s to challenge the international financial institutions which frame the rules of global trade, can be described as development education in practice. Angus McBrian, an eyewitness to the high-profile protests at the World Trade Organisation's (WTO) Ministerial Council meeting in Seattle in November 1999, suggested that 'the events in Seattle found their greatest success as an endeavour in development education'.[10] The issues under discussion at WTO meetings are complex, technical and difficult to process into public campaigns and therefore the protesters engaged in what McBrian described as 'self-education' initiatives involving 'teach-ins, workshops and seminars'.[11] This methodology corresponds with Freirean 'problem-posing education' and co-investigation in dialogue.

REFLECTIVE ACTION

Freire's work is noted for its articulation of the needs of the oppressed and those living in absolute poverty. He aimed to break what he described as the 'culture of silence' of those who were dispossessed, through a union of theory and praxis. This process encompassed an analysis of the social relations and power structures (media, government, cultural elitism) which entrapped the masses in a state of domination. For Freire, the process of liberation should be characterised by the same principles and actions which underpin a transformed society liberated from the bonds of colonialism. The revolutionary process advocated by Freire involved reflective action encompassing measured and contemplative dialogue within the dominated class as part of a meaningful act of liberation. Freire regarded reflection without an active outcome as mere 'verbalism' and action without reflection as pure 'activism' (action for action's sake). His concept of 'dialogical action' was clearly influenced by Marx's 'dialectical materialism' whereby 'the combination of materialism with dialectics transforms both'.[12]

Both Marx and Freire believed that the masses should participate in the revolutionary process to surmount the anti-dialogical praxis of the dominant elites. As Freire puts it: 'The unity of the elite derives from its *antagonism* with the people; the unity of the revolutionary group grows out of *communion* with the (united) people.'[13] The main concern of the ruling elite is to maintain the status quo of social relations by undermining any alteration to the social order. Freire cautioned against 'communiqués' or entreaties from the ruling class offering to enter into dialogue with those they dominate. This process, he believed, was not dialogical praxis but an attempt to quell the formations of action that threatened the power base of the elite. For example, the conquest of Latin America by colonial powers was superseded by an equally oppressive neo-colonial process of corrupt oligarchies and 'democracies' that were in fact executors of power bestowed by the old colonial masters. Thus, indigenous rulers did not alter the social, economic and political forces that underpinned poverty and social exclusion. Freire, therefore, considered the revolutionary process as a liberating experience for both the oppressors and the oppressed, in the struggle to reconstitute socio-economic relations on the principle of equality rather than that of domination.

CULTURAL SYNTHESIS

Another key Freirean concept is that of cultural synthesis, which is also a dialectical process based on the notion that culture can either transform social reality or maintain the old hierarchical order. Freire described cultural synthesis as 'a mode of action for confronting culture itself, as the preserver of the very structures by which it was formed'.[14] Dialogical cultural action is based on relations of 'permanence' and 'change' that can be transcended through a new social structure. Cultural synthesis recognises the value of diversity and engenders an enthusiasm to learn from the values and traditions of others rather than imposing one cultural form on another. The colonial conquest of developing countries was attended by a 'civilising' project intended to impose Westernised cultures and faiths on indigenous populations. Indeed, the conquest of the Americas some five centuries ago represented the securing of new markets and resources in the guise of a Christian crusade. The invading Spanish conquistadors were engaged in cultural supremacy, not synthesis, seeking to eradicate, rather than learn from, indigenous traditions.

Placed in the contemporary context of globalisation, Freire's anti-dialogical theory of cultural domination resonates loudly in the economic activities of transnational corporations and developed countries. McDonald's, Starbucks, Nike and Coca-Cola are totems of a cultural invasion of developing countries that has accompanied economic dominance. The *Human Development Report 1999* makes this point clearly when it states that 'today's flow of culture is unbalanced, heavily weighted in one direction, from rich countries to poor'.[15] The report adds that the United States' most profitable export is Hollywood films which, in 1997, grossed more than $30 billion and eclipsed domestic film markets throughout the world. This US-driven cultural invasion of developing countries creates an appetite for Western commodities and conjures up images of a superficially attractive path to development that masks massive levels of underlying poverty in developing and developed countries (including the US). As Freire suggests, anti-dialogical action – cultural permanence toward social stasis – is constructed upon conquest, division and manipulation. Cultural action, therefore, aims to 'supersede the dominant alienated and alienating culture. In this sense, every authentic revolution is a cultural revolution.'[16]

DEVELOPMENT EDUCATION PRACTICE

In assessing the impact of Freire's educational philosophy on the activities of contemporary educational practitioners, Ann McCollum identified a significant gap between the theory and practice of development education. McCollum's critical analysis of the development sector, particularly in Britain and Ireland, concluded that the radical vision of Freire's work had been moderated by development educators to accommodate the dominant liberal ideology and practice in the education sector. She suggested that 'Freire's ideas have been misappropriated within development education leading to dilemmas in relation to the theory and practice of development education which must be recognised and resolved'.[17] McCollum believed that the 'central assumption' of development education – that raising individual awareness of development issues would logically result in social action – was fundamentally flawed. Freire regarded education as an agent of societal change whereas liberal education focuses on the development of the individual. McCollum argued that development education was not engaging with major social and economic structures and relations as advocated in Freire's radical social theory. Development education lacked the 'conceptual space' to engage with the theoretical questions posed by Freire that underpinned action toward social transformation. Instead, development educators had embraced Freire's active learning methodology without addressing 'the wider implications of the sociology of knowledge'.[18]

McCollum also identified problems within the wider operations of development NGOs that limited their impact as development education practitioners. She described the development community as speaking 'only to itself' and, thereby, limiting its influence within the education system and civil society. However, McCollum acknowledged the difficult context in which development NGOs have to operate. The development education sector in developed countries has been chronically underfunded with government support normally representing a small percentage of the overall development aid budget. The UN set a target for developed countries of 0.7 per cent of Gross National Product (GNP) for overseas aid budgets, and most Western governments have fallen well short of this meagre contribution. Thus development education expenditure in most Western countries is a fraction of overall aid expenditure that itself falls short of the UN target. A notable exception to this trend is Sweden which in 2001 contributed 0.8 per cent of its overall aid budget to development education. This compares with 0.04 per cent in France, 0.19 per cent in Britain and 0.008 per cent in the United States. Development education practitioners have consequently found it difficult to operate in such a harsh economic climate.

Over the past 30 years, development education has largely been financed by development NGOs (such as Christian Aid, Oxfam and Save the Children) with limited funding also coming from other sources, such as government departments, trust funds, local authorities and charities. Development agencies were largely instrumental in the establishment of some 50 Development Education Centres (DECs) in Britain and Ireland from the 1970s onward with the remit of delivering specialist development education services such as resource provision and training workshops. Whilst some DECs have prevailed through an uncertain financial climate, others have struggled and been unable to enhance their organisational capacity. Moreover, as McCollum suggests, 'DEC activities are dominated and circumscribed by government whether it be in terms of education policy or practice.'[19] Development agencies and DECs have a remit that includes challenging government policies when they believe that they exacerbate poverty. However, this role can be compromised when an NGO is overly reliant on government funding to support its activities. Project funding or running costs often come with an attendant policy agenda that can lead the work of an NGO rather than the organisation pursuing its own objectives.

DEVELOPMENT EDUCATION POLICY: BRITAIN – A CASE STUDY

The development education policy environment has changed considerably in Britain since McCollum compiled her constructive critique of the gap between theory and practice. The election of a New Labour government in 1997 resulted in the establishment of the Department for International Development (DFID) which superseded the Overseas Development Administration (ODA) as the ministry responsible for oveseas aid, policy development and development education. In November 1997, DFID published a White Paper which was the first 'definitive statement' by the British government on international development for over 20 years. The White Paper represented a renewed engagement by the government in international issues following two decades of underfunding and a gaping policy vacuum.[20] Indeed, DFID candidly accepted that:

> For much of the last 20 years, the UK government has attached little importance to development education work in the UK, leaving others, particularly the network of Development Education Centres and others in the voluntary sector, to take the lead in promoting greater awareness and understanding.[21]

Clare Short, the Secretary of State for International Development, also commended the role of DECs in promoting development education, although she identified a need for strategic direction in the development sector:

> I want to pay tribute to the work of the 50 or so Development Education Centres spread around the UK. Often run on a

shoestring, they have delivered both materials and expertise to many schools ... But DECs would be the first to admit that their reach and resources are limited. We have increased our support for their work but also need to look strategically at this area.[22]

A key objective of the White Paper was that: 'Every child should be educated about development issues, so that they understand the key global considerations that will shape their lives.'[23] DFID established a Development Awareness Working Group (DAWG)[24] to discuss how this objective would be delivered and subsequently produced a strategy document for development education.[25] DFID's strategic aims for development education included:

- Reversing the decline in development education spending
- Reaching out to new sectors in securing their support for development awareness – trade unions, business, adult education, churches and faiths, etc.
- Promoting development education resources in education sectors (schools, youth groups, community organisations, etc.) more effectively
- Influencing schools' curriculum review processes in England and Wales, Scotland and Northern Ireland
- Enlisting the support of other government departments for development education

The results of this process have been mixed. The development education budget has increased dramatically from a paltry £700,000 under the Conservative government (1996–97) to £6.5 million in 2001–02.[26] Britain's total aid contribution, however, in 2002 stood at 0.31 per cent of GNP – which is less than half of the UN's overseas development aid target. Moreover, it is questionable how far DFID's development education objectives can be achieved with a limited budget of £6.5 million to finance activities in England, Scotland, Wales and Northern Ireland.

Despite DFID's accession to full cabinet status in 1997, it has yet to secure the co-operation of other key ministries in adopting an integrated approach to development. Government development policies should include environmental protection, financial support for development from the exchequer, reduced spending on defence and tighter enforcement of arms export controls, ethical investment criteria, and an enhanced development education content in the statutory schools curriculum – in short, a 'joined-up' approach to sustainable development that has the full support of appropriate ministers and civil servants. In assessing progress made to date in achieving this aim, the DEA states that:

> Sustainable development is supposedly at the heart of the work of the UK Government and the devolved administrations, but there is, as yet, little evidence to show that there is effective co-ordination in the delivery of these agendas across Government departments.[27]

The arms trade, for example, illustrates the disjointed nature of New Labour policies in respect to eradicating poverty in developing countries. The DFID *Departmental Report* (1999) stated that 'A major obstacle to the eradication of poverty is the persistence of violent conflict, or its legacy, in many of the poorest countries. Reducing the incidence, duration and effects of armed conflict is essential.'[28] This position, however, was completely at odds with that of the Department of Trade and Industry (DTI), which approved 2,181 arms export licences to 35 countries from 1997, 21 of which were engaged in high- or low-intensity conflicts, the majority being low- or middle-income developing states.[29] The contradictions in government development policy are mostly rooted in the competing demands for the DTI to create jobs and investment, and for DFID to establish an effective, integrated government programme for development. However, development NGOs have become increasingly uneasy with the gap between government rhetoric and policy implementation. New Labour's interventions (with the US) in the former Yugoslavia and, more recently, in Afghanistan, combined with ongoing sanctions and aggression against Iraq since the Gulf War, undermines its efforts to build partnerships within civil society to promote development education and effective support for developing countries.

In development education policy, DFID has delivered on promises to increase support for practitioners. Moreover, it has recently embarked on a new strategic initiative, Enabling Effective Support (EES), designed to increase development education practice in schools. Organised on a regional basis, EES aims to pull together key statutory education and NGO representatives into a steering group with the remit of identifying gaps in existing development education practice and establishing an action plan to address identified weaknesses in provision. The strategic thinking underpinning EES offers development education a more solid platform for influencing the mainstream education sector. This strategy, however, will have a limited impact without cross-departmental commitment to development issues, which is underpinned by actions as well as rhetoric.

FORMAL AND NON-FORMAL EDUCATION

Development education practitioners have made significant headway in enhancing awareness about development issues in the formal and non-formal sectors, particularly over the past decade. Development agencies, DECs and statutory education bodies have developed models of good practice in training provision and resource production that have encouraged educators to incorporate development issues into their teaching practice. Increased funding into the development sector in recent years has enhanced the professionalism of the services provided by NGOs and enabled them to promote their work more effectively through information technology. Moreover, the widespread recognition within the education sector that globalisation necessitates the development of a global perspective among young people from an early age has added weight to the argument for the increased resourcing and practice of development education.

Development educators have traditionally focused their activities on the formal (schools, colleges, universities) and non-formal (youth groups, community organisations, adult education, trade unions, women's groups, etc.) education sectors. Formal sector work can include teacher training, Initial Teacher Education (student teacher training), workshops with students, and advocacy work aimed at integrating development education into mainstream education practice. Activity in the non-formal sector is less constrained by statutory curricula and is targeted at a wide range of groups in civil society that have an interest in broadening the global perspective of their constituents. The methodology applied in both sectors is based on the Freirean active learning approach, although the content of training events can be tailored to meet the needs of target groups – for example, trade unions are likely to be most interested in the impact of trade and globalisation on workers in developed and developing countries.

The limitations of development education practice have often resulted from the misperceptions of learners as to how this form of education relates to them and what the concept actually means. The sources of this confusion include: the breadth of development education content, which can overwhelm the learner; the various labels pertaining to development education, which can dilute its impact; the notion that development issues have a global context that is somehow removed from the learner's own experiences and reality; and the concern that development education is an additional subject area to be foisted on already overburdened teachers and educators rather than an area of study that complements their teaching practice. Of course, the misperceptions of learners can often result from the failings of development education practitioners to adequately promote their work, strategically align their activities to mainstream education needs, and build alliances with statutory education bodies. Development NGOs have acknowledged weaknesses in their practice but can point to some of the mitigating factors discussed above – inadequate funding, fragmented government policies on development issues, and competing priorities for their resources (campaigning, fundraising, overseas aid, development education).

Operational difficulties for development NGOs have been compounded by the education system's failure to provide an adequate infrastructure to facilitate enhanced learning about development issues. Development NGOs have always stressed the capacity of development education to support learning in a wide range of subject areas – Mathematics, English, Geography, History, Science, etc. – in the formal sector. However, curriculum managers and government education departments have not realised the full potential of development education for teachers by providing them with opportunities to explore development issues through these subject areas. Instead, the contemporary education debate in Britain and Ireland has focused on making curriculum provision for Citizenship as a subject area that can tackle issues such as racism, cultural diversity, conflict, homelessness and development issues. Thus, development education could continue to suffer from piecemeal curriculum provision that will maintain its marginal position in formal education. This scenario has serious implications for the provision of teacher training and the production of resources. The reality of formal-sector education dictates that if development education does not form an explicit and substantial component of statutory curriculum content, then development issues will not be taught in classrooms, thereby making the need for training and resources redundant.

EVALUATION

A key problem in assessing the effectiveness of development education has been in identifying appropriate methodologies to measure its impact on learners. Development education aims to instill values and attitudes in the learner that should be reflected in transformative action both locally and globally. Therefore, some of the outcomes of development education are not immediately evident and require time to gestate. However, this is an area of activity assuming increasing importance if development education is to demonstrate its value to learners and the wider education system. McCollum argues that evaluation has often suffered from the pressured working environment of NGOs, where emphasis has been on 'getting the job done' rather than assessing its contribution to stakeholders. She suggests that: 'There has been inadequate development in areas such as measuring intangible performance parameters, measuring organizational effectiveness and judging synergetic factors in effectiveness.'[30] Evaluation enables the teacher or facilitator to improve practice through dialogue with the learner by determining the strengths and weaknesses of the learning process. Dialogue between the teacher and learner is consistent with the concept of reflective learning, which offers opportunities for experimentation that will underpin new approaches to education.

The growing trend of funding development education work through three-year project cycles often frustrates meaningful evaluation because of the limited 'conceptual space' available to reflect on project activities. Development NGOs, therefore, need to evaluate their work as part of a broader, ongoing organisational review process to ensure that activities correspond with the organisation's aims and objectives. McCollum argues that regular discussion with target groups and partners in education combined with constant reference to 'long-term goals', and 'ultimate objectives' will inform a meaningful evaluation process. Moreover, evaluation techniques and approaches should reflect the active learning and participative methodologies underpinning development education. The active participation of learners in the evaluation process is equally important to their engagement with development education activities – they are part of the same continuum.

EDUCATION FOR SUSTAINABLE DEVELOPMENT

The concept of education for sustainable development (ESD) dates back to the Brundtland Commission's report in 1987, but it really gathered momentum after the 1992 United Nations Conference on Environment and Development (UNCED) in Rio de Janeiro. The significance of ESD for development education is its conscious aim of addressing environment and human development concerns in a holistic, educational context. Proponents of ESD suggest that environment and development organisations share common concerns in regard to the sustainability of the planet and its people and, therefore, make natural bedfellows in the field of education. Development and environment groups also share the pedagogical practice of participative learning and encourage active citizenship in promoting sustainability. There is also some overlap in the content of environment and development education – models of economic growth, the use of natural resources, the quality of life, etc. – that lends itself to a more complete understanding of sustainable development issues. In contrast, some development educators have argued that ESD is not a partnership of equals, with the more public-friendly environment message eclipsing or minimising the importance of human development. They also argue that ESD is not a simple hybrid of environment and development education, and adopting such a perspective can traduce their respective agendas for change.

However, the concept of ESD has fast become part of the development lexicon in Western countries since the Rio conference despite its addition to the myriad labels and acronyms that plague the development sector. The term has become even more consolidated in the public consciousness following the World Summit on Sustainable Development (WSSD) held in Johannesburg from 26 August to 4 September 2002. The summit was a follow-up to the Rio conference, with the aim of agreeing targets and timetables for addressing key environment and development concerns such as global warming, lack of sanitation and clean water in poor countries, the spread of HIV/AIDS and the eradication of natural wildlife and plants. Although the summit's plan of action fell woefully short of agreeing concrete and measurable steps for addressing its main agenda points, the event's international media coverage galvanised a worldwide discussion on sustainable development issues. Thus, development and environment issues will become increasingly integrated in the strategising and policy making of governments and NGOs in the future.

It is, therefore, worth considering one of several definitions of ESD which, like development education, encompasses a wide range of issues and outcomes:

Education for Sustainable Development is about the learning
needed to maintain and improve our quality of life and the quality
of life of generations to come. It is about equipping individuals,
communities, groups, businesses and Government to live and act
sustainably as well as giving them an understanding of the
environmental, social and economic issues involved. It is about
preparing for the world in which we live in the next century, and
making sure that we are not found wanting.[31]

This definition formed part of a report by an ESD panel to the
Department of Education and Employment and the curriculum
authority in Britain during the last review of the schools' curriculum.
This panel 'secured recognition of sustainable development within
the school curriculum', which suggests that there is a strategic value
in the environment and development lobbies forming alliances
under the ESD banner to promote their common agenda.[32]
Moreover, the practice of ESD reinforces the need for healthy and
vibrant development and environment sectors rather than threatening their very existence. ESD could represent a significant
opportunity for development education to secure a stronger foothold
in mainstream education as part of a broader set of strategic
relationships with statutory and non-statutory partners.

CONCLUSION

The acceleration of globalisation in the post-Cold War era has
increased the importance and necessity of development education
both within the education system and in wider civil society. The
anti-globalisation protest movement is a reflection of societal
concern about a range of development and environment issues that
impact on all our lives. The extent to which development education
has informed, or even underpinned, the anti-globalisation protests
is difficult to discern, but the activities of development NGOs have
undoubtedly contributed enormously to public education on a range
of sustainable development issues. However, development education
still remains on the margins of mainstream education provision in
many developed countries, particularly in the US, where the events
of 11 September 2001 were visited on an insulated population largely
bereft of the global awareness necessary to comprehend why these
horrors transpired. The leadership role taken by the US in the
globalisation process has not been sufficiently scrutinised from
within the country by its citizens, further underlining the need for

development education practice and methodologies to ensure participative democracy where people are at liberty to engage in political debate and actions.

Within the European Union (EU), development education practice is uneven and this is partly explained by the inadequate funding of the development sector by most EU member states. Other factors include the lack of strategic alliances formed by development educators with key education providers, shortcomings in planning, delivery and evaluation, and a piecemeal adoption of Freirean educational philosophy. Recently, there have been encouraging indications in Britain and Ireland that the development sector has started to think strategically about how it can best impact on the formal and non-formal education sectors. These new initiatives can build on the renewed professionalism that has characterised development education training and resource production in recent years, and the wealth of experience garnered by committed practitioners in the sector. It is essential, however, that good practice in development education should be informed whenever possible by partnerships within the developing world. Development education should not constitute or advocate a Westernised path to development, but should rather be receptive to and prepared to learn from the experiences and practices of developing countries. The challenges of globalisation also necessitate that development education should engage with civil society in a learning process that is genuinely transformative, embracing Freire's vision of education as a means of empowerment.

NOTES

1. UNDP, *Human Development Report 2001* (New York: United Nations, 2001). The *Human Development Report* is produced annually and ranks countries on a Human Development Index (HDI) that provides a more balanced assessment of their social and economic performance over the previous year. The HDI is based on four main criteria: life expectancy at birth, adult literacy, combined gross school enrolment and Gross Domestic Product (GDP). The aim of the index is to reflect the extent to which countries address the social and economic needs of their people rather than relying exclusively on the GDP criterion favoured by the World Bank and other international financial institutions.
2. UNDP, *Human Development Report 2001*.
3. Lynn Davies, 'Global Goals and Own-Goals in Education' (Birmingham: Teachers in Development Education, 1998).
4. Audrey Osler (ed.), *Development Education: Global Perspectives in the Classroom* (London: Cassell, 1994).

5. The Development Education Association (DEA) is a national umbrella body established in 1993 to support and promote the work of 'all those engaged in bringing about a better public understanding in the UK of global and development issues'. The DEA has 250 members including 40 local Development Education Centres (DECs).
6. DEA, 'Measuring Effectiveness in Development Education' (London: DEA, 2001).
7. Paulo Freire, *Pedagogy of the Oppressed* (London: Penguin Books, 1972), p. 47.
8. Freire, *Pedagogy of the Oppressed*, p. 54.
9. Freire, *Pedagogy of the Oppressed*, p. 45.
10. Angus McBrian, 'The Battle in Seattle: Mass protest as development education', in *The Development Education Journal*, Vol. 7, No. 2 (London: DEA, March 2001), pp. 32–3.
11. McBrian, 'The Battle in Seattle', pp. 32–3.
12. Tom Bottomore (ed.), *A Dictionary of Marxist Thought* (Oxford: Blackwell, 1991).
13. Freire, *Pedagogy of the Oppressed*, p. 140. Author's emphasis and brackets.
14. Freire, *Pedagogy of the Oppressed*, p. 147.
15. UNDP, *Human Development Report 1999* (New York: United Nations, 1999).
16. Freire, *Pedagogy of the Oppressed*, p. 147.
17. Ann McCollum, 'Bridging the Gap between Theory and Practice', a paper presented to the Network of Development Education Centres and Groups (NODE) conference, 'Development Education in Ireland Today' (Dublin, 25 May 1996).
18. McCollum, 'Bridging the Gap'.
19. McCollum, 'Bridging the Gap'.
20. DFID, *Eliminating World Poverty: A Challenge for the 21st Century*, a White Paper on International Development published by the Department for International Development (London: HM Stationery Office, November 1997).
21. DFID, *Building Support for Development*, a Department for International Development Strategy Paper (London: DFID, April 1999).
22. Clare Short, 'Education and Our Global Future', speech at the Annual Conference of the Secondary Heads Association, Brighton, 24 April 1999 (London: DFID, 1999).
23. DFID, *Eliminating World Poverty*, p. 77.
24. The Development Awareness Working Group (DAWG) was chaired by the Minister of State for International Development (George Foulkes, 1997–2001; Chris Mullen, January–May 2001) and comprised representatives of statutory education bodies, development agencies (from England, Scotland, Wales and Northern Ireland), Development Education Centres, youth organisations, black and ethnic groups, the media, and other sectors interested in development education work.
25. DFID, *Building Support for Development*.
26. DEA, 'The Case for Development Education: Why it should be funded and supported' (London: DEA, 1996); DEA, 'Global Perspectives in

Education: The contribution of development education' (London: DEA, 2001).

27. DEA, 'Global Perspectives in Education', p. 15.
28. DFID, *Departmental Report 1999* (London: DFID, 1999).
29. Saferworld, a parliamentary briefing titled 'Lack of Transparency in Government Figures Raises Grave Questions About British Arms Export Policy' (London: Saferworld, 1998).
30. Ann McCollum, 'Evaluating to Strengthen Partnership: Engaging schools in development education' (Birmingham: Development Education Centre, 1999).
31. 'Education for Sustainable Development in the Schools Sector' (London: A Report to DFEE/QCA, 14 September 1998).
32. DEA, 'Global Perspectives in Education', p. 5.

WEB SITES

Development Education Association	www.dea.org.uk
Department for International Development	www.dfid.gov.uk
Development Education Unit (Ireland Aid)	www.ncde.ie
One World Centre (NI)	www.belfastdec.org
Teachers in Development Education	www.tidec.org
United Nations publications	www.un.org/publications

Part IV

The Global Cost of Development

11   Asylum Seekers, Refugees and Racism

Iris Teichmann

In the wake of the Second World War, an estimated 30 million people became refugees in Europe alone. Since then the numbers have steadily increased with the proliferation of regional conflicts around the globe. The twenty-first century in turn is witnessing an un-precedented number of people becoming refugees, either in their own region or seeking asylum in developed countries. The United Nations High Commissioner for Refugees (UNHCR), the UN agency charged with protecting and assisting refugees around the world, estimates that there are around 20 million refugees worldwide today. Although the majority of these refugees are concentrated in less developed countries – in Asia, Africa and the Middle East – there has been a marked increase in the number of people seeking asylum in developed countries in North America and Europe, as well as Australia, particu-larly since the mid-1980s. The topic of refugees and asylum seekers has consequently become one of the most politicised in the developed world and their plight is a dominant issue on government agendas in both domestic and intergovernmental debates.

The European Union (EU) is the most controversial example of governments taking measures to harmonise their asylum procedures across member states, building what has been labelled by aid agencies as 'Fortress Europe' – a wealthy regional alliance limiting the import of commodities and the immigration of people from developing countries. Increasingly, the EU is moving towards the implementation of restrictive immigration practices resembling those already employed by the United States of America (US). The debate on asylum in developed countries, therefore, usually focuses on immigration and border controls, restricting access to asylum determination procedures, and tightening asylum decision-making processes. Crucially, the debate fails to address the complex factors that compel people to flee their home and country to seek security and sanctuary elsewhere. This chapter outlines the global refugee context and the international protection framework, setting out some of the key causes of refugee movements and assessing the response of Western governments to asylum seekers. The chapter also considers the impact that Western governments' asylum policies have on individual asylum seekers in their host country.[1]

THE GLOBAL REFUGEE CONTEXT

Wars, military coups, dictatorships, and ethnic and religious conflicts are some of the factors that force people to flee their country and seek sanctuary elsewhere. Many people have become refugees because of ethnic, religious or territorial conflicts that have not been resolved for generations – for example, the events surrounding the ongoing dispute over Kashmir between India and Pakistan, and the similarly protracted civil war and factional fighting in Somalia since 1988. Domestic and international conflicts are likely to arise in other countries in the future despite international co-operation and peace agreements, resulting in the movement of unquantifiable numbers of refugees. The proliferation of conflict situations exacerbates refugee movements and yet this is often overlooked as a cause of the displacement of large numbers of people.

Conflicts within national borders, or between two countries, impact on civilians today on a greater scale than in previous generations. For example, during the First World War, the overwhelming majority of casualties were soldiers in combat rather than civilians, whereas during the Second World War there were mass casualties and displacements of civilians. During the Cold War era, developed countries like the US, West Germany and Britain pointedly accepted refugees who fled communist regimes to find freedom and democracy. Welcoming those refugees presented a political means for Western governments to undermine socialist regimes and promote their own ideology. However, since the end of the Cold War many Eastern European countries and former Soviet Union satellites have undergone enormous political and socio-economic changes that have generated immense poverty and social inertia. These economic and political upheavals have resulted in increasing numbers of people seeking employment, prosperity or refuge from conflict by entering Western Europe. The upsurge in nationalist conflicts in the former Yugoslavia in the early 1990s created large numbers of refugees as various ethnic groups sought greater autonomy or independence in countries like Slovenia, Croatia, Bosnia-Herzegovina and Macedonia. The recent increase in refugee movements toward developed countries has, therefore, partly emanated from post-Cold War turmoil in Eastern Europe as well as from ongoing underdevelopment in the Third World. Today's asylum seekers from Eastern Europe are finding Western countries less receptive to their request for refuge.

Other causes of refugee movements are rooted much further back in history. Colonialism in the nineteenth century left many less developed countries, particularly in Africa, struggling for independence and embroiled in territorial disputes, power struggles, political instability and corruption. Decolonisation also generated disputes between ethnic or religious minorities trying to establish political and economic dominance within newly independent countries, often resulting in military conflict. Post-colonial intervention has sometimes led developed nations to influence the outcome of a civil war or conflict between two countries to serve their own economic or strategic needs, while leaving a legacy of social and economic chaos in the affected regions. For example, in 2001, the US, together with Britain and other European allies, supported the Northern Alliance in Afghanistan in ousting the Taliban regime. This intervention led to the mass displacement of civilians in a country already devastated by civil war and occupation by the former Soviet Union during the 1980s.[2] Prior to the US-led invasion, Afghanistan was already the source of more refugees than any other country. This situation was greatly exacerbated as a result of the war in 2001.

It is not just internal and international conflicts and wars that force people to flee from their home and country. Many governments and non-state factions, such as rebel groups or paramilitaries, have been increasingly disregarding the human rights of their citizens. According to Amnesty International, currently there is an unprecedented level of human rights violations occurring in over 130 countries around the world.[3] Moreover, population growth, combined with increased poverty often caused by the effects of globalisation and a lack of sustainable development, are also issues that exacerbate refugee situations. They are factors that create serious political instability and often result in conflict. Poverty can also be caused by corruption and maladministration in developing countries. Haitians, for example, have fled in large numbers for years from the dire poverty levels caused directly by a succession of corrupt and self-serving governments. In global terms, the number of refugees has increased over the last few decades to staggering proportions. In 1976, there were approximately 3 million refugees. This number increased to over 8 million in 1980. By 1992 there were almost 18 million refugees, rising to 20 million in 2002.[4] The UNHCR estimates that there are millions around the globe who are internally displaced within the borders of their own country, because they are either unable to gain access to safe refuge in another state, or they simply do not want to leave their country, despite the dangers to their personal safety during ongoing conflict situations.

THE INTERNATIONAL FRAMEWORK FOR REFUGEE PROTECTION

An indication of the current imbalances in the asylum debate in the West is reflected in the biased use of terminology, by media and government representatives alike, to describe people forced to flee their country. The usual sequence in media reporting is one in which 'asylum seekers' become 'refugees', 'refugees' become 'migrants' and 'migrants' become 'illegal immigrants'. The term *asylum* has been associated with safety, security, and sanctuary, yet legally it means much more than that. The right of asylum is a fundamental human right set out in the 1948 Universal Declaration of Human Rights, a set of principles formulated immediately after the end of the Second World War.[5] Article 14 of the Declaration states that 'everyone has the right to seek and to enjoy in other countries asylum from persecution'.[6] However, a person who has committed a non-political crime and flees their country to avoid prosecution, or has acted in any way that contravenes the purposes and principles of the United Nations, is unable to benefit from the right to seek asylum.

Importantly, however, the universal right to flee one's country to seek asylum in another does not automatically oblige the host country to grant asylum. Not everyone fleeing danger, human rights abuses, famine, a natural disaster or an economic crisis in their country is a *refugee* under international law. The 1951 United Nations Convention Relating to the Status of Refugees (usually referred to as the 1951 Refugee Convention or the Geneva Convention) defines *refugee* status and outlines the international standards for protecting internationally recognised refugees.[7] All developed countries that are UN member states have signed the Refugee Convention. Switzerland, which has only recently become a UN member, has been a signatory for some time. Pakistan, however, which hosts large numbers of refugees, mainly from Afghanistan, is not a signatory. According to Article 1 of the Convention, a refugee is someone who has:

... a well-founded fear of being persecuted for reasons of race, religion, nationality, membership of a particular social group, or political opinion, is outside the country of his nationality, and is unable to or, owing to such fear, is unwilling to avail himself of the protection of that country.[8]

'Asylum seekers', by default, are people who have been admitted to an established asylum determination procedure and are awaiting a decision by the host country on whether they are considered to be refugees under international law. The term 'migrant' is usually applied to people who go abroad to work or find work.

The Refugee Convention does not oblige signatories to grant asylum or refugee status (in some countries, the *asylum* status carries fewer rights than *refugee status*). State signatories of the Refugee Convention commit themselves to the meaningful protection of recognised refugees and are obliged to ensure that they have the same rights as citizens of their country. The standards for refugee protection outlined in the 1951 Refugee Convention were expanded by the 1967 Protocol Relating to the Status of Refugees, to pertain not only to European refugees but refugees worldwide. There are other provisions in the Convention which aim to defend the right of asylum. Articles 32 and 33 of the Convention require signatories not to expel or return (referred to using the French term *non-refoulement*) an asylum-seeker to a country where his or her life or freedom would be threatened, even if the person entered the country illegally. Article 31 of the Convention asks signatories not to impose any penalties on people who seek asylum illegally – provided they present themselves as soon as possible to the authorities and can give satisfactory reasons as to why they entered illegally.[9]

Another important principle of protection to refugees is temporary asylum, often also referred to as 'temporary protection'. When a country absorbs a particularly large group of asylum seekers (for example, as a result of conflict in a neighbouring state), that country is obliged to offer the group temporary asylum. This is normally provided in co-operation with the international community under the auspices of the UNHCR. During the Kosovo crisis in 1999, the UNHCR together with other international organisations encouraged the international community to offer temporary protection to thousands of Kosovar refugees to ensure their welfare and safety until the conditions were created that would allow them to return home. It is often the case, however, that poor or underdeveloped countries can have their resources stretched to the limit when required to take responsibility for the welfare of large numbers of refugees.

One of the myths of development is that the majority of the world's refugees are 'flooding' into developed countries from the Third World. In fact, only a minority of refugees from developing countries – about 20 per cent of the global total of 20 million – find sanctuary in the developed world.[10] The overriding majority of refugees are, therefore, offered sanctuary in the developing world by countries that often have to contend with internal social and welfare problems of their own. Signatories of the 1951 Convention must grant refugee status to anyone who meets the definition of a refugee as outlined in the articles of the Convention. However, the definition of a refugee is far from precise and, although there are UNHCR guidelines on how to apply the Convention, some Western countries apply the Convention's principles more liberally than others. It is normally government departments that decide on asylum applications – with the exception of Canada, which has an independent refugee board deciding on individual asylum applications. Developed nations have set up their own domestic asylum determination procedures and governments' interpretations of the refugee definition still vary considerably, although the European Union aims to harmonise the asylum procedures of its member countries by 2004.

Migration has reached unprecedented levels in recent years primarily because of the need for migrants to find work, or join family members already abroad as immigrants with the intention to settle. The Refugee Convention makes it clear that people who leave their country in order to improve their economic situation are not to be considered refugees. In recent years, however, it has become increasingly difficult to distinguish between a refugee and a migrant, as the factors that underpin economic migration are often the direct result of political instability or violence. In order to be granted refugee status, asylum seekers have to prove that they would be subject to persecution if returned to their country of origin. They have to provide evidence that their government is unable to, or has no interest in, protecting them.

The displacement of refugees often results from conflict, violence or human rights abuses that may be general characteristics of their country's regime. In such circumstances, developed countries have resorted to granting people temporary humanitarian status, which may eventually lead to permanent status, if government authorities are satisfied that an individual would be placed at risk (though not necessarily individual persecution) if returned home. Some agencies, such as Amnesty International and Human Rights Watch, have argued that the Refugee Convention is outdated, given that so few asylum seekers are able to meet its strict definition criteria.

It is clear, however, that given the increasing numbers of people who flee from generalised violence or conflicts, the international community needs to implement the articles of the Refugee Convention fully and generously. The immigration policies of developed countries are becoming increasingly restrictive, as the number of refugees worldwide looks set to increase. By tightening their border controls and criteria for asylum and refugee status, Western countries are exacerbating poverty levels in the developing world, where the majority of refugees are located. Moreover, many refugees are victims of the policies and interventions of developed countries in the Third World, whether these take the form of military campaigns, economic programmes that result in debt and dependency, or unfair trade rules foisted on poor countries by the World Trade Organisation (WTO). To alleviate these complications for refugees, NGOs have argued that Western governments should commit greater resources and introduce more flexible legislation in dealing with refugees and asylum seekers.

THE WESTERN RESPONSE

During the 1980s, the number of refugees worldwide increased markedly, but Western governments further tightened legal immigration channels. As the globalising economy has increased migration levels, the main legal route to residency in a Western country has become that of joining family members who have already settled abroad. People migrating for business or work purposes often only settle in a new country for a limited period of time. Despite the introduction of increasingly restrictive immigration policies, the numbers of individuals applying for asylum and entering asylum determination systems in developed countries has grown significantly since the 1970s and especially from the mid-1980s. Western governments and societies increasingly distinguished between asylum seekers from developing countries and the refugees that had been created during and after the Second World War. As more refugees and asylum seekers have become visible in the developed world, Western governments have focused on preventing people from arriving at their borders to apply for asylum, or have sought to deter future arrivals by minimising access for asylum seekers to welfare services.

Some of the measures adopted by Western governments to stem the flow of asylum seekers include imposing visa restrictions on many refugee-producing countries. This can effectively put refugees' lives at risk if they have to apply for a visa in their home country. Moreover, EU governments, in particular, have introduced strict controls at ports and airports, and have even increased checks at airports abroad, to detect 'illegal' immigrants. Airlines and other carriers now risk heavy fines if they carry passengers to an EU country without proper documentation. These measures have increased the levels of harassment of ethnic or non-Caucasian travellers in the developed world. The EU summit held in Seville in June 2002 considered proposals tabled by the British and Spanish governments 'to cut aid to countries such as Turkey and Bosnia that refuse to crack down on asylum seekers passing through their borders'.[11] The Anglo-Spanish plan aimed to tie aid donations to compliance with hardline EU policies on asylum and immigration but was vetoed by France and Sweden when a unanimous vote was required. Despite the defeat of this proposal, it reflects the direction in which EU immigration policy is moving and demands concerted efforts by civil liberties and human rights groups in EU member states to ensure that such draconian measures are not introduced in the future.

Western governments have increasingly gravitated toward treating people who arrive illegally and without proper documentation with suspicion. For example, the UK introduced new asylum legislation in 1996 which divided asylum seekers into two groups: people who apply immediately on arrival for asylum – so-called 'port applicants' – and those who apply once they are already in the country, described as 'in-country applicants'. In-country applicants are denied entitlements to welfare benefits, whereas port applicants can apply for state support. The assumption underlying this policy is that in-country applicants are less likely to be successful with their asylum cases than port applicants. Yet the majority of applicants who are granted refugee status continue to be in-country rather than port applicants, making this arbitrary policy an infringement of human rights that adds to the poverty and marginalisation already experienced by the majority of asylum seekers in the UK.

Asylum seekers, particularly those entering illegally, are often detained on arrival and can be denied proper access to asylum determination procedures. For example, Hungary routinely detains asylum seekers who have entered illegally, while German border guards at the German–Polish border are known to prevent Eastern European 'illegal' entrants from applying for asylum. In Australia, all asylum applicants are detained on arrival and the Canberra government, led by Prime Minister John Howard, has appeased extreme right-wing opinion by becoming increasingly tough on asylum seekers and refugees. On 26 August 2001, a ferry carrying 430 (mainly Afghan) asylum seekers sank off the coast of Australia. The asylum seekers were rescued by a Norwegian freighter, the *Tampa*, but the Australian and Indonesian governments refused to allow them to disembark and they remained stranded at sea in appalling conditions for more than three weeks. John Howard decided to use the asylum seeker issue as a political football in the midst of a general election campaign and demonstrated his government's refusal to become a 'soft touch' for refugees. The asylum seekers were eventually transferred to an Australian troopship before being taken to Nauru, an impoverished and isolated pacific island, while some were accepted by New Zealand. Some of the refugees on the *Tampa* were from the village of Ejan in north-east Afghanistan, where living conditions were 'so wretched that only 50 families remained in a village that once housed 500'.[12]

The asylum procedures of developed countries fail to take into account the trauma and hardship that has forced the majority of refugees to flee their countries of origin. Many refugees have experienced human rights abuses, torture, undernourishment and the dehumanising lifestyle associated with an all-pervading poverty only to encounter further social degradation and marginalisation in developed countries. In the north of Ireland, for example, some asylum seekers are detained in prison while their asylum applications are assessed and yet 'none has committed a criminal offence and none faces trial'.[13] Many asylum seekers arrive having left their family and home in their country of origin under extremely trying circumstances to face imprisonment in a regime where they have little access to translation facilities, language material, culturally appropriate food, recreational facilities, or even appropriate health provisions.[14]

The treatment of asylum seekers in Australia and the EU needs to be examined in the international context of refugee movements. For example, the overwhelming majority of Afghanistan's 3 million refugees are living in Pakistan and Iran – developing countries – while only about 150,000 Afghans have applied for asylum in Western Europe over the past ten years.[15] As Ruud Lubbers, the UN High Commissioner for Refugees, has suggested to Western governments: 'You cannot complain about the huge number of people moving around the world if you are not prepared to give the money that is needed for solutions in the regions where refugees come from.'[16]

The culmination of the restrictive immigration practices operative in most developed countries is undoubtedly the undermining of legal mechanisms that can enable asylum seekers to find sanctuary in Western states. Asylum seekers can be detained if they are unable to establish their identity. Many asylum seekers are consequently being forced into the hands of smugglers (also referred to as 'agents'), who often belong to large internationally organised criminal networks involved in human trafficking. Smugglers are often paid large fees to secure false travel documentation for asylum seekers or to arrange highly dangerous journeys to Western countries, which can result in fatalities, or in detection, with the strong possibility of deportation. Those smuggled may even end up in the hands of people traffickers and be forced to work in slave-like conditions in developed countries. While most asylum seekers do not carry false documentation, those found in possession of illegal documents are normally refugees fleeing persecution from their own government and, therefore, unable to obtain the legal travel visas or passports required to reach a safe country.[17]

When the UN adopted the 1951 Refugee Convention, it urged signatories to consider the factors that often lead asylum seekers to use illegal means to escape persecution and seek safety. Article 31 (1) of the Convention emphasises that as long as asylum seekers, or other people seeking protection, have good reasons for trying to enter countries illegally, this should not put them at a disadvantage.[18] In 1990, EU countries agreed in the Dublin Convention that member states can opt to send a prospective asylum seeker back to the first safe EU country s/he has travelled through. However, the country where asylum seekers make their claim for refuge must first check whether there are any compelling reasons for that state taking responsibility for the applicant's request for asylum. Asylum seekers may have family members already resident in the country or a strong community support network, which might not be available in another EU country. In fact, the right to flee one's country does not include the right to choose a country of asylum. The reality for most refugees is that in the first instance they will flee to neighbouring countries or other countries in their region. However, there is no requirement in the 1951 Refugee Convention that obliges asylum seekers to remain in the first safe country in which they arrive. People who flee across the borders of their country may still feel unsafe if placed in a refugee camp in a neighbouring country, or may not receive humanitarian assistance from other countries in their region. These circumstances could compel them to seek refuge in a third country.

A key cause of instability in refugee camps is the phenomenon of militarisation. Refugee camps can be open to attack from factions in neighbouring countries, particularly if they are situated close to the border. During the late 1990s, for example, rival Hutu gangs killed thousands of Congolese Tutsi in refugee camps in Rwanda. Mixing military forces and civilians in a camp can also create chaos and instability. In East Timor, an estimated 230,000 persons were thought to have been forcibly removed to refugee camps in West Timor during the carnage and chaos that followed a popular referendum in August 1999 that paved the way for East Timorese independence from Indonesia. Indonesian militias and military forces seized control of camps in West Timor and denied UN personnel access to refugees. As a consequence, 'Thousands were declared killed and/or unaccounted for, following reports and testimonies from witnesses, survivors and refugees.'[19] Refugees can, therefore, be exposed to human rights abuses and, in the case of East Timor, to retribution and revenge from military forces that were ultimately ousted from the territory following the popular vote for independence.

In some cases, ethnic refugee groups may not be welcome in the host country. Pakistan, for example, did not want to accept large numbers of non-Pashtun (and therefore anti-Taliban) Afghan refugees across its borders following the US-led intervention in Afghanistan in 2001. Nonetheless, most people seek asylum in neighbouring countries rather than try to seek sanctuary in the West. Guinea is an example of a developing country with a population of less than 7 million, and yet it supports 500,000 refugees from Sierra Leone and Liberia. The world's poorest countries continue to support the largest numbers of refugees, which in turn can cause internal instability and economic difficulties in the host countries – as was the case in countries neighbouring Rwanda and the former Yugoslavia in the 1990s.[20]

The Refugee Convention requires that asylum cases should be decided on their individual merit, yet many countries have resorted to refusing asylum applications from nationals of countries outright, without looking into the individual cases in detail. This is particularly evident in the cases of nationals who have come from a country with a history of immigration into the host state, such as Turkish nationals into Germany or Latin Americans into the US. In 1996, the UK government introduced new asylum legislation that established a 'White List' of countries from which asylum applications should be refused. This policy was subsequently abolished five years later. Many Western countries have also introduced a series of asylum bills designed to accelerate asylum determination processes and use detention both to deter further arrivals and to speed up the removal of unsuccessful asylum applicants. In Hungary, the detention of asylum seekers who have entered illegally has increased dramatically in recent years and, as a result, the authorities have turned open community shelters for asylum seekers into closed detention centres.

The increasing confinement of asylum seekers is also prevalent in many Western countries, making it more difficult for applicants to access legal advice. Despite most European countries recognising in their domestic laws the right of asylum seekers to legal assistance, the majority of applicants are finding it extremely difficult, if not impossible, to exercise that right. This has an adverse effect on the quality of decision making regarding asylum claims and ultimately ensures that a greater number of applications are refused. Western countries need to recognise that restrictive asylum laws and faster asylum determination procedures are unlikely to reduce the number of people applying for asylum. Ultimately, reducing asylum applications could be realised more effectively by addressing the underlying socio-economic and human rights conditions that create refugees in the first place.[21]

ASYLUM AND RACISM

It is clear that many developed countries, particularly in Europe, have found their asylum procedures to be overloaded in recent years. A considerable backlog of asylum seekers has formed, necessitating the allocation of additional resources to tackle the problem. However, an increase in the number of requests for asylum does not justify endangering the lives of applicants, who may be returning to life-threatening situations should their applications be refused. For example, Western governments have tended to refuse refugee status to Tamils and Kurds on the grounds that they would not suffer persecution as individuals if returned home, despite serious ongoing conflict in their countries of origin. In some cases, governments have granted humanitarian status – a status often carrying fewer rights than refugee status – to individuals in danger of persecution. Other nationals, who are found not to have any grounds for refugee or humanitarian status, can prove difficult to deport as many countries do not accept the return of citizens without adequate proof of citizenship.

These procedures have cast serious doubt in the public's mind about the effectiveness of asylum systems and governments' capacity to regulate them effectively. As a result, governments have devised ever more restrictive asylum laws and adopted a very narrow interpretation of the Refugee Convention. In some cases, such as Australia, France and the Netherlands, governments are responding to an increase in support for extreme right-wing political movements that promote a zero-tolerance policy in regard to immigrants from developing countries. Rather than challenge the anti-immigration platforms of the extreme right in developed countries, many governments have tried to appease their constituencies by tightening immigration procedures. Most developed countries today deny asylum seekers access to their welfare systems and offer them the most basic means of subsistence support. In the UK, asylum seekers receive 70 per cent of the country's normal benefit levels in the form of cash vouchers.[22] Other countries provide support only during the first few months after the asylum seeker's arrival.

In many countries, asylum seekers are not allowed to work until they are granted refugee status and are often confined to specifically designed reception centres or accommodation facilities. The Sangatte detention centre in north-west France became infamous for the numbers of people being detained and the conditions which the detainees had to endure. Most governments disperse asylum seekers to different parts of the country and house them where accommodation is available. In Germany, asylum seekers are sent to small towns in the regions, which take an annual quota of asylum applicants, where they are often the only foreigners living in the area. The UK has recently changed its asylum laws to send asylum seekers in groups to remote areas in the country. Sometimes this has meant housing them in poor, isolated areas, located large distances from town centres or in high-density inner-city estates where they are increasingly vulnerable to racist attacks and racial harassment. The dispersal system used by the UK and other developed countries is a clear attempt to isolate asylum seekers from wider society, which ultimately threatens their personal safety and well-being, and undermines the potentially valuable contribution they can make to society. In most developed countries, asylum seekers find themselves at the margins of society in terms of access to social services, health, education and even the capacity to communicate with state authorities.

Asylum decision-making processes can span several months or even years, with applicants being denied the opportunity to use this time to improve their language skills or enhance their personal development through education or vocational training. As a consequence many asylum seekers experience physical or mental health problems, such as depression and a diminishing sense of their own self-worth and self-esteem. In fact, a large number of asylum seekers are qualified professionals, and eager to employ their skills in developed countries, but are prevented from doing so by asylum legislation. Moreover, asylum seekers often have to contend with mistrust and even resentment among the local population as their cultural and ethnic composition is so diverse and often so far removed from indigenous faiths and cultures that it can cause division and friction at a local level. For example, Roma gypsies from Eastern Europe have been at the forefront of racist abuse and attacks across several European countries.

Elements of the mainstream media have been culpable in generating misinformation in regard to the asylum issue and in a number of instances 'cheerleading' some of the more negative attitudes and actions against asylum seekers. The media, on occasion, have described refugees as 'flooding' into developed countries, conjuring up images of 'scrounging' immigrants living off the welfare system, or taking jobs that could ease unemployment levels in host countries. The fact that asylum seekers in the UK are prevented from working, and receive only 70 per cent of the value of welfare benefits in vouchers, goes largely unreported. Moreover, refugees that are granted leave to remain in a host country have immense problems in assimilating into the local culture and society. They find difficulty in accessing the most basic services, such as opening a bank account, registering with a General Practitioner or attending an educational institution.[23] Rather than considering the value of diversity and welcoming new cultural traditions, developed countries largely treat asylum seekers and recognised refugees with distrust, and alienate them from wider society.

In the aftermath of 11 September 2001, there has been increasing suspicion in Western countries directed at immigrants and residents with origins in the Middle East. In the US, 'tens of thousands of illegal immigrants have been rounded up, detained and deported' while in Britain 'the government rushed through the Anti-terrorism, Crime and Security Act, which allows internment without trial and suspends obligations under the European Convention on Human Rights'.[24] The response of EU states and the US to 11 September has exacerbated the refugee problem in both the developed and developing worlds. The US-led invasion of Afghanistan dramatically increased the number of internally displaced Afghan refugees and those forced into refugee camps in neighbouring countries like Pakistan. While the rapid introduction of emergency legislation, particularly in the US and Britain, has further undermined the legal protection afforded refugees and asylum seekers, it has also reflected increased levels of racism directed against individuals granted refugee status. The events of 11 September 2001 and, indeed, the Bali massacre on 12 October 2002, have enabled developed countries to introduce more severe asylum assessment procedures under the guise of their 'war against terrorism'.

CONCLUSION

Refugees and asylum seekers are victims of oppression or under-development rather than opportunists simply attempting to improve their lifestyles under the guise of refugee status. Statistical evidence produced by the United Nations High Commissioner for Refugees underlines the fact that the overwhelming majority of refugees are living in developing countries rather than seeking sanctuary in North America or Europe. Furthermore, most of the asylum seekers that have sought refugee status in Western countries have fled per-secution, human rights abuses or grinding poverty. They are then often subject to media and political bias in the Western states in which they have sought refuge. NGOs, such as the UK Refugee Council, argue that the media should enforce a properly monitored code of conduct in regard to their reporting of the issue of refugees and asylum seekers. Nick Hardwick, Chief Executive of the UK Refugee Council, commented that 'when we talk about "floods" or "swamps" of asylum-seekers and refugees, we de-humanise the individual experience and this makes it easier to ignore'.[25] Many refugees have fled their families, homes and countries of origin in order to escape the tyranny of oppressive regimes and yet are confronted with detention on arrival in developed countries. As Hardwick suggests:

> Detention is the hardest thing to understand. It is fundamentally wrong to detain people without going before a court, without telling them how long they will be detained for, without them even being suspected of anything. For asylum seekers, being detained is upsetting in itself, but for those who have been through trauma in their home countries, this can bring back very painful memories.[26]

Even when granted status as a refugee, the stigma associated with this term can remain with a person for the rest of their life. The factors that force individuals to leave home and country rarely inform the immigration procedures of developed countries, yet they urgently need to be incorporated into a wholesale review of asylum assessment measures. Meanwhile, NGOs dealing with refugee issues continue to work for a situation where Western countries treat asylum seekers with compassion rather than accentuating their trauma with detention or imprisonment.

NOTES

1. A useful reference resource on the issue of refugees is *The State of the World's Refugees* produced by United Nations Refugee Agency (Oxford: Oxford University Press, 2000), particularly chapters 6, 7 and 11. The complete text is available on <www.unhcr.ch/pubs/sowr2000/sowr2000toc.htm>. The United Nations Development Programme, *Human Development Report 2001* (Oxford: Oxford University Press, 2001), provides an overview of development in an international context and contains helpful statistics, and information on the factors underpinning increases in the number of refugees worldwide.
2. New Internationalist, *The World Guide 2001–02* (Oxford: New Internationalist Publications, 2001), pp. 67–9. Also see Elazar Barkan and Marie-Denise Shelto (eds), *Borders, Exiles, Diasporas* (Stanford, Calif.: Stanford University Press, 1998).
3. Amnesty International, *Amnesty International Report 2002* (Oxford: Amnesty International Publications, 2002).
4. United Nations Refugee Agency, *The State of the World's Refugees* (Oxford: Oxford University Press, 2000). Also see Refugee Action Group, 'Forced To Flee' (Belfast: Refugee Action Group, 2002); and Refugee Council, *Asylum By Numbers: Analysis of Available Asylum Data from 1985 to 2000* (London: Refugee Council, February 2002).
5. See the Universal Declaration of Human Rights adopted and proclaimed by the United Nations General Assembly on 10 December 1948 in the

Amnesty International Handbook (London: Amnesty International Publications, 1992), p. 123.

6. Article 14 of the Universal Declaration of Human Rights is quoted in full in Henry Steiner and Philip Alston, *International Human Rights in Context* (Oxford: Oxford University Press, 2000), p. 137. This provides a useful overview of the human rights obligations of signatories to the declaration.

7. The full text of the 1951 United Nations Convention Relating to the Status of Refugees can be found on the UN Refugee Agency web site <http://www.unhcr.ch/cgi-bin/texis/vtx/home>.

8. The gender-biased language is a feature of the original document.

9. For further information on the Convention and the 1967 Protocol see the UN Refugee Agency web site <http://www.unhcr.ch/cgi-bin/texis/vtx/home>.

10. Anne Bernstein (ed.), *Migration and Refugee Policies: An Overview* (London: Pinter, 1999).

11. *Observer* (23 June 2002).

12. A full account of the refugees rescued from the *Tampa* can be found in the *Amnesty International Report 2002* (Oxford: Amnesty International Publications, 2002), p. 11.

13. Refugee Action Group, 'Forced to Flee' (Belfast: Refugee Action Group, 2002).

14. Robbie McVeigh, *Northern Ireland: A Place of Refuge?* (Belfast: Refugee Action Group, 2002).

15. *Amnesty International Report 2002*, p. 11.

16. Ruud Lubbers is quoted in the *Amnesty International Report 2002*, p. 11.

17. European Council on Refugees and Exile, *Study on the Availability of Free and Low-Cost Legal Assistance for Asylum Seekers in European States* (Brussels: EC, November 2001). Also see Tony Kushner and Katharine Knox, *Refugees in an Age of Genocide: Global, National and Local Perspectives during the Twentieth Century* (London and Portland: Frank Cass, 1999).

18. See web site: <www.unhchr.ch/html/menu3/b/o_c_ref.htm>.

19. Paul Hainsworth and Stephen McCloskey (eds), *The East Timor Question: The Struggle for Independence from Indonesia* (London and New York: I.B. Tauris, 2000), p. 204.

20. For the politics of the refugee issue, see Peter van Kriek (ed.), *Refugee Law in Context: The Exclusion Clause* (The Hague: Asser, 1999). Also see Jennifer Hyndman, *Managing Displacement: Refugees and the Politics of Humanitarianism* (Minneapolis: University of Minnesota Press, 2000); US Committee for Refugees, *World Refugee Survey 2000: An annual assessment of conditions affecting refugees, asylum seekers, and internally displaced persons* (New York: Immigration and Refugee Services of America, 2000).

21. For a good overview of how developed countries have been adapting their policies to the new global political situation see Bernstein, *Migration and Refugee Policies: An Overview*.

22. NICEM, 'Asylum Seekers and Refugees' (Belfast: Northern Ireland Council for Ethnic Minorities, 2001).

23. See Jennifer Moore, 'Whither the Accountability Theory? Second-class status for third-party refugees as a threat to international refugee

protection', *International Journal of Refugee Law*, Vol. 13, Nos 1–2 (2001), pp. 32–50. Also see Gil Loescher, *Beyond Charity: International Cooperation and the Global Refugee Crisis* (Oxford and New York: Oxford University Press, 1993).

24. *Guardian* (11 March 2002).

25. NICEM, 'Asylum Seekers and Refugees'. Also see Arthur Helton, 'The State of the World's Refugees: Fifty years of humanitarian action', *International Journal of Refugee Law*, Vol. 13, Nos 1–2 (2001), pp. 269–74.

26. NICEM, 'Asylum Seekers and Refugees'.

WEB SITES

International Organisation for Migration (IOM)	www.iom.int
United Nations (UN)	www.un.org
United Nations High Commissioner for Refugees	www.unhcr.ch
Anti-Slavery International	www.antislavery.org
Australian Refugee Council	www.refugeecouncil.org.au
British Refugee Council	www.refugeecouncil.org.uk
Canadian Council for Refugees	www.web.net/~ccr
Danish Refugee Council	www.drc.dk
Electronic Immigration Network	www.ein.org.uk
European Council on Refugees and Exiles	www.ecre.org
National Immigration Forum	www.immigrationforum.org
Pro-Asyl in Germany	www.proasyl.de
The US Committee for Refugees	www.refugees.org
Australian Department of Immigration and Multicultural Affairs	www.immi.gov.au
Citizenship and Immigration Canada	www.cic.gc.ca
UK Home Office Immigration and Nationality Directorate	www.homeoffice.gov.uk
United States Immigration and Naturalisation Service	www.ins.usdoj.gov

12 The Environmental Costs of Development

Mary Louise Malig

A decade ago, the world witnessed the momentous Earth Summit in Rio de Janeiro, where it was decided that the only way to achieve a truly sustainable kind of development was by protecting the environment and preventing the over-exploitation of the world's natural resources. The tenth anniversary of the Earth Summit provides a useful opportunity to assess progress toward protecting the environment in the context of globalisation. Many pledges were made in the interests of environmental protection, along with declarations and conventions on sustainable development which were signed into law. A decade later most of these agreements represent little more than empty rhetoric.

This chapter will examine why many of the Rio proclamations and agreements did not materialise into progressive state practice. The chapter will also outline recent policy developments in regard to protecting the environment in the context of globalisation, before addressing key issues and recent concerns around environmental denudation. It will also discuss how the empty rhetoric of Rio crystallised during the World Summit on Sustainable Development (WSSD) in Johannesburg in September 2002. It will conclude by offering recommendations for progressive action in the future.

FROM BRUNDTLAND TO RIO

The environment has always been a secondary consideration to matters of economic growth and the liberalisation of the global market in commodities. Developed countries have largely prioritised the values of neo-liberalism over sustainable lifestyles and eco-friendly means of production. Protecting biodiversity and the natural environment has, however, long been a primary concern of non-governmental organisations (NGOs) and environmentalists rather than of state agencies. Environmental protection agencies, operating under the auspices of the state, have introduced reforms largely on terms acceptable to business and industry leaders, rather than taking meaningful measures that could address the underlying causes of environmental destruction. The developed world has thus operated on the basis of the maxim 'develop now, pay later', on the mistaken assumption that natural resources are inexhaustible. In this policy context the environment has been systematically marginalised within the process of development.

It was in 1987 that the environment – long abused and disregarded – first entered the lexicon of development, when an independent commission, the World Commission on Environment and Development (led by Gro Harlem Brundtland) presented its landmark report, *Our Common Future*, to the United Nations General Assembly. The Brundtland report, as it is now known, offered the first definition of sustainable development to the world by suggesting that 'development is sustainable when it meets the needs of the present without compromising the ability of future generations to meet their own needs'.[1]

Brundtland suggested that development should facilitate a form of economic growth that ensured environmental protection and an equitable distribution of wealth and resources while raising the quality of life for everyone. The Brundtland report led many to recognise that rainforests, minerals and the rest of the world's natural resources were finite and that many species and animals had already been made extinct as casualties of development. This dire environmental situation was more pronounced in developing countries, where rainforests had suffered massive denudation over the past 30 years and many rivers lay biologically dead. In the Philippines alone, the annual rainforest denudation rate was 87,556 hectares, leaving only 700,000 hectares of virgin forest by 1991.[2]

Despite the alarming findings of the Brundtland report, developed countries remained hesitant about taking affirmative action to protect the environment. There were, however, two exceptions to the general antipathy towards eco-protection: the Montreal Protocol on environmental protection and the Inter-Agency Committee on Climate Change. The latter recognised and highlighted among other things:

> ... that all countries, especially developing countries, need access to resources required to achieve sustainable social and economic development and that, in order for developing countries to progress towards that goal, their energy consumption will need to grow taking into account the possibilities for achieving greater

energy efficiency and for controlling greenhouse gas emissions in
general, including through the application of new technologies
on terms which make such an application economically and
socially beneficial.[3]

It was not until the convening of the Earth Summit in Rio in 1992
that a meaningful debate linking the environment and economic
development was held to discuss the concerns raised by the Inter-
Agency Committee. The Earth Summit, or the United Nations
Conference on Environment and Development (UNCED), held in
Rio de Janeiro from 3 to 14 June 1992, took bold steps in raising a
global awareness of environmental issues. Debates stressed the need
for a departure from the prevailing neo-liberal model of economic
growth to a more sustainable form of development. Over 100 heads
of state and government attended the summit, along with an
estimated 2,400 representatives of NGOs. The outcomes of the
summit included agreements designed to protect the environment
for future generations while addressing the social needs of poor
countries. The agreements reached in Rio included: Agenda 21, the
Rio Declaration on Environment and Development, the Statement
of Forest Principles, the United Nations Framework Convention on
Climate Change, and the United Nations Convention on Biological
Diversity. To ensure the implementation of these declarations,
monitoring mechanisms were established which included the
Commission on Sustainable Development, the Inter-Agency
Committee on Sustainable Development and the Advisory Board on
Sustainable Development.

The rhetoric of the summit was progressive and stressed the need
for a reassessment of the existing model of economic development.
It specifically focused on the effects of the depletion of natural
resources, and air and sea pollution. Two clear causes of environmental destruction were identified at the summit – the excessive
consumption of natural resources by developed countries and
increased global poverty directly related to resource depletion. It was
agreed that any environmentally friendly form of sustainable development would necessitate a change of lifestyles in developed
countries based on reduced consumption and responsible stewardship of natural resources.

Before the end of the summit, however, developed nations,
particularly the United States of America (USA), insisted that their
'lifestyles' could not be subject to negotiation. After negotiations and

compromises, the blueprint on sustainable development, Agenda 21, became diluted and severely weakened. Maurice Strong, the Conference Secretary-General, admitted that Agenda 21 had been weakened by compromise and negotiation – mostly at the behest of developed countries.[4] Nevertheless, the document was hailed as the most progressive and comprehensive agreed at the summit, with its promises of equitable growth and sustainable development. World leaders concurred in the view that with proper implementation Agenda 21 could become the summit's most effective programme of action. Since then, the rhetoric of sustainable development has been introduced into the sphere of economic development, with governments and businesses having to justify their operations, and policies being assessed on the basis of their environmental impact by adhering to the principles of Rio and the declarations of Agenda 21.

Agenda 21 encompassed social and economic management schemes and the conservation of resources to enhance a policy culture of sustainable development – in short, it assumed the appearance of a blueprint for a sustainable means of development. It promised to accelerate sustainable development in developing countries through international co-operation and, more importantly, to combat poverty and 'enable the poor to achieve sustainable livelihoods'.[5] In practice, though, this blueprint did not alter the existing world economic order established by the international financial institutions (IFIs) – the World Bank, the International Monetary Fund (IMF) and the World Trade Organisation (WTO). These organisations were effectively dictating economic policy to developing countries through their control of multilateral and bilateral lending programmes and by formulating the rules of world trade. As a consequence, the environmental policies of developing countries were subject to adverse conditions imposed on them by the IFIs.

CONTRADICTIONS AND DOUBLESPEAK

A glaring omission from the Earth Summit agreements was a commitment to address the fundamental inequalities in economic relations between developed and developing countries. While environmental destruction was tacitly linked to excessive consumption of natural resources, most notably in the developed world, the summit delegates did not establish an effective programme to redress the imbalance in resource consumption and its underlying causes. Thus, rather than tackling the rapacious character of market competition which creates widespread human poverty and threatens the world's finite supply of natural resources, the summit ultimately chose to focus on the symptoms of the world's malaise (unfettered trade and globalisation) rather than diagnosing a cure. Developing countries have extensively documented the causes of poverty and the over-exploitation of resources as directly relating to the IMF's structural adjustment programmes (SAPs – imposed in over 70 developing countries for over 15 years with devastating effects). This criticism has merely been acknowledged by governments and IFIs, rather than acted upon.

SAPs are neo-liberal reform programmes, enforced by the IMF, that are attached to loans to developing countries. Accessing loans from the IMF necessitates that Third World countries drastically reduce their expenditure on education, health, welfare and other key social services. Loans have attendant conditions which require that countries channel their resources into export-led means of production to increase their inflow of hard currency, rather than investing in indigenous industries that would benefit the economy over the longer term. Thus SAPs are directing governments to dramatically roll back their involvement in managing their own economies and are thereby facilitating greater private ownership of public services. Given the spiralling poverty levels in developing countries, SAPs have proved disastrous for the world's poor as government support of many primary services has been dismantled or dramatically reduced. As a consequence SAPs have had a disastrous effect on the environment.

Furthermore, the export-led economic growth dictated by SAPs necessitates a greater investment of natural resources in commodity production in the agricultural sector. Sustainable lifestyles based on the production of food crops have been abandoned to facilitate the cultivation of cash crops for export. This method makes increasing demands on the local environment and involves the intensive use of pesticides rather than natural and traditional farming methods. The denudation of vast tracts of rainforest in South-East Asia and Latin America, for the purposes of cattle grazing and the export of hardwoods to developed countries, is the clearest example of natural resources being consumed to satisfy the demands of the global market in commodities. The experience of the Philippines is an example of the correlation between environmental destruction and structural adjustment. The findings of a study carried out by the

World Resources Institute on environmental destruction in the Philippines states that:

> Adjustment created so much unemployment that migration patterns changed drastically. The large migration flows to Manila [the capital] declined, and most migrants could only turn to open access forests, watersheds and artisanal fisheries. Thus the major environmental effect of the economic crisis was over-exploitation of these resources.[6]

The problems created by SAPs have been exacerbated by a drive towards recklessly exploiting natural resources to fuel trade in commodities. This has resulted in a severely ravaged environment.

Despite all the laudable rhetoric on sustainable development and equitable growth on the world stage, development still adheres to the three basic principles of the free market formula: liberalising, privatising and deregulating. These principles have underpinned the agenda of the IMF in its dealings with debtor countries, regardless of social, economic, political or environmental conditions. The IMF's adjustment programmes have a 'one-size-fits-all' ideology which means that the same neo-liberal economic approach underpins its dealing with all developing countries irrespective of their stage of economic development or the extent to which they have stripped away their natural resources. Designed to lift countries out of poverty, the SAPs have instead institutionalised and exacerbated poverty and economic stagnation (or regression) in the Third World, with the environment being the first casualty.

The report of the International Financial Institution Advisory Commission, better known as the Meltzer report after its chairman Alan Meltzer, assessed the impact of IMF policies on developing countries. Among the claims made by the report are the following:

- Instead of promoting economic growth, the IMF institution- alises economic stagnation – with an astounding 65–70 per cent failure rate of its projects in the poorest countries
- The World Bank is marginal rather than central to the elimination of global poverty
- Both institutions are largely driven by the interests of key political and economic institutions in the G8 (Group of Eight leading industrialised countries) – particularly, in the case of the IMF, the USA government and its financial interests

- The dynamics of the World Bank and the IMF are not driven
  by the external demands of poverty alleviation or promoting
  growth, but from the internal imperative of expansionism or
  empire building – as most resources have been distributed to
  developed countries, thereby contradicting the IMF's avowed
  mission of global poverty alleviation[7]

This contradiction between the IMF's stated goal of equitable and
sustainable growth, and its structural adjustment doctrine on the
liberalisation of economies (that creates immense inequality) has
emerged as a solid obstacle on the road to achieving pro-Third World
sustainable development. This was the key issue that the Earth
Summit failed to address ten years ago and remains an underlying
problem as governments and NGOs deal with the outcomes of the
follow-up to Rio, the WSSD, held in Johannesburg from 26 August
to 4 September 2002.

FROM RIO TO JOHANNESBURG

The ten years following the Rio summit saw the appropriation of the
rhetoric of sustainable development by economic strategists and the
IFIs. 'Greenwashing' became a regular practice for corporations
seeking good publicity on the basis of their environmental record
or, at least, the way in which it was portrayed in glossy promotional
literature and annual reports. Private corporations used the
terminology of sustainable development to greenwash their activities
and pass themselves off as responsible corporations and 'good
citizens' in relation to the environment. The practice has been particularly notable in the oil industry, which is renowned for its
pollution of the natural environment in the countries where it
operates. For example, the Shell Corporation was strongly criticised
for the impact of its operations in Ogoniland, Nigeria, where its
pipelines spoiled the local environment and created health problems
for the indigenous Ogoni people. Saving or conserving the environment is a proclamation espoused by many transnational
corporations (TNCs), but their practice rarely matches the rhetoric of
their eco-friendly literature.

There have also been disappointments at national governmental
level in terms of implementing existing environmental protocols –
many of which are modest in their aims and limited in their
implementation. Following years of negotiation for poisonous
emissions control, the US negated decades of progress by state and

non-governmental organisations alike by deciding not to sign up to the Kyoto Protocol, which aimed to reduce emissions. This decision was taken by the US's Bush administration, which has cultivated strong financial ties with the oil industry. Indeed, the oil lobby is on record as opposing environmental protocols that limit its operations and profits through adherence to measures designed to conserve resources and reduce pollution emissions. Oil companies have often disregarded the national environmental laws of developing countries or, alternatively, have been offered an opt-out from compliance with domestic legislation to facilitate their investment.

The Bush government includes senior cabinet officials – including the vice-president, Dick Cheney, and the president himself – who have business histories within the oil industry and have maintained these links throughout their presidential election campaign and period in office. Political commentators speculated on the possible policy implications of the Bush campaign team receiving substantive donations from the oil industry should the Bush–Cheney team be elected into office. Two years on, the worst fears of environmentalists have been realised with the administration's reneging on the Kyoto Protocol and setting its face against other international agreements which restrained US financial or strategic interests. The Bush administration is reluctant to curb the activities of TNCs to ensure that they comply with environmental legislation in either national or international contexts. The United States – which has around 4 per cent of the world's population yet consumes over a third of the world's energy resources – needs to realise that it has a responsibility along with the rest of the world for sustainable development.

The main benchmarks used by NGOs in assessing a country's state of sustainable development are the reduction of poverty and inequality, and the protection of the environment and natural resources. The factors are interrelated. However, the income share of the global rich over the past ten years has steadily increased, while poverty and unemployment in developing countries has worsened. In 1998, three industrialists, Bill Gates, Warren Buffet and Paul Allen, received a combined income that was in excess of the total income of the 600 million people that live in the world's 48 least developed countries.[8] Statistical evidence suggests that the poverty gap is widening at national and international levels, while the wealth and market share of TNCs is ensuring that they have an increasing influence on negotiations toward international agreements on the environment.

The World Summit on Sustainable Development worked on a series of difficult issues related to global finance and trade. However, if international agreements are to have a meaningful impact in redressing environmental destruction, global warming, and air and sea pollution, resources and finance must be invested in protecting the environment in the vulnerable areas of the Third World and not only the green belts of the First World. Controversially, Kofi Annan, the UN Secretary-General, facilitated the participation of 50 large corporations in the decision-making process at the summit. Such a move did not augur well for the outcomes of the summit, with the values and priorities of TNCs and developed countries dominating the agenda. Developed countries needed to listen to the concerns raised by NGOs and activists from the Third World, who represent the majority of the world's poor, and who bear the greatest burden of environmental destruction resulting from unfettered global trade.

The depletion of natural resources and pollution of the environment are threatening biodiversity – literally millions of plants and animal species could become extinct at current rates of global warming, air pollution, and rainforest destruction. Moreover, many indigenous cultures, lifestyles, traditions and values are being sacrificed through the destruction of natural habitats throughout the developing world. Poverty and environmental destruction are closely intertwined and must be addressed through an integrated and – as the environmental NGOs at the World Summit were to point out – committed approach from the business sector *and* developed countries.[9]

CORPORATE-DRIVEN DEVELOPMENT

The IFIs tried, tested and failed economic model of privatisation, liberalisation and deregulation, has been detrimental to progress on environment issues. An unwavering faith in the free market and the prescriptive policies of the IMF have prioritised economic growth and development based on foreign direct investment (FDI). When confronted with the reality of flagging domestic industries in developing countries, due to inward competition from foreign investments, developed governments have described this scenario as healthy competition. Thus, the main impact of structural adjustment or liberalisation policies in poor countries has been the development of a strong private sector and a weak state. This leaves natural resources unprotected by the state and ripe for exploitation by private companies.

In addition to the IMF's neo-liberal policies, the new global order has been constructed upon trading inequalities between rich and poor countries under the auspices of the WTO. The WTO enables wealthy states to access unlimited natural resources from the Third World, while denying access to their own markets to commodities produced by poor countries. Developing countries are denied full participation in the decision-making procedures of the WTO and are often bullied into accepting agreements that favour developed countries. While WTO decisions are in theory reached by consensus among its member organisations, the reality is that strong-arm tactics are regularly employed by wealthy states and TNCs to dominate negotiations. As representatives of some 80 per cent of the world's population, developing countries should hold sway in WTO negotiations but, in fact, negotiations are monopolised by the wealthiest countries, who exploit their immense economic clout in their dealings with the less developed nations.

The WTO was sold to the global public as the linchpin of a multilateral system of economic governance that would provide the necessary rules to facilitate the growth of global trade and a more equitable distribution of wealth. But in its five years of operations, the WTO has consistently arrived at agreements that are detrimental to the environment and to the poor in the developing world.[10] The damaging agreements include:

- The Agreement on Trade Related Investment Measures (TRIMs), which meant that many developing countries signed away their right to use trade policy as a means of industrialisation
- The Agreement on Trade Related Intellectual Property Rights (TRIPs), which enables hi-tech TNCs like Microsoft and Intel to monopolise innovation in the knowledge-intensive industries, and provides biotechnology firms like Novartis and Monsanto the opportunity to privatise the fruits of aeons of creative interaction between human communities and nature – such as seeds, plants and animal life
- The Agreement on Agriculture (AOA), which opens the markets of developing countries to cheap agricultural imports while allowing the developed countries to consolidate their system of subsidised agricultural production that was leading to the massive dumping of surpluses in the Third World – a process that was, in turn, destroying smallholder based agriculture

The WTO represents a legal system that enshrines the priority of free trade over the environment, justice, equity and community development. WTO policies, therefore, run contrary to the model of sustainable development agreed at Rio and promoted by Agenda 21. Trading inequities that penalise developing countries have led to the impoverishment of millions of people in the Third World. Moreover, the onerous debt cycle exacerbates economic problems in developing countries where the repaying of a national debt to the IFIs (particularly the World Bank and the IMF) necessitates cuts in important services like health, housing, social welfare, land distribution, and environmental protection. The Third World debt crisis, orchestrated by the World Bank and the IMF since the 1970s, effectively prevents meaningful development in underdeveloped countries, many of which channel as much as 50 per cent of their Gross National Product (GNP) into debt repayments. This leaves them open to further pressures from TNCs.

The economies of many developing countries are, therefore, caught in an ongoing debt crisis combined with the trading inequalities overseen by the WTO. Poor countries are thereby forced to use their natural resources to engage in the global trading system and earn sufficient hard currency to sustain basic social services. For example, the Philippines was forced to open its markets to foreign investors as a direct result of the neo-liberal policies pursued by IFIs and multilateral development banks. The financial doctrine espoused by the IFIs consists of the aggressive privatisation of public services, economic liberalisation and currency deregulation (so-called tight money). In the mining industry in the Philippines, liberalisation policies have ensured that foreign investors have been allowed 100 per cent ownership of domestic mining interests together with tax holidays, exemption incentives and legal opt-outs. Moreover, if local communities reside on land with proven mineral reserves they are required by law to give way to the interests of foreign investors.

The environmental destruction caused by an industry such as mining is often written off by the governments of developing countries desperate to attract investment at any cost. One example of environmental pollution caused by the mining industry is that of the mine tailings spillage in the Boac river, Marinduque, a small island in the Philippines. The Marcopper Corporation was guilty of corporate irresponsibility in leaking toxic chemicals into the Boac, and yet proved itself bereft of corporate accountability in failing to redress the problems caused by the spillage. In this instance, Marcopper went unchecked by the state authorities, which, of course, invited other corporate investors to similarly disregard domestic environment protection laws. The Boac river, however, has yet to be dredged of its toxic pollutants and lethal mine tailings and as long as this situation persists the more widespread will be its effects and damage to the island's habitat and people.

The entire island of Marinduque has been biologically devastated because of Marcopper's negligence and yet the corporation has largely been shielded from claims of environmental damage by its mother company – Placer Dome – a powerful Canadian mining operation. This is just one example among many in South-East Asia where communities have been displaced, entire forests destroyed, and the air and sea polluted by negligent industries. The agencies of global governance, the UN and the G8, are not addressing the issue of how large corporations can be regulated and local environments protected from the activities of TNCs. It is no longer sufficient to rely on self-monitoring codes of conduct introduced and enforced by the TNCs themselves. TNCs should be regulated by a body independent of the WTO, with sufficient authority and power to enforce international guidelines governing how TNCs operate in developing countries. Moreover, developed countries should become more proactive in monitoring TNCs based in their jurisdiction and operating in developing countries. Large corporations are becoming increasingly responsible for environmental pollution and should be properly policed.

THE WORLD SUMMIT

The agenda of the WSSD largely reflected the economic programmes of the IFIs and reflected the influence of corporate interests over the proceedings. The summit began ominously with the unwarranted arrest of peaceful marchers from the National Land Council and the Landless People's Movement of South Africa. The summit was also drawing similar protests to those organised by trade justice groups at WTO, G8 and IFI meetings. The influence of big business on the event was further evidenced by the overwhelming display of corporate billboards, advertisements and marketing paraphernalia that littered the summit complex. In fact, the summit attracted the largest business presence ever assembled at a UN conference – with

700 business executives, 200 companies and more than 100 chief executive officers (CEOs) of TNCs attending. The corporate influence on the summit seemed to reflect the UN's new approach to eradicating poverty through public–private partnerships (PPPs) in what was described as a 'Global Compact'.

Private interests came to compete for ownership of public services in developing countries and sectors such as water, energy, health care, agriculture and biodiversity. However, as the NGOs urgently pointed out, entrusting TNCs with the world's resources can only worsen poverty levels in the South given the lack of effective legislation and of political will to bring large corporations to task for environmental disasters – such as the 16,000 deaths caused by toxic emissions from the Union Carbide factory in Bhopal, India, or the biological devastation caused by Marcopper in the Philippines. By the end of the summit, civil society organisations, social movements and several development NGOs were expressing dismay and frustration over the way corporations had hijacked the UN and had turned the summit into a farcical TNC gold rush. As one delegate commented, the summit was not Rio plus 10 but rather Rio minus 20 – meaning that the protection of the environment had been set back 20 years.

SUSTAINING DEVELOPMENT

In recent years civil society organisations in both developed and developing countries have become more engaged and vigilant in campaigns which specifically seek to regulate the activities of corporations and prevent environmental malpractice. The objective of many of the NGOs has been to ensure that national and international legislation works towards protecting ecosystems and that biodiversity as a policy is properly enforced by governments and multilateral organisations such as the UN and its environment agencies. However, increasingly it is the developed countries which have been relegating environment issues to marginal and underfunded agencies, while pursuing neo-liberal policies that undo much of their work. Arguably, sustainable thinking needs to permeate government departments to ensure that both development and environmental issues are considered central to a 'joined-up' and ecologically sound programme of government. Trade and economic issues tend to dominate government agendas with environmental policies developing in the unsympathetic context of a neo-liberal ethos. However, mounting concern about erratic weather patterns, global warming, air pollution and 'dirty' industries should be reflected in urgent international action to recognise the causes of these effects. Furthermore, governments have to be persuaded of the links between growing poverty levels in developing countries and the irresponsible exploitation of the natural environment that is pushing the most vulnerable individuals, families and communities below subsistence thresholds.

Realising the responsibility of governments to pursue these actions, though, does not mean that they alone should be held accountable for their promises and actions. The private sector also has a responsibility to implement the highest possible standards in safeguarding the environment. Moreover, IFIs have considerable influence and credibility and should be pushed to use this responsibly for the benefit of the world's poor.

As we initiate implementation of the WSSD action plans, it is imperative that civil society movements prevent a private-sector agenda from assuming control of the development and environmental debate, thus further marginalising the voices of the poor and dispossessed in both developed and developing countries. Progressive environmental movements, such as Greenpeace and Friends of the Earth, cannot achieve this by themselves. It is important and urgent for governments to form alliances with civil society to work toward the regulation and control of private interests and corporate-led globalisation. The goal is a global order that is built on a partnership that respects and enhances the diversity of human communities while protecting our natural resources. The two processes have to be taken together. More importantly, a global order that facilitates an effective sustainable form of development needs to be a priority for investment – one that meets the needs of present generations without compromising the ability of future generations to meet their own needs. The reality is that the world's poor and their environment cannot afford to wait for development to become sustainable.

NOTES

1. The Brundtland report, *Our Common Future*, can be found at <www.un.org/documents/ga/res/42/ares42-186.htm>. Also see Don Hinrichsen, *Our Common Future: A Reader's Guide* (London: Earthscan, 1987); Michael Decleris, *The Law of Sustainable Development: General Principles* (Luxembourg: Office for Official Publications of the European Communities, 2000); Department for International Development,

Achieving Sustainability: Poverty Elimination and the Environment (London: DFID, 2000).

2. Victor Ramos, *They Fought for the Forest* (Quezon City, Philippines: DENR, 2000), p. 10. Also refer to the seminal text by Vandana Shiva, *Monocultures of the Mind* (London: Zed Books, 1993).

3. *United Nations Framework for the Convention on Climate Change* (New York: United Nations, 1992). Also see David William Pearce, *Economics and Environment: Essays on Ecological Economics and Sustainable Development* (Cheltenham: Edward Elgar, 1998).

4. The Earth Summit, at <www.un.org/geninfo/bp/enviro.html>.

5. *Agenda 21*, Chapter 3: 'Combating Poverty Programme Area'. For the full document visit <www.un.org/esa/sustdev/agenda21.htm>.

6. Owen Lynch, Kirk Talbot and Marshall Berdin, *Balancing Acts: Community-Based Forest Management and National Law in Asia and the Pacific* (Washington, D.C.: World Resoures Institute, 1995). Also see <www.wri.org/wri/index.html>.

7. See the Meltzer Report at <www.house.gov/jec/imf/imfpage.htm>; also Walden Bello, *The Future in the Balance: Essays on Globalization* (London: Food First Books, 2001).

8. Bello, *Future in the Balance*. Also see J.K. Boyce, *The Political Economy of the Environment* (Cheltenham: Edward Elgar, 2002).

9. See the Greenpeace and Friends of the Earth web sites at <www.greenpeace.org> and <www.foei.org>.

10. Bello, *Future in the Balance*.

WEB SITES

Earth Summit	www.un.org/geninfo/bp/enviro.html
Statistics for environment and development	www.ids.ac.uk
Sustainable development in environmental terms	www.sustainable-development.gov.uk
International Institute for Environment and Development	www.iied.org
The Hunger Site Campaign	www.thehungersite.com
Greenpeace	www.greenpeace.org
Friends of the Earth	www.foei.org
International Institute for Sustainable Development	www.iisd.ca
Econet	www.igc.org/igc/econet
Agenda 21	www.un.org/esa/sustdev/agenda21.htm
Focus	www.focusweb.org
Meltzer Report	www.house.gov/jec/imf/imfpage.htm

13 Globalisation and Development: Charting the Future

Gerard McCann

Anticipating the expansion of the market-driven society, the nineteenth-century social economist Karl Marx foresaw 'the entanglement of all peoples in the net of the world market', a place where human interaction and culture would be shaped by world-encompassing financial structures.[1] Developed countries have seen this new globalised world order transform their societies into a homogeneous, brand-dominated market place. Alternatively, the developing world has been targeted by the governments of the richest countries and transnational corporations (TNCs), with ever-increasing pressures to integrate into the global economy within an all embracing neo-liberal model of development. While this globalised system is multidimensional in form, covering all aspects of human development, it also contains fundamental fault lines which expose and accentuate the gaps between advantaged and disadvantaged peoples within countries and across the globe. Globalisation has constructed a number of alternative futures within its developmental process, which at best has closed the technological space between regions, but at worst has condemned the poorest regions to continual underdevelopment. To conclude this study of development, this chapter will assess the possibilities that globalisation holds, looking at the options that have evolved in the light of new ideologies and technologies, and the political economy that accompanies its progression.

DEFINING THE NEW WORLD ORDER

The globalised market system has introduced an epoch in which social inequalities are aggravated by the extent of economic growth in some developed countries and the increasing exclusion of the poorest regions. It is a system in which:

- A quarter of the world's population are consigned to abject poverty
- A wealthy elite of 250 people own a combined wealth which is equal to the annual income of 50 per cent of the world's population
- World trade increased by 50 per cent over the past six years and is now worth over $17 billion a day
- One-third of world trade consists of the movement of goods between different parts of the same corporations
- Of the 100 largest economic entities in the world, 51 are corporations
- Non-oil primary commodity prices (the basic foods and raw materials produced by the Third World) fell by 50 per cent in real terms over the past 20 years
- Conflict and war are presented in some cases as opportunities to facilitate market growth
- One-fifth of the world's people live out their life experiences through high-technological interaction, while the poorest fifth endure an existence little removed from that of the dark ages[2]

The polarisation that currently exists between the richest and poorest of nations is as stark today as it has ever been, and the dynamics which have carried the global society to this point of difference are as advanced as any preceding them. The process of globalisation, ultimately, represents a system of power which is filtered through the economic, political and cultural elements of each society, and – as with all such systems of power – involves dysfunction and conflict.

Globalisation has generated both academic and ideological disputes over the form and definition of the new world order and has spawned a raft of new debates on the types of change taking place and the future that is opening up. Perhaps the most authoritative statement on the nature of the globalised system is offered by David Held, when he states that:

> ... globalization can be thought of as a process (or set of processes) which embodies a transformation in the spatial organisation of social relations and transactions – assessed in terms of their extensity, intensity, velocity and impact – generating transcontinental or interregional flows and networks of activity, interaction, and the exercise of power.[3]

Anthony Giddens defined globalisation as 'the intensification of worldwide social relations which link distant localities in such a way that local happenings are shaped by events occurring many miles away and vice versa'.[4] Alternatively, Robert Keohane stated simply that globalisation was 'the intensification of transnational as well as interstate relations'.[5] The global economic order has been shaped in many ways by its own internal or semi-autonomous dynamics that continually widen its interests and are driven by investment patterns, trade, technological innovation, migration and shifts within global culture. As a consequence, societies and their economies are induced to reframe and constantly renew their societies in order to keep apace with the economic order, with many regions around the world having to reconstitute total interregional working relations to accommodate the changes. Even governmental institutions are having to continually adapt to comply with the new rules, with local cultures being encouraged to mirror the patterns of this globalised system.

Post-Cold War international relations have been conceived, to a large extent, through the mechanisms of globalisation, and have been noticeable for the forcefulness of developments such as TNC access to markets, debt reclamation or coercive trading relations. The emerging structures are arguably manifesting themselves as empires have done in the past, transcending political borders, reducing fiscal constraints, promoting a monolithic cultural identity, and, under the auspices of new technologies, developing at a speed that is almost unmanageable. Globalisation is communication driven and credit based, binding both developed and developing countries as participants in a unilinear global market place. Susan Strange, a lifelong student of global economic development, envisaged the future of the global system as being dominated by 'the impersonal forces of world markets' that will be 'more powerful than the states to whom ultimate political authority over society and economy is supposed to belong'.[6] The new millennium has already witnessed a realignment of political and cultural forms to facilitate the more predatory intentions of corporate strategies and global finance. The dominant influence of transnational financial powers has been largely unhindered by political constraints, thereby requiring the various state and governmental agents to conform to the mandate which the enterprise demands. In short, corporate enterprise and its political agents enact and practice globalisation while the rest of the world is subjected to it.

This new economic order has its architects and managers, committed to the acceleration of globalisation, operating under the direction of the main international financial institutions (IFIs) and transgovernmental bodies: the World Bank, the World Trade Organisation (WTO), the International Monetary Fund (IMF) and the Group of Eight leading industrialised countries (G8). Together they provide an enabling framework for the design, advising, investing, and where necessary 'disciplining' of economies in regions around the world. Their initiatives and programmes confer the detail of the system, with the promise of participation, economic growth and financial incentives. It is at this level that the ideology underpinning the economic and political structures of globalisation is practiced and enforced. The basic tenets of neo-liberalism dominate the language and form of this globalising process, an ideology which places competition, the cultural homogeneity of postmodernity and laissez-faire economics, at the centre of human development. In effect, it has meant that post-Cold War global development has been shaped by increasingly aggressive market competition.

The upshot of the integration of economies around the globe under neo-liberalism is that there will be losers as well as winners. The World Bank has recognised that enhancing market potential through transnational competition results in economic divergence and increases the poverty gap between the global rich and poor. Indeed, the World Bank itself estimates that some 2 billion people around the world are systematically excluded from the process of development.[7] The IFIs seem to accept that 'progress' and increased incorporation into the global economy will also create more pronounced social and economic divisions, between and within the developed and developing regions. The World Bank's policy document *Globalization, Growth and Poverty*, represents the views of many pro-globalisation advocates, where it suggests that far from constantly requiring competitive, exploitative pools of human resources, TNCs view underdevelopment as caused by '... weak governance and policies in the non-integrating countries, tariffs and other barriers that poor countries and poor people face in accessing rich country markets, and declining development assistance'.[8] Stripped back, this seems to subscribe to a form of Malthusian theory that blames poverty on the poor, while reasserting an understanding of the world as being market formed – where peoples either participate or are left underdeveloped. Thus, the future of neo-liberalism, as ideology and practice, is tied fundamentally to the future of globalisation. A further aspect of this 'trickle-down' system of global economics is its life-defeating constraints on the least developed countries. A leading forum monitoring the process, the World Development Movement (WDM), highlighted this point in its challenge to the British government's policy on globalisation when it inferred that Western governments and TNCs were operating a system which was 'anti-poor'.[9]

THE NEW GOVERNANCE

The chief characteristic of the new global economy is the speed at which it has reshaped international power relations to become more concentrated and focused on common development goals. Rather than promoting the concepts of interdependence and mutuality, globalisation has constructed a 'one-world' model that utilises global communications to forge a single market culture. The main beneficiaries of renewed linkages have been the TNCs, largely at the expense of indigenous, localised, traditional and community-oriented spheres of human interaction. Those peoples who do not concede to the system remain outside, impoverished and marginalised. The telecommunications revolution that propels globalisation has had an unprecedented capacity to impact on all levels and facets of human activity. The technology and linkages have come to influence human society in a pervasive manner, ranging from the production of toys by Chinese child workers for a children's market in the USA to the deforestation of Indonesia to produce furniture for European homes. Thus global development is attended by an extreme manifestation of uneven development at local and global levels. In many ways globalisation depends on increasing interdependence between regions that are developing, because the very processes of expansionism ensures a constant competitiveness. In neo-liberal theory, competition and untapped markets open up new consumers, resources and profitable opportunities.

Some theorists have argued that globalisation has had an impact that transcends the economic domain and constitutes a process which is manifested through unlimited technological and cultural change. Manuel Castells, in *The Rise of the Network Society*, introduced an interpretation of the modern world which was ideological in its intentions but technological in its methods. In practice what has emerged in recent years has been a new way of communicating, particularly in the developed world, and a new interpretation of human society that crosses traditional spatial, cultural and political boundaries. The main complication with this new means of communication has been that those who are networked into it are increasingly detached from those who are not and vice versa.

Globalisation has also altered the way in which regions and groups within society engage politically. Developed countries have been progressively consolidating a consensus-driven liberal democracy where pluralism and stakeholding have become the central means of governmental organisation. Diverse pressure groups, from NGOs to TNCs operating on an international basis, compete for patronage and influence. In turn, parliamentary institutions – from the UK's parliament to the Russian Duma – have been reformed to ensure compliance with the globalised vision of participatory democracy. The changes are encouraged and to an extent managed by the various transnational institutions headed by the G8. These policy forums are backed up through investment promises from TNCs, which have economic and political influence as powerful as many of the constituent states in the G8 itself. In effect, new codes of governance are emerging to manage the development of the global political economy and in this restructuring there has also evolved a stratified order which continually places the less developed countries at a disadvantaged and differential position vis-à-vis the wealthy core leadership of the Organisation for Economic Co-operation and Development (OECD). In the developed regions, the new democratic order has seen the growth of pressure groups and new social movements which feed into the ever increasing dialogue on political, ethical, and moral issues. This has helped to open up the debate on globalisation and has created the impetus for worldwide pressure groups against the more destructive processes of the system. Alternatively, in many developing countries, exclusion and a decoupling from the mechanisms of development have led to the proliferation of fundamentalist movements and a growing resistance to the cultural dominance and politics of the developed world. For many in the developing world, perpetual exclusion from the new wealth generated by globalisation has engendered increasingly reactionary responses from those dispossessed in this 'new world order'.

As the institutions of government have been altered to adapt to the pressures of globalisation, national and international law have similarly struggled to keep apace of these developments. In the European Union, for example (which dominates the G8), there has been an integration of legal systems, with tougher immigration laws,

the strengthening of external borders and an increase in protectionist trade and competition policies. Western states are moving
toward a harmonisation of policies to ensure that trade liberalisation
is facilitated by changes to competition law. What has also been
notable in the globalisation process in Europe and the US has been
the growing drive for foreign and security policies which will unite
their military capabilities in confronting international threats –
primarily from developing countries. For example, since 2001 the
EU has been working on a single constitution, an EU military force,
and the institution of a unitary European presidency. The new era of
globalisation, and its impact on the developing world, was
commented on by Romano Prodi (the President of the European
Union's Commission) in July 2001, when he suggested that: '... the
problem of poverty cannot be resolved by less globalisation, if
anything we need more ... a model for the world as regards
protection and has the capacity to intervene beyond its borders to
generate prosperity and growth in the emerging countries as well'.[10]
The EU Commission subsequently went on to preside over some of
the toughest anti-immigration and anti-third country trade laws in
its history.

The legal and state network which has been emerging with the
evolving globalisation process has been compliant with economic
developments, and carries with it a new vision of governance which
is more international than ever before. It has also reconstituted the
concept of democratic representation and political self-determin-
ation. The apparatus of global governance has reformed the manner
in which developed states interact and supplants conventional
notions of sovereignty. Ulrich Beck views this change as an alteration
in the very concept of national governance, highlighting: '... the
processes through which sovereign national states are criss-crossed
and undermined by transnational actors with varying prospects of
power, orientations, identities and networks'.[11]

Two significant changes have occurred in world governance since
the end of the Cold War and the rise of TNCs into the political
sphere of influence. The first has been the emergence of semi-
secretive gatherings between the leaders of the Organisation for
Economic Co-operation and Development (OECD) and the
executives of TNCs, through the Bilderberg conferences, the World
Economic Forum, the Paris Club, the Mont Pelerin Society and the
Trilateral Commission.[12] The focus of these meetings has been to
direct and integrate global finance policies and to facilitate political

adaptation to this configuration. The second is the accelerated networking and policy integration of new methods of governance which may be sensitive to, but not always limited by, spatial or cultural constraints. This is particularly obvious with the symbiotic relationship that has emerged within international diplomacy and large media conglomerates where issues and interests have become blurred and events, such as war, can be confused, trivialised or ignored (the 'invisible wars' in Somalia, Colombia, Chechnya and Algeria being typical examples).

In the networking of political, cultural and economic interests this 'open' system of human interaction has brought forward different worldviews which may no longer be confined to the local, but do not fully embrace the complexities of global society. The attacks of 11 September 2001 presented the ultimate paradox of this new global system – where Saudi terrorists, trained in Afghanistan, Pakistan and the US, based in Paris and London, attacked strategic financial and military targets in the US. The attack was relayed live around the world by the US media, to become, perversely, the most watched media event ever. In a way, with this single event the global village was shocked into its citizenship – 'a virtual community, perhaps an incipient community-in-the-making, whose members have become complexly involved in one another's lives, if only as prospective auditors and spectators'.[13] The integration of economies, policies and futures has taken shape at a speed and with a dynamism that is difficult to comprehend, and could become difficult to sustain. While the communication industries have acquired an unprecedented influence on political power – as is most clearly evident in the US, Britain, Australia and Italy, where so-called 'media moguls' have become key patrons or leaders of government parties – they have collectively offered an opaque vision of the world where the only noticeable developments are the global patterns of wealth generation. The process of intercommunication which accompanies this type of globalisation carries with it a vision that is profoundly biased in its interpretation of other cultures, identities and societies. Media-driven cultural imperialism offers little to those outside the developed world.

Alternatively, some analysts of globalisation believe that harnessing the energy of globalisation, and directing it in a more constructive manner to address social needs, is the only way of ensuring sustainable development. Nobel Laureate Amartya Sen has described contemporary forms of development as having misanthropic and destructive tendencies.[14] He suggests that if the more malign aspects of globalisation could be removed by a commitment to controlling the system's market fundamentalism, it could possibly be adapted to enhance economic benefits for the poor, strengthen democracy on a global plane, and act as a deterrent to political corruption. Progressive change, from Sen's point of view, has been characterised by access and adherence to democratic structures and society. Thus, what is required from the new order is a reigning in of the new financial and communication exchanges through democratic checks and balances. For Sen, democratic freedom is about the deliverance of human agency – our right to control our own destiny – and the ability to direct individual human futures through accountable global governance. In effect, globalisation could become a vehicle for integrating democracy and not merely enforcing markets. Freedom needs to be politically reasserted so that it does not merely accommodate the exclusively economistic spheres of human interaction. Sen suggests that:

> Development consists of the removal of various types of unfreedom that leave people with little choice and little opportunity of exercising their reasoned agency ... The intrinsic importance of human freedom, in general, as the preeminent object of development is strongly supplemented by the instrumental effectiveness of freedoms of particular kinds to promote freedoms of other kinds ... For example, there is strong evidence that economic and political freedoms help to reinforce one another, rather than being hostile to one another ... Similarly, social opportunities of education on health care, which may require public action, complement individual opportunities of economic and political participation and also help foster our own initiatives in overcoming our respective deprivations.[15]

THE PRIMACY OF POLITICS

The method of using economic growth rates as a measure of the level of global economic convergence lies at the heart of the relationship between private companies, TNCs and governments in the developed world. Policy making has altered significantly to facilitate competition and free access to markets among companies on a global basis. Attempting to achieve a level playing field for production and trade in commodities has become the backbone of the global system, in an infrastructure within which governments negotiate to accommodate foreign direct investment (FDI) and stock trading. The relaxation of trade, investment and competition legislation has ensured easier movement, greater incentives and ultimately better profitability across the globe. Recent trade liberalisation has promoted a pattern of development which has been similar to that advocated by the monetarists of the early 1980s and the type of 'open' economy encouraged by theorists such as Friedrich Hayek, Theodore Schultz and Milton Friedman.[16] In this model of 'development', states seek to reduce their involvement in the economy, contribute to enterprise by providing company incentives, reduce taxes, privatise state assets, and comply where possible with the access and competition strategies of companies. The politicians become merely the agents of corporate strategies. FDI has become a functional means of activating local economies into the global network. Giving primacy to this type of development has led, in recent years, to TNCs having unrestricted access to many developed and developing regions without political accountability or social responsibility. Profit can be made without recourse to the social costs or political censure, and, where necessary, even working conditions can be adapted to reduce restrictions on capacity-driven productivity.

A central problem in global finance is the failure to incorporate social needs and development issues into trade, investment negotiations and policy structures. In particular, there remains a weakness in the system of global finance in that it overlooks and often ignores key development issues – such as human rights or equality. Thus, in the business of rationalisation and market innovation, human development issues become incidental to the equation. James Wolfensohn, the president of the World Bank, reinforced this notion in 1999 when he commented that 'at the level of people, the system isn't working'.[17]

Global finance exploits regional commercial activity through transnational operations. Its methods include the recurrent rationalisation of production targets in order to work profitably, while avoiding restrictions on competition. The speculation involved in this form of international exchange depends on regional stability and state political collusion with the system. From the perspective of the IFIs, states which opt out (such as Cuba and Venezuela) are excluded; and rejecting this model of globalisation (as Iran and Libya have done) leads to dysfunctional financial relations and limited market access, contributing to a series of restricting effects. The system is also sensitive to global financial trends, as witnessed in the contagion that afflicted many of the East Asian markets in the late 1990s, or the collapse of the Argentine economy in 2001. What the architects of globalisation have failed to recognise is that development is often primarily political and cultural, with the economy secondary. This inversion can react against the political culture of countries in the developing world to whom the new global governance is alien in its form and seems to be seeking to resume a neo-colonial influence over them. For many regions, the outcome of this marginalisation has been reaction, in the form of fundamentalism, revolution or popular upheaval.

The current OECD consensus on development, as framed by the World Bank, the G8 and the IMF, is designed for a specific type of economic growth which contains fault lines that require debt, borrowing, expanding transnational companies, the targeting of developing countries, and in many regions of the world, political conformity. In practice, the weaker regions are forced to facilitate the massive growth of TNCs and global finance. Indeed, the World Bank recently highlighted 24 developing countries that were recognisably integrating more fully into the 'world economy' – as measured by the countries' economic growth rates. It also mentioned that some 2 billion people (a third of the world's population) – 'particularly in sub-Saharan Africa, the Middle East, and the former Soviet Union – live in countries that are being left behind'. It noted that while 'these countries have been unable to increase their integration with the world economy, their ratio of trade to GDP either remained flat or actually declined'.[18] In effect, according to the World Bank's own weighting of globalisation, less developed countries were getting poorer and more politically disaffected. From the point of view of the World Bank, significant sections of the developing world are not in a position to comply with the demands set by the developed world for integration within this new system. Many developing countries are unable to satisfy the economic indicators of growth advocated by the World Bank and are, thereby, unable to integrate into the new global financial order. This model and advocacy of globalisation also draws into question the worth of the World Bank and the IMF to the developing world, and undermines the structural adjustment policies which enforce economic compliance and which obviously have a disintegrating effect on the weakest countries.

The ongoing pattern of development that is typified by increased social and economic divergence between developed and developing countries leaves scant evidence to suggest that the gap between the rich and the poor worlds is closing. The new post-Cold War global system, indeed, has brought forward a different paradigm of global development, where the poorest are deliberately excluded. In anticipating the rise of this excluded 'fourth world', outside the mechanisms of global capital, Manuel Castells commented:

Thus, overall, the ascent of informational, global capitalism is indeed characterized by simultaneous economic development and underdevelopment, social inclusion and social exclusion, in a process very roughly reflected in comparative statistics. There is polarization in the distribution of wealth at the global level, differential evolution of intra-country income inequality, and substantial growth of poverty and misery in the world at large, and in most countries, both developed and developing.[19]

In a way, this marks a return to a situation that was prevalent in the 1970s, when uneven development between the northern and southern hemispheres was having a destabilising effect on the political equilibrium existing at the time. It also means that vast numbers of the most vulnerable around the globe are being systematically forced into subsistence living standards and marginalisation from decision-making processes, while those in the richest regions enjoy unprecedented privilege. What is evident from the first years of the new millennium is the increasing volatility of international relations at the behest of an aggressive economic development. The developing world is, consequently, urged to step into line and globalise to meet the needs of the developed countries, or become another of the ever increasing number of 'outsider' states. As the process continues those excluded in economic, community and cultural terms are seeking ever more desperate measures of redress.

CONCLUSION

The changes within the process of globalisation since the end of the Cold War have been monumental, not least in the IFIs' interpretation of development. The development practices which are tied to neo-liberalism have given rise to a whole series of concerns which have had an adverse effect on the developing world in general and the poorest regions in particular. The divisions between the rich and the poor are growing faster than at any time in human history and the exploitation of poorer peoples has become more pronounced and globalised. The ideology underwriting this type of neo-liberal development is, however, only one vision of the future of globalisation. NGOs, many of whom have been at the forefront of the anti-globalisation protests at World Bank, EU, G8 and IMF summits, have offered a different vision of development based on progressive inclusion and equitable relations between the rich and poor.

The form of globalisation that many of the NGOs are demanding is premised on a concept of justice which places meaningful development through economic growth as a political priority designed to meet social needs. One of the leading organisations in this movement for harnessing globalisation is the World Development Movement. In its statement of intent on government policies regarding development and globalisation, it commented: 'We consider that governments have a crucial role to establish fair and sustainable economies nationally and internationally, rather than assuming that the market will produce outcomes that are equitable. Unless governments assume their responsibilities to establish a fair framework for markets to operate in the public interest, the problems will worsen.'[20] Ultimately, it is up to governments to recognise their responsibility to a sustainable and equitable global development process, and a just relationship between the developing and developed worlds which gives priority to inclusive and sustainable strategies. If Western governments accept this responsibility to promote the principle of global democracy, and are genuine about poverty alleviation, they will ultimately need to respond with a pro-poor concept of global development.

NOTES

1. Karl Marx, quoted in Paul Cammack, 'Attacking the Poor', *New Left Review*, Vol. 13 (January/February 2002), p. 125. Also see Karl Marx, *Marx on Globalisation*, edited and selected by David Renton (London: Lawrence and Wishart, 2001).
2. See Clare Short, 'Speech to the World Trade Organisation's Ministerial Meeting', *Development*, Vol. 9, No. 1 (2000), pp. 10–11. Also see UNDP, *Human Development Report 2001* (Oxford: Oxford University Press, 2001), p. 9. Statistics also taken from 'Where Did All the Protesters Go?', *Observer* (14 July 2002).
3. David Held et al., *Global Transformations* (Cambridge: Polity Press, 1999), p. 16.
4. Anthony Giddens, 'The Globalizing of Modernity', in David Held and Anthony McGrew (eds), *The Global Transformations Reader* (Cambridge:

Polity Press, 2000), p. 92. Also John Beynon and David Dunkerley (eds), *The Globalisation Reader* (London: Athlone, 1999).

5. Robert Keohane, 'Sovereignty in International Society', in Held and McGrew, *The Global Transformations Reader*, p. 109. Also see Jeff Faux and Larry Mishel, 'Inequality and the Global Economy', in Will Hutton and Anthony Giddens (eds) *On the Edge* (London: Jonathan Cape, 2000), pp. 93–111.

6. Susan Strange, *The Retreat of the State: The Diffusion of Power in the World Economy* (Cambridge: Cambridge University Press, 1996), p. 4. Also see Ash Nahrain Roy, *The Third World in the Age of Globalisation* (London: Zed Books, 1999).

7. World Bank, *Globalization, Growth and Poverty* (New York: World Bank, 2001), pp. 17–22. Also see the Department for International Development, *Eliminating World Poverty: Making Globalisation Work for the Poor; White Paper on International Development* (London: DFID, 2000); OECD, *Economic Globalisation and the Environment* (New York: Organisation for Economic Co-operation and Development, 1997); OECD, *Globalisation, Migration and Development* (New York: OECD, 2000), and Marina Wes, *Globalisation: Winners and Losers* (London: Institute for Public Policy Research, 1996).

8. World Bank, *Globalization, Growth and Poverty*, pp. 20–1, <www.worldbank.org/research/global/slides/prr/index.htm>, p. 1. Also see Robert Kuttner, 'The Role of Governments in the Global Economy', in Hutton and Giddens, *On the Edge*, pp. 147–63.

9. World Development Movement, *Making Globalisation Work for People* (London: WDM, 2000), p. 2. Also see B. Gavin, *The European Union and Globalisation* (Cheltenham: Edward Elgar, 2001).

10. Romano Prodi, 'Globalisation', European Commission Statement (Brussels: EC, 20 July 2001), p. 1. Also see George Soros, *On Globalization* (Oxford: Public Affairs Ltd, 2002).

11. Ulrich Beck, 'What is Globalisation?', in Held and McGrew, *The Global Transformations Reader*, p. 101. Also Ray Kiely and Phil Marfleet, *Globalisation and the Third World* (London: Routledge, 1998).

12. See Beck, 'What is Globalisation?'. Also see Anthony Bende-Nabende, *Globalisation, FDI, Regional Integration and Sustainable Development: Theory, Evidence and Policy* (Aldershot: Ashgate, 2002).

13. Clive Kessler, 'Globalisation: Another false universalism?', *Third World Quarterly*, Vol. 21, No. 6 (2000), p. 932. Also see Zygmunt Bauman, *Globalization: The Human Consequences* (Oxford: Polity Press, 1998).

14. Amartya Sen, *Development as Freedom* (New York: Alfred Knopf, 1999).

15. Sen, *Development as Freedom*, p. xii.

16. See George DeMartino, *Global Economy, Global Justice: Theoretical Objections and Policy Alternatives to Neoliberalism* (London: Routledge, 2000). Also, Patricia Marchak, *The Integrated Circus: The New Right and the Restructuring of Global Markets* (Dublin: McGill-QUB, 1991).

17. James Wolfensohn, quoted in Faux and Mishell, 'Inequality and the Global Economy', p. 93.

18. World Bank Report, *Globalization, Growth, and Poverty*, introductory brief <www.econ.worldbank.org/prr>, p. 1; pp. 17–22. Also see

<www.twnside.org>; Federico Mayor, *The World Ahead* (London: Zed Books, 2001), pp. 57–100; and Will Hutton, *The World We're In* (London: Little Brown, 2002), particularly the chapter titled 'Greed Isn't Good For You', pp. 118–48.

19. Manuel Castells, 'The Rise of the Fourth World', in Held and McGrew, *The Global Transformations Reader*, p. 352. Also Charles Oman, *Globalisation and Regionalisation: The Challenge for Developing Countries* (New York: OECD, 1994).

20. World Development Movement, *Making Globalisation Work for People*, p. 6. Also, see Lance Taylor (ed.), 'Sustainable Development: Macroeconomic, environmental and political dimensions', *World Development*, Vol. 24 (Special Issue 1996), pp. 215–405.

WEB SITES

World Bank Statistics	www.econ.worldbank.org/prr
Third World Network	www.twnside.org
DFID	www.globalisation.gov.uk
World Trade Organisation	www.wto.org
United Nations	www.undp.org
World Bank	www.worldbank.org
Organisation for Economic Co-operation and Development	www.oecd.org/dac
One World	www.oneworld.org
Transparency	www.transparency.org
Development Research	www.comminit.com
Centre for the Study of Global Governance at LSE	www.lse.ac.uk/Depts/global
Centre for the Study of Globalisation and Regionalisation (CSGR), University of Warwick	www.warwick.ac.uk/csgr
Economic Policy Institute: Trade and Globalisation	epinet.org/subjectpages/trade
International Forum on Globalisation	www.ifg.org
Global Policy Forum	www.globalpolicy.org

Contributors

Dr Purnaka L. de Silva is the head of leadership programmes in North America at the United Nations Leadership Academy (UNU/LA). He was lecturer and advisor of studies at the School of Politics/Centre for the Study of Ethnic Conflict at Queen's University, Belfast. He is a specialist on political violence and its disruptive effects on the development process. His most recent publications are *Political Violence and its Cultural Constructions* (Palgrave, 2002), and *Postmodern Insurgencies: Political Violence, Identity Formation and Peacemaking in Comparative Perspective* (Macmillan and St. Martin's Press, 2000).

Eimear Flanagan has worked in the field of development education for both Save the Children and Trócaire. She has a particular interest in the rights of the child and is currently working in the Middle East.

Dr Paul Hainsworth is a senior lecturer in politics at the University of Ulster. He is Amnesty International UK's Asia world region co-ordinator, is the founder and chair of the East Timor Solidarity Campaign and is a member of the management board of the One World Centre (NI). His recent publications include: *The Politics of the Extreme Right* (editor, 1998); *Divided Society* (Pluto Press, 1998); and *The East Timor Question* (edited with Stephen McCloskey, I.B. Tauris, 2000). He is also editor of the journal *Regional Federal Studies*.

Maura Leen is a lecturer in the Centre for Development Studies in University College, Dublin, in the theories and strategies of economic development. She was previously Trócaire's co-ordinator of Policy and Research. Prior to that, she was Trócaire's Asia Projects Officer from 1992 to 1995. Between 1989 and 1991, she worked as an economist and project officer in the Ministry of Economic Development in Belize. She has also lectured in equality studies and development studies in University College, Dublin. She is vice-chair of the Debt and Development Coalition and is a member of the NGO/Department of Foreign Affairs Joint Standing Committee on Human Rights. She has been editor of Trócaire's *Development Review* journal since 1995. Recent publications include: 'EU Development Policy beyond 2000: Putting policies into practice' (with Bob van

Dillen), in *Development Review* (December 2000); 'Human Rights: The crisis and the challenge', *Irish Quarterly Review* (Summer 1999); and *Refugees and Asylum Seekers: A Challenge to Solidarity* (with Jerome Connolly, Irish Commission for Justice and Peace/Trócaire, 1997).

Dr Madeleine Leonard is a lecturer in the Department of Sociology and Social Policy at Queen's University, Belfast. She is the convenor of two modules: 'Development and Change', which is concerned with the relationship between the developed and developing worlds; and 'Women in Irish Society', which examines feminist theories in the local and global context. Her publications include: *Invisible Work, Invisible Workers: The Informal Economy in Europe* (Macmillan, 1998); *Women in Irish Society: A Sociological Reader* (co-editor, Pale Publications, 1997); *Informal Economic Activity in Belfast* (Avebury, 1994).

Mary Louise Malig is a research associate at Focus on the Global South based in Manila, the Philippines. She graduated from the University of the Philippines with a degree in sociology. As well as writing reports and monitoring development policy she also is a contributor to a number of Asian newspapers and magazines.

Dr Gerard McCann is a lecturer in European Studies at St Mary's College, Queen's University, Belfast. He is chairperson of the Institute for Popular Economics and was the former chairperson of the Belfast Development Education Centre. He is a founder member of the Ireland–Palestine Cultural Links Project. He is also author of *Theory and History* (Ashgate, 1997) and is editor of *The Rights Debate* (WBEF, 2001) and *The Equality Duty* (WBEF, 2001).

Stephen McCloskey has been the Director of the Belfast-based One World Centre (NI) since 1995. He has an MSc in development and environment education (South Bank University) and a BA in philosophy (Queen's University). He has contributed numerous articles to development education journals and publications and is the co-editor (with Paul Hainsworth) of *The East Timor Question: The Struggle for Independence from Indonesia* (I.B. Taurus, London and New York, 2000). He is also Chair of Cuba Support Group (Belfast) and Secretary of the East Timor Solidarity Campaign (NI).

Professor Denis O'Hearn is both an economist and a sociologist. He was educated at the Universities of New Mexico and Michigan. For several years he taught at the University of Wisconsin, Madison, where he was associate professor of sociology. Currently, he is professor in sociology and social policy at Queens University, Belfast. He is the editor of the *Irish Journal of Sociology* and chair of the West Belfast Economic Forum. His recent books include: *The Altantic Economy* (Manchester University Press, 2001); *Inside the Celtic Tiger* (Pluto Press, 1998); and *Critical Development Theory* (edited with Ronaldo Munck, Zed Books, 1999).

Dr Paula Rodgers is a regional policy and research manager with Save the Children. She was formerly a research fellow in the Department of Sociology and Social Policy, Queen's University, Belfast. She has extensive experience of qualitative research and her research interests include: the educational experiences of young mothers, the employment experiences of children in local and global contexts, policies towards young people with disabilities, and young people's involvement in public decision making. Her publications include: 'Save the Children's Position on Child Labour', in *No Time to Play* (One World Centre, 1997); 'Single mothers in the Republic of Ireland', in *Single Mothers in an International Context* (edited by S. Duncan and E. Edwards, UCL Press, 1997); and *Crime in Ireland 1945–1995* (with J. Brewer and B. Lockhart, Clarendon, 1997).

Jean Somers is the co-ordinator of the Debt and Development Coalition, Dublin – an NGO campaigning for debt cancellation. Her recent articles include: a review of the *World Bank's World Development Report 2000/2001*, in *Development Review* (December 2000); 'A Debt-Free Start to the New Millennium?', *World* magazine (January/February 2000); 'Bolivian Blend: Poverty reduction strategy paper approach to Bolivia', *Focus* magazine (Issue 63, Winter 2000); 'Rehashing failed plan will not solve debt trap', *Irish Times* (2 October 1999); and a chapter on debt in *75:25* (edited by Colm Regan, Dochas, 1996).

Andy Storey is a senior lecturer at the Development Studies Centre, Kimmage Manor, Dublin. He previously worked for Trócaire and is currently chair of the campaigning NGO Action from Ireland (AfrI). His recent publications include: 'Post-Development Theory', *Development* (Vol. 43, No. 4, 2000); 'The World Bank, Neo-Liberalism and Power', *Development in Practice* (Vol. 10, Nos 3 and 4, 2000); 'Globalisation and the African state', *Development Review* (1999); and

'Economics and Ethnic Conflict: Structural adjustment in Rwanda', *Development Policy Review* (Vol. 17, No. 1, 1999).

Iris Teichmann is a senior editor at the Refugee Council in London, and has worked on UK asylum issues since 1995. She is currently a member of the Electronic Immigration management committee and has recently published a schools resource entitled *Asylum and Immigration* (Franklin Watts).

Index

Compiled by Sue Carlton